AF644490

Evolution of Indian Philosophy

Andhra University Philosophical Studies

Andhra University Philosophical Studies contain comprehensive works oriented to the traditions of Socrates and Śaṅkara. With the motto, 'Global Understanding with Vedāntic Spirit' initiated by S. Radhakrishnan at Andhra University these volumes reflect ethics, social ideals and cultural values, embodied both in secular society and religious thought. Apart from brief texts on the Buddha and Śaṅkara, volumes on Saints and Gurus, Social Relevance of Philosophy and Philosophical Teaching have been released. Volumes published under the series are:

1. Life and Teachings of Ādi Śaṅkarācārya; by P. George Victor (ISBN 81-246-0194-1)
2. Saints and Gurus: Perspectives on Spiritual and Social Renaissance in Contemporary India; edited by P. George Victor and S.D.A. Joga Rao (ISBN 81-246-0203-4)
3. Social Relevance of Philosophy: Essays on Applied Philosophy; edited by P. George Victor (ISBN 81-246-0204-2)
4. Teaching Philosophy in the Twenty-First Century; edited by P. George Victor (ISBN 81-246-0205-0)
5. Studies in Vedānta: Essays in Honour of Professor S.S. Rama Rao Pappu; edited by P. George Victor and V.V.S. Saibaba (ISBN 81-246-0350-2)
6. Discourses in Buddhist Classics; by V.V.S. Saibaba (ISBN 81-246-0360-X)
7. Hinduism and its Development; by K. Satchidananda Murty (ISBN 81-246-0383-9)
8. Evolution of Indian Philosophy; by K. Satchidananda Murty (ISBN 81-246-0393-6)

Andhra University Philosophical Studies, no. 8

Evolution of Indian Philosophy

by

K. Satchidananda Murty

With an Introduction by

M.N. Roy

D.K. Printworld (P) Ltd.
New Delhi

Cataloging in Publication Data — DK
Courtesy: D.K. Agencies (P) Ltd. <docinfo@dkagencies.com>

Satchidananda Murty, K. (Kotta), 1924-
Evolution of Indian philosophy / by K. Satchidananda Murty ; with an introduction by M.N. Roy — 2nd rev. ed.
p. 23 cm. — (Andhra University philosophical studies ; no. 8)
Includes bibliographical references (p.)
Includes index.
ISBN 8124603936 (hardbound)
ISBN 8124603944 (paperback)

1. Philosophy, Indic. I. Title. II. Series: Andhra University philosophical studies ; no. 8.

DDC 181.4 22

ISBN 81-246-0393-6 (hardbound)
ISBN 81-246-0394-4 (paperback)
First published in 1952 under the title *"Evolution of Philosophy in India — A brief sketch."*
Second revised edition published in 2007
© K. Satchidananda Murty

All rights reserved. No part of this publication may be reproduced or transmitted, except brief quotations, in any form or by any means, electronic or mechanical, including photocopying, recording, or any information storage or retrieval system, without prior written permission of the copyright holder, indicated above, and the publishers.

Published & printed by:
D.K. Printworld (P) Ltd.
Regd. Office: 'Sri Kunj', F-52, Bali Nagar
New Delhi-110 015
Phones: (011) 2545-3975; 2546-6019; *Fax*: (011) 2546-5926
E-mail: dkprintworld@vsnl.net
Website: www.dkprintworld.com

Foreword

I AM grateful to Sri K. Satchidananda Murty for giving me an opportunity of going through the typescripts of his interesting book on the evolution of philosophy in India. I have found this very fascinating, because the standpoint taken up is something fresh and original even to the extent of being unconventional for an Indian. As a typical example of his approach I shall recount what he writes "Nor do I see any reason why one should use those hazy terms, "spiritual" and "other worldly" instead of the plain "irrational" and "unworldly"; for to be spiritual is to be not intellectual and to be other worldly is to be unworldly. It might be objected that to be spiritual is to be supranational. It must be remembered that whatever is not rational is irrational whether it is supranational or subrational." I am not sure that this statement will be taken by all at its face value; but I cannot but admire the courage of the man, who makes this statement not in any dogmatic fashion, but with arguments culled from anthropology and sociology, psychology and philosophy.

The book is not likely to be popular with people who mistake words for arguments and patriotism for truth. That is why I am inclined to echo whole-heartedly the famous words of Voltaire: "I disagree with every word you say; but I shall fight to death for your right to say it." Mr Murty has had his say, and it would do a lot of good especially to people who disagree with him, if at least they are honest enough not merely to repeat old worn-out texts against him, but to resubmit their own thinking to clear-cut logic. They may then discover that Mr Murty has considerable justification for departing from the old shibboleths and beginning his study of Indian philosophy with a new approach. My congratulations to him; and I have so thoroughly enjoyed reading it, found in it so much that I have said myself on several occasions, and I have learnt so much from it that the least I can do is to accede gracefully to his request for a foreword from my humble pen. The book is sure to be welcomed by all, who love truth and a freshness of approach. I welcome it as a very valuable contribution to the development of Indian philosophy.

Professor A.R. Wadia
Pro Vice-Chancellor
MS University, Baroda

Preface

THIS is an attempt to trace the evolution of philosophy in India in relation to socio-political conditions. Developments in psychology and sociology of knowledge have established that truth like error is dependent on the prevalent conditions of social and physical environment. No thinker and philosophy can be considered in the abstract, they being the products of their social milieu. No historian of Indian philosophy has kept this fact in mind. Again, the histories of Indian philosophy fail to distinguish between religion and philosophy. Philosophy is the search of the intellect for truth, while religion is the cry of the heart for salvation.[1] The point of departure for a history of philosophy is the distinction between philosophy and religion.

Critics governed more by sentiment and feeling than by reason may object to some passages in this book; while those who have not got over the confusion of philosophy with religion and are in the clutches of the belief that Indian thought is the best that has been ever produced and will be produced will be shocked by the views expressed herein. While none can have greater regard and love for Indian culture and the Indian way of life than me, I am for viewing things objectively and scientifically, unclogged by misplaced patriotism and love for the past. It is not popular opinion and patriotism that should guide one in assessing the value of philosophical systems. I

1. Gilbert Murray, *Five Stages of Greek Religion*, p. 117.

have in my enquiries followed the maxim of that great Italian poet, Dante: *Segui il tuo corso, e lascia dir le genti* (follow your own course, and let people talk).

In view of the vast stretches of time covered and the many currents and cross-currents of thought and action, this book is a very brief treatment of the subject, and does not arrogate to itself the status of more than an imperfect introductory essay. Apart from the original Sanskrit texts, I have derived the greatest benefit from the works of European savants. Works of Indian authors lack critical spirit and are devoid of historic sense in the method of writing. There are some academicians like Jha, Bhandarkar and Vidyabhusan among the old guard and Humayun Kabir and Wadia among the contemporary scholars, who are exceptions to this. Professor Wadia's writings exhibit the penetrating thought of a genius; his Calcutta lectures are masterpieces of a brilliant mind. The dazzling radiance of style and the clear and logical way in which Dr Kabir analyses and discusses a problem have ever been the objects of admiration and envy to me.

I must herein recall with gratitude the kindness and encouragement, which I am constantly receiving from Vice-Chancellor V.S. Krishna; but for his benignity my work as a whole would have been far less in quality and quantity. Mr M.N. Roy has done me the honour of writing the introduction. I owe my thanks to this great son of India. I am indebted to Professor A.R. Wadia for the foreword. It has not been possible to remove the numerous misprints, as the author could not go through the proofs.

Andhra University, **K. Satchidananda Murty**
April 1952

Preface to the Second Edition

MAHAMAHOPADHYAYA K. Satchidananda Murty is the most thought-provoking philosopher of our times, whose books on Indian philosophy, culture, religion — particularly Vedānta — contain "an instructive and penetrating analysis," and fill the gaps left by famous writers, insisting on the relevance and the forgotten dimension of philosophical learning in India. This work, which was originally entitled *Evolution of Philosophy in India* and printed at St. Michael's Industrial School Press, Guntur of Andhra Pradesh in 1952 did not enjoy a wide circulation. It is now brought out under the modified title, *Evolution of Indian Philosophy* for the benefit of students and researchers to keep as a reference book.

One can appreciate this work, if one is familiar with Bertrand Russell's *History of Western Philosophy* and the history of India, through which one can learn that life and thought are invariably interconnected with polity and persons, economy and environment. The sections of this text were originally chapters, but now have been rearranged in accordance with the popular pattern of writing Indian philosophy. In this edition no single sentence has been added, however too many references and complex narratives have been reduced. As a whole a few sentences here and there in a chapter or two in the entire text have been deleted; thus the original text has been kept alive, both in spirit and content.

The first chapter demonstrates the socio-political, geographical and racial causes for the formation of human thinking, followed by a chapter on what philosophy is and the nature of Indian philosophy. The Vedas and Upaniṣads, the *Bhagavad-Gītā*, and about five schools of Vedānta, including Kāśmīra-Śaivism were discussed at length in three different chapters. Another three chapters on Cārvākas, Jainism and Buddhism; and one on Sāṁkhya and Vaiśeṣika were dealt with; however this book does not contain any chapter or section on the systems of Nyāya, Yoga and Mīmāṁsā. Probably Professor Murty might have been influenced by the writings of Max Müller, Paul Deussen and Garbe, assuming that the Mīmāṁsā as scriptural exegesis of the ritualistic portion of the Vedas, Yoga as a form of discipline of meditation, and Nyāya as the science of logic, have little philosophy.

When the philosophical circles throughout the world are being swept away by the cyclone of epistemological analysis, and the tsunami of metaphysical speculations, the "Andhra University Philosophical Studies" series reoriented to the traditions of Socrates and Śaṅkara, which were initiated by S. Radhakrishnan and P.T. Raju at Andhra University followed by K. Satchidananda Murty, with the motto "Global Understanding with Vedāntic Spirit" wherein the Department of Philosophy and Religious Studies inculcates in its curriculum ethics, social ideals and cultural values, embodied both in secular society and religious thought. As such *Evolution of Indian Philosophy* is the eighth volume in the "Andhra University Philosophical Studies Series," which was started a few years ago.

The foreword written by Professor A.R. Wadia from Baroda and the introduction by honourable M.N. Roy written from Dehradun respectively on 20th and 30th April in the year

1952 reveal the method and spirit in which the book is written. This book is dedicated to Professor V.S. Krishna, the then Vice-Chancellor of Andhra University. Having been directed by Professor Murty for our doctoral researches on Vedānta and Buddhism, and being associated as his younger colleagues in the Department of Philosophy and Religious Studies, we feel proud in presenting to the seekers of truth, the insights of Professor K. Satchidananda Murty with reference to the evolution of philosophy in India. In this context, we are thankful to Professor K. Ramesh of the Department of IRPM in Andhra University, the youngest son of Professor K. Satchidananda Murty for permitting us to undertake the second edition. We are grateful to Shri Susheel K. Mittal, Director of the D.K. Printworld for publishing this under the "Andhra University Philosophical Studies" series.

Andhra University
August 2006

P. George Victor
V.V.S. Saibaba

Key to Transliteration

VOWELS

अ *a*	आ *ā*	इ *i*	ई *ī*	उ *u*	ऊ *ū*
(but)	(palm)	(it)	(beet)	(put)	(pool)
ऋ *ṛ*	ए *e*	ऐ *ai*	ओ *o*	औ *au*	
(rhythm)	(play)	(air)	(toe)	(loud)	

CONSONANTS

Guttural	क *ka*	ख* *kha*	ग *ga*	घ *gha*	ङ *ṅa*
	(skate)	(blockhead)	(gate)	(ghost)	(sing)
Palatal	च *ca*	छ* *cha*	ज *ja*	झ *jha*	ञ *ña*
	(chunk)	(catch him)	(john)	(hedgehog)	(bunch)
Cerebral	ट *ṭa*	ठ* *ṭha*	ड *ḍa*	ढ* *ḍha*	ण* *ṇa*
	(start)	(anthill)	(dart)	(godhead)	(under)
Dental	त *ta*	थ *tha*	द *da*	ध* *dha*	न *na*
	(path)	(thunder)	(that)	(breathe)	(numb)
Labial	प *pa*	फ* *pha*	ब *ba*	भ *bha*	म *ma*
	(spin)	(philosophy)	(bin)	(abhor)	(much)
Semi-vowels	य *ya*	र *ra*	ल *la*	व *va*	
	(young)	(drama)	(luck)	(vile)	
Sibilants	श *śa*	ष *ṣa*	स *sa*	ह *ha*	
	(shove)	(bushel)	(so)	(hum)	
Others	क्ष *kṣa*	त्र *tra*	ज्ञ *jña*	ळ* *ḷ*	ॠ* *ṝ*
	(*kṣatriya*)	(*triśūla*)	(*jñānī*)	(*play*)	

अं (◌ं) *ṁ anusvāra* (nasalization of preceding vowel) like *saṁskṛti*

अः *visarga* = *ḥ* (aspiration of preceding vowel) like (*prātaḥ*)

ऽ *Avagraha* consonant #'consonant (like:- *ime 'vasthitā*)

Anusvāra at the end of a line is presented by m (म्) and not ṁ

* No exact English equivalents for these letters.

Contents

Introduction

M.N. Roy

THIS book is a substantial contribution to the attempt to write a history of Indian philosophy. In a short compass, the author has covered certain aspects of the subject ignored in other more imposing works. The earlier chapters outline the sociological, anthropological, ethnological and psychological approaches to the problems of historical research. Though the treatment may not always be quite convincing, these chapters are of great importance methodologically, and as such constitute the more valuable part of a commendable work of scholarship. While the "effects of geographical environment on thought" are undeniable, "race mind" is an assumption, which not only lacks empirical basis, but also is fraught with dangerous cultural tendencies. However, in this respect the author's conclusions seem to be tentative. On the whole, his approach is rational and critical, which is sure to guide the seeker of truth in the right direction. The author's realization that an agreed definition of philosophy is the precondition for any fruitful enquiry into the history of philosophy, introduces freshness in his treatment of the subject. A courageous rejection of the conformist, conventional and patriotic view in favour of the objective, scholarly and critical has enabled the author to discover that Indian philosophy was never differentiated from Theology. It may be added that, owing to the peculiar features of what is generally known as Indian philosophy, even modern philosophers tend to be rather believers than thinkers.

But in ancient India, philosophy revolted against religion. The philosophical heritage of India has still to be discovered and properly evaluated. A philosophical reaction is the outstanding feature of the intellectual life of India, which is dominated by religious revivalism — a vain attempt to rationalize the irrational.

By her own effort, India never emerged from the intellectual twilight of her Middle Ages, which followed the downfall of Buddhism. In the sixteenth and seventeenth centuries, individual religious reformers preached devotionals which would dispense with the priestly-intermediary between God and his devotees. But their influence was local and transitory. India experienced neither a Renaissance nor a Reformation. The intellectual stagnation lasted until the middle of the nineteenth century, when a faint echo of the modern rationalist and liberal thought reached India, to disturb it partially. During the latter half of the century, the intellectual life of the country was influenced by a number of men who preached revolt against religious orthodoxy, intellectual parochialism and social injustice. There was no great philosopher amongst them. They were social reformers. None of them thought of going behind the twilight of the Middle Ages in search of India's philosophical heritage. The attitude of the more advanced amongst those forerunners of an Indian Renaissance towards her past was negative. They drew inspiration from the West and held that India as a whole must do the same in order to emerge from medievalism.

Unfortunately, the impact of modern Western thought came in the wake of the British conquest. It made some headway until discontent and then hatred against the foreign political rule became the predominating passion of the educated classes. Then all Western influence was decried as denationalizing materialism to be opposed and rejected in favour of the spiritual genius of Indian culture. Speculative thought of any kind had been for centuries eclipsed by priestly bigotry, superstitious ritualism and practice of social injustice, such as the caste system, untouchability, etc. which passed as religion. In that atmosphere, the democratic simplicity of Christianity had a strong appeal not only for the victims of social injustice, but also for many liberal intellectuals.

A movement of religious reform and of revival of the spiritualist philosophy of India were the reaction to that process of the disintegration of an intellectually stagnant society. Return to the pristine purity of Vedic ritualism was the religious reform advocated. The orthodoxy of the reformers was more bigoted than the current variety. Such a reactionary movement being incapable of meeting the situation, the modern prophets of India's spiritual mission, who sought to provide a philosophical sanction for a religious revivalism, reinforced it. It was discovered in the post-Buddhist scholastic theology, which had expounded Vedānta as the quintessence of the philosophical thought of ancient India.

To have found the unity in diversity is claimed as the greatest merit of orthodox Hindu philosophy. But, as a matter of fact, the unity was not found. It was simply assumed or imagined. It is an ideal conception which brushes aside the problems to be solved. Since the rise of the material world out of the assumed immaterial root-causes is not logically possible, dualism persists, defying all metaphysical verbal jugglery. From the Upaniṣadic *ṛṣi*s down to Śaṅkarācārya, no orthodox Hindu speculative thinker was able to prove how the diversities of nature could arise from a common cause. The sheer impossibility of the task ultimately drove Indian speculation to the monumental absurdity of the *māyā-vāda*. Vitiated by the baffling, but obstinate problem of dualism, the speculation about the origin of the world must necessarily come back again and again to the good old conception of an anthropomorphic god, whose venerable appearance casts a sinister shadow on the sublime light of philosophy. Śaṅkarācārya's laboriously constructed Advaita-vāda solved the problem of the world by the simple contrivance of declaring it to be a dream. Nevertheless, it could not get rid of a personal god. And a personal god is utterly incompatible with the philosophical conception of unity in diversity.

The various currents of philosophical thought of ancient India, as distinct from religious, eventually contributed to the rise of Buddhism. Thus, it grew out of a background of the subordination of the faith in the supernatural to human reason. Buddhism, though counted as one of the Great Religions of the world, was not a religion in the strictest sense. Therefore, it could not fill up the spiritual vacuum created by the disintegration of the early Vedic natural religion. On the one hand, it flourished as an intellectual movement (the Hīnayāna school) with a limited scope; and on the other, it compromised with the vulgarities of the decayed natural religion. In this bitter form, it could not hold its own against the rationalized religious revival buttressed upon Śaṅkarācārya's scholasticism.

The downfall of Buddhism buried its philosophical foundation in the ruins of time. The triumphant Brāhmanical reaction not only falsified ancient philosophical thought, which had dared deny the authority of the Vedas and even the existence of God, so as to combat it conveniently; but the blasphemous works of atheists, materialists and nihilists were mostly destroyed. India entered her Middle Ages, during which theology, scholastic as well as anthropomorphic, dominated the thought. What has come down as orthodox Hindu philosophy was elaborated in that period of intellectual reaction. Being primarily concerned with the nature of God, which conception was taken for granted, of the soul and how the latter could return to its transcendental home, it was not philosophy but theology.

But like ancient Greece, India also had known naturalist, secular and rationalist currents of philosophical thought. Jacques Maritain may still believe that theology is the queen of sciences; but more than two thousand years ago the founder of the Sāṁkhya system of philosophy, Kapila, denied the existence of God because there was no evidence. And Kapila's agnostic naturalism was preceded by the materialist (atomist) rationalism of the Nyāya-Vaiśeṣika system expounded by Kaṇāda and Gautama.

As against the ancient system of truly philosophical thought, which had resulted from the metaphysical speculations fragmentarily recorded in the Upaniṣads, Śaṅkarācārya picked up the pantheistic theology of the Vedānta to oppose Buddhism, which had inherited the rationalist and atheist traditions of the ancient Indian thought. As the name suggests, the Vedānta system is conventionally believed to be the quintessence of the Vedas; and therefore, since Śaṅkarācārya's time, it has been regarded as the Hindu philosophy. But criticism must doubt the philosophical validity of a system which draws authority from the scriptures. Although traditionally Vedānta is counted among six systems of the philosophy of ancient India, there is ground for doubt about its authenticity as such. The alternative theory that it was formulated on the basis of older religious beliefs to combat

Buddhism, and that Śaṅkarācārya himself was the author, appears to be quite plausible. The *Vedānta-sūtras* are open to any kind of interpretation. They provided the authority also for qualified monist and out-and-out dualist theologies. The *Bhagavad-Gītā* is believed to contain the most authoritative (because it was preached by God Incarnate) elucidation of the Vedānta philosophy. It is a part of the epic — the *Mahābhārata*, which evidently is a compilation of contradictory pieces written at different times. The *Bhagavad-Gītā* must have been a very late, most probably post-Buddhist, interpolation.

In any case, the six systems of philosophy, whether they belonged to the same period or not, fall into two distinct categories, both resulting from the metaphysical and theological speculations quickened by the decay of the Vedic natural religion. The earlier three — Vaiśeṣika, Nyāya and Sāṁkhya — record the development of naturalist and rationalist thought, which disputed the divine authority of the Vedas, rejected the belief in creation and therefore the idea of God, and preached rebellion against the priesthood. The other three — Yoga, Uttara Mīmāṁsā and Pūrva Mīmāṁsā — did not break away from the Vedic tradition, relied on the scriptural authority and constructed a partly anthropomorphic, partly impersonal, monotheistic religion superimposed upon the earlier polytheism. The last three systems, one of which deals with Vedic-ritualism, collectively came to be subsequently called the Vedānta. The suggestion was that the earlier three did not flow from the Vedas, and therefore were not recognized as part of Indian intellectual heritage. Yet, they constitute India's contribution to philosophical thought, as distinct from religious doctrines and theological speculations.

Whatever record exists about the various schools of philosophical thought in ancient India bears testimony to the fact that dissatisfaction with the Vedic natural religion gave rise to speculations about the origin of the world, which inevitably developed tendencies to explain the world in physical terms. In India also, physics preceded metaphysics. Much of the really philosophical thought of ancient India has unfortunately been lost. But from the fragmentary evidence on record, the forgotten chapter of the spiritual history of India can be reconstructed. As everywhere, originally, in India also, philosophy was Materialism. The materialistic outcome of the speculations of the rebels against the Vedic natural religion, contained in the three systems of philosophy proper, namely, Vaiśeṣika, Sāṁkhya and Nyāya, provided the inspiration for the greatest event in the history of ancient India — the Buddhist Revolution. The spiritual development of India during nearly a thousand years, beginning from the seventh century BC, was very largely dominated by materialist and rationalist tendencies. It is highly doubtful if the Vedānta system was formulated before the end of that Golden Age of Indian history. Internal evidence tends to prove the opposite case. The main purpose with which Vedāntic pantheism developed was to combat the materialist systems of Kaṇāda and Kapila as well as the revolutionary doctrines of Buddhism and the unsettling logic of Jainism.

Śaṅkarācārya constructed his rigidly logical, but philosophically ambiguous, system of monism for combating Buddhist Idealism. But the real enemy he has to contend with was the materialist traditions of the pre-Buddhist philosophy. Śaṅkarācārya was the ideologist of the Brāhmanical reaction and patriarchal society which were re-established on the ruins of the Buddhist Revolution. But his effort for liquidating the traditions of the really philosophical thought of ancient India was a failure. It is obvious from a critical study of

Śaṅkarācārya's work that he failed to meet the materialists on their ground. He could not refute their arguments. He had to fall back on the authority of the scriptures, the repudiation of which had been the starting point of all philosophical thought in ancient India. Of all the great ancient rationalists, Kapila alone had admitted scriptural testimony as evidence. But that was only a formal concession. While declaring that the existence of God could not be proved, because there was no evidence, Kapila does not take scriptural testimony into account. Even the *Vedānta-sūtras* themselves do not accept the scriptures as answering all the questions raised by those dissatisfied with the dogmas of natural religion.

So highly developed and powerful were the materialist and naturalist schools combated by Śaṅkarācārya that, whenever he tried to refute their arguments logically, he was driven to take up an essentially materialist position. His pantheistic monism is inverted materialism. The *māyā-vāda* is a shamefaced recognition of the reality of the external world. The unreality of the phenomenal world is the fundamental dogma of the Vedānta system. But in order to refute the idealistic schools of Buddhism, Śaṅkarācārya himself rejected the very dogma. Therefore, his more orthodox opponents called him a "Prachanna Bauddha" (camouflaged Buddhist).

Dissatisfaction with the Vedic natural religion gave rise to the speculation about the origin of the world. The Upaniṣads contain fragmentary records of the early spirit of enquiry. Indeed, out and out atheism and materialism can be found; in some of them naturalist heretical thought seems to have developed even earlier in the Vedic age. There are hymns which invoke the wrath of the gods against unbelievers. The *svabhāva-vādin*s (naturalists), mentioned in the earlier Upaniṣads and the Vedas, must have been the pioneers of Indian philosophy. They not only disputed the existence of gods and scoffed at the pretensions of the priests, but were empiricists holding that perception was the only source of knowledge. Therefore they were called *dārśanika*s; subsequently the term came to mean philosophers. The Lokāyata-vāda expounded by those early fathers of Indian philosophy held that perception was the only authority; earth, water, fire and air were the primordial elements; there was no other world; and enjoyment was the only purpose of human existence.

The authorship of the Lokāyata-vāda was traditionally attributed to Bṛhaspati, the legendary preceptor of the gods. The tradition suggests that the forerunners of Indian philosophy were held in high esteem. So much that the authorship of the out and out materialist Cārvāka system was also attributed to the preceptor of the gods. This proves that for more than a thousand years, until the fall of Buddhism, Indian philosophical thought was sceptical, naturalistic, empirical and materialistic.

Although the fundamental principles of ancient Indian materialism were stated originally in the Vaiśeṣika system of Kaṇāda, the dominating position in the intellectual life of that period came to be occupied by the Sāṁkhya system of Kapila. The latter deviated largely from the strictly materialist ground, and developed rather as a rational-naturalist system of metaphysics. Nevertheless, Kapila elaborated the physical principles of materialism philosophically. He is known as an atheist who maintained that the existence of God could not be proved by logical evidence. But the real merit of his philosophy is the recognition of the objective reality of the physical world. The Sāṁkhya system decidedly rejects the doctrine that the external world has no objective existence, and that nothing exists but thought.

The long process of the development of naturalist, rationalist and sceptic, agonistic and materialist thought in ancient India found culmination in the Cārvāka system, which can be compared with Greek Epicureanism, and as such is to be appreciated as the positive outcome of the intellectual culture of ancient India.

The Cārvākas laughed at the notion that the Vedas were divinely revealed truth; they held that truth could never be known except through the senses; therefore, the idea of soul was a delusion. Anticipating modern ultra-empiricism, they held that even reason was not to be trusted, because every inference depended for its validity not only on accurate observation and correct reasoning but also upon the assumption that the future would behave like the past, and of this there was no certainty. But the Cārvākas were not mere nihilists, agnostics and sceptics. They developed an elaborate system of positive philosophical thought, which can be summarized as follows:

> All phenomena are natural. Neither in experience nor in history do we find any interposition of supernatural forces. Matter is the only reality; the mind is matter thinking. The hypothesis of a creator is useless for explaining or understanding the world. Men think religion is necessary only because, being accustomed to it, they feel a sense of loss and an uncomfortable void when the growth of knowledge destroys faith. Morality is natural; it is a social convention and convenience not a divine command. There is no need to control instincts and emotions; they are commands of nature. The purpose of life is to live; and the only wisdom is happiness.

The author of this book seems to have drawn his inspiration from the boldness of the philosophical thinkers of ancient India.

Let his scholarship and critical attitude inspire the younger generation to cultivate the spirit of enquiry, which is rewarded with ever increasing knowledge; and the empirical content of knowledge is the only truth within human reach. Anything supposed to be beyond that has no bearing on human existence; it is a mere figment of imagination which only deludes one into the dreamland of hallucination.

1

Being and Thinking

Sociology of Knowledge and its Effects

WESTERN sociology has revolutionized the methods of interpreting history and philosophy, according to which knowledge is socially conditioned. Though this was one of the epoch-making discoveries of Karl Marx, it was not entirely unknown previously. To give an example, Bacon long ago wrote: "The human understanding is no dry light, but receives an infusion from the will and affections, whence proceed science which may be called 'sciences as one would'."

In different periods of history, different ideas, theories and views are dominant. The origins of these are not to be found solely within thought but in extra-cognitive existential factors, namely the different conditions of life, stages of society and periods of history. The social being of men determines their thought.[1] As far as Marx was concerned, he functionalized the ideas by locating them within the class structure.[2] But he is careful to add that persons belonging to a certain class may identify themselves with another class and give rise to ideas which are not appropriate to the class to which those persons actually belong.[3] Many a people have misunderstood Marx,

---

1. Marx and Engels, *Selected Works*, vol. I, p. 300.
2. Karl Marx, *Capital*, vol. I, p. 15.
3. Marx and Engels, *Selected Works*, vol. I, p. 216.

thinking that he has postulated a one-sided perspective of social conditions on the origination and formation of ideas and theories. Marx is aware of the significance of ideas and theories and the potent force which they possess in breaking up long-established social and political institutions and in giving rise to new social factors and conditions. "Theory becomes a material force as soon as it has gripped the masses."[4] Some critics of Marxism, like Bertrand Russell in his *History of Western Philosophy,* have tried to find fault with it on the ground that it puts economic factors as the sole determinant of philosophy, religion and science. In fact, though Marx is vague about this, Engels has stated that only and "ultimately" economic factors influence philosophy, religion and science, while the pre-existing body of knowledge and beliefs directly influences them.[5] Engels goes to the length of saying that political, philosophical and religious developments "react upon one another and also upon the economic base. It is not that the economic position is the cause and alone active."[6] Marx gives a different status to natural science, which is so precise and so objective that though its "matter" and "aim" be determined by social conditions the validity of its concepts is not impaired thereby.[7] It stands on a different footing from political, religious and philosophic theories.[8]

Thus Marxism holds that thinking is not a mere "reflection" of the socio-economic conditions, but also changes the social conditions. Further, socio-economic conditions do not strictly

---

4. Vide: *History of the CPSU,* p. 184.
5. Marx and Engels, *Selected Works,* vol. I, p. 386.
6. Ibid., p. 392.
7. Marx and Engels, *The German Ideology,* p. 36.
8. Karl Marx, *A Contribution to the Critique of Political Economy,* p. 12.

determine ideas, in the sense that they regulate the range of ideas but not their sole sufficing causes. In turn, ideas make history, and ideas which do not fit in with the existing socio-economic structure fail to be effective.

These facts put forward by Marx and Engels have great consequences for understanding the development in thought, whether in philosophy or in religion. Even other sociologists who do not agree with the theories of Marxism, like Schiller, Mannheim, Durkheim and others — have shown that no system of ideas is self-contained, and none advances a theory without reference to the social structure. Keynes, for example, has observed that Darwin's "Principle of the Survival of the Fittest" could be regarded as one of the generalization of the Ricardian economics.[9] Bertrand Russell has remarked upon the fact of animals used in psychological research displaying the national characteristics of the observer. Animals studied by Americans rush about frantically with an incredible display of hustle and pep, and at last achieve the desired result by chance. Animals observed by Germans sit still and think, and at last evolve the solution out of their inner consciousness.[10] A.N. Whitehead has pointed out that the conception of God of the theologians of Alexandria and Antioch "was sublimation from its barbaric origin. He (God) stood in the same relation to the whole world as early Egyptian or Mesopotamian Kings stood to their subject populations. Also the moral characters were very analogous."[11] The fundamental social organizational changes in Nazi Germany have shown that the direction and extent of scientific work depends upon the prevalent socio-

9. See Talcott Parsons, *The Structure of Social Action*, p. 113.

10. Bertrand Russell, *History of Western Philosophy*, pp. 29-30.

11. A.N. Whitehead, *Adventures of Ideas*, p. 199.

economic structure. Sorokin has observed that centres of military power tend to be the centres of scientific and technologic development.[12] Possibly the paucity of original scientific work in India is due to this reason. The pressure towards techniques and away from serious thought and the emphasis on the statistical method as opposed to the reflective has much to do with the jazz-loving, coco-cola drinking, and gum chewing Americans rather than with the English or the Germans. The stereotyped contemporary literature of Russia is closely related to the regimented harsh organization of Soviet life.

I think these facts are enough to show that knowledge is socially conditioned, while again in its turn, it influences social organization. The social origins and conditions of an idea do not and cannot help to pronounce any judgement upon the value or validity of that idea. For example, would the teaching of the Buddha or Christ be invalidated, if the economic and social conditions in their respective societies are ascertained? The answer can neither be fully in the negative nor in the positive. Christianity arose amidst "the Galilean peasantry who having regard to their climate and simplicity of life, were neither rich nor poor: they were protected from disturbances, from within or from without, by the guardian structure of the Roman Empire. They had no responsibility for the maintenance of this complex system. Their own society was of the simplest; and they were ignorant of the conditions requisite for its efficiency, and of the conditions necessary for its preservation."[13] Moreover the end of the world was believed to be at hand by the founders and early followers of Christianity. It was in these conditions that Christianity arose.

---

12. *Social and Cultural Dynamics*, vol. IV, pp. 249-51.

13. A.N. Whitehead, *Adventures of Ideas*, p. 26.

So necessarily the ethics of Christianity was found to be impracticable, for "in the real world of the Herods and the Roman Empire sevenfold forgiveness touched upon the impracticable"[14] Jesus' knowledge was really limited by the conditions of his earthly life, in particular his period, nationality and education. Some try to guard themselves by declaring that any errors to which he was liable to concerned only his non-religious beliefs, such as matters of geography and physical science, and did not affect his teaching about God. But this attempt to salvage as much as possible for the doctrine of his omniscience is not satisfactory. Jesus' beliefs were part of what was inculcated upon him in the course of his education, just as were his beliefs about the physical world and past history.[15] There is no need to point out the greater impracticability of Christian ethics at present as nobody believes that the end of the world is at hand, nor do we have such a simple contented community as the Galilean peasantry. But this does not point out the validity or invalidity of Christian ethics. In fact, no question of validity arises. The Golden rule of Christ simply means this: I wish (or command) everyone to behave towards his neighbours as he expects them to behave towards him. This sentence is not a proposition, it is a wish or command and can neither be deduced from knowledge of facts nor can it be verified by an observation of facts. It is therefore meaningless to ask whether it is true or not.

Let us take another example, that of the six systems of Indian philosophy. Somewhere in the second century these schools took definite shape.[16] The prevalent tendency in the

---

14. Ibid., p. 27.
15. See C.J. Cadoux, *The Life of Jesus*, pp. 216-17.
16. See J.N. Farquhar, *Outline of the Religious Literature of India*, p. 123.

first and second centuries was to seek an approach (or escape?) from actual facts to an eternal realm of peace. The whole world was made out to be: a great shipwreck. The one important thing was considered to be the saving of oneself from this chaotic world. A morbid suppression of all interest in life and an indifference to all the affairs of the world was the prevalent tendency. The narrowly negativistic and gloomily pessimistic interpretation of the Buddha's doctrines together with Aśoka's propagation of pacifism and vegetarianism debilitated and emasculated the people. It cannot be decisively said whether it was this condition of the people which explains why they succumbed to the Indo-Bactrian, the Indo-Parthian and the Kuṣāṇa invasions or whether, it was these invasions which aggravated this condition. However it was in such circumstances, when salvation was looked upon as the *summum bonum* and when the world was looked upon as a hindrance to it, that the six systems of Indian philosophy took definite shape. The need for salvation — to get away from this world of impermanence and imperfection, gave rise to the six schools. All this shows how the socio-economic conditions of northern India at that time prompted a desire for deliverance. All the schools take it as axiomatic that the world is the cause of bondage, that perfection and freedom lies somewhere beyond the world. It can be seen that this view is couched in factually meaningless expressions. They are emotive expressions containing extra-logical terms which cannot be experientially or operatively defined and they assume systems of which they are a part. As such this presumption with which the six systems start is one which is neither true nor false; it is simply meaningless. Another consideration arises. At present no large group of people either in India or elsewhere is yearning for salvation or trying to escape from this world. What then is the relevance of these schools of thought to the present day?

They contain ideas which originated from and hence are relevant to a certain sociological sphere. With the vanishing of that sphere, they lose their relevance and as for truth they never contained it nor were they devoid of it. They were and are meaningless. Jawaharlal Nehru on September 12, 1952 in Lucknow said:

> In this world of fast changing phases, it is not possible to find a solution for problems by adopting methods which had become out-of-date. If India had to make progress the solution for her various complex problems which are so interrelated to one another, should have to be found in the context of new ideologies. The Ideology of Hindu *Dharma* and Hindu Rashtra is completely out of tune, with the present times. If it took root in India it would smash the country to pieces.[17]

It is therefore to be concluded that "the function of the findings of sociology of knowledge lies somewhere in a fashion hitherto not clearly understood, between irrelevance to the establishment of truth on the one hand, and entire adequacy for determining truth on the other."[18] Determination of the truth or otherwise of sets of propositions is the prerogative of science. Nevertheless the sociology of knowledge shows us that developments in thought are conditioned by the prevalent social structures. Not only the problems selected by theology, philosophy and sciences are so determined; but also the socio-cultural context goes to make up the concepts and categories of thought. Further, sociology of knowledge exhibits the irrelevance of certain ideas and theories as soon as it is shown that the socio-cultural set-up which gave rise to them is no longer present. Also certain words acquire fresh

17. *The Hindu*, September 16, 1952.

18. See Karl Mannheim, *Ideology and Utopia*, p. 256.

meaning in course of time and to describe facts still in terms of such words involves the question of understanding the meaning given to that word when at first applied and whether we may still continue to apply that word in the same sense or, whether we should find a different word in view of the original meaning being obsolete. The word "father" has significance to the Romans of the early republic which is different from that it has to Americans of today. For the former it recalled a stern dominating person, for the latter a tender benevolent one. Now when the conception of the fatherhood of God is put forward, in which sense is it to be understood?[19] So no philosophy could be understood in vacuum, it must be studied in relation to the sociological framework in which it has risen and the conceptual patterns current then.

Developments in Psychology and their bearing

Knowledge is socially conditioned. But anthropologists have noted the fact that social organization has a twofold aspect. "On the one hand and perhaps primarily, it is an organization of the food-quest. On the other hand, hardly less fundamentally, it is an organization of marriage."[20] Finally it may be inferred that knowledge, like everything else is conditioned by the elemental factors of hunger and sex.[21] Thus a reconciliation of both Marx and Freud is found.

Psychology has established the fact that the primary motive forces of human nature are instincts; that all human activity, mental and physical, is the resultant of the prompting of instincts to satisfy themselves. "The instincts are the prime movers of all human activity. All the complex intellectual

---

19. See A.N. Whitehead, *Religion in the Making*.
20. See R.R. Marett, *Anthropology*, p. 159.
21. F.H. Allport, *Social Psychology*, p. 167.

apparatus of the most highly developed mind is but the instrument by which these impulses seek their satisfaction."[22] While McDougall postulates a plurality of these basic forces, Freud conceives of an unconscious. The mind is supposed to consist of two parts, the conscious and the unconscious. The contents and workings of the conscious part are the expressions of forces within the unconscious. The existence of society requires the suppression of many unconscious desires. All intellectual activity is a compensation for thwarted instinctive activity. The child finds itself in a hostile world and tends to rely on its father for guidance and protection. But as the child grows up the father unaccountably fails it, due to want of power and also want of interest in the child. So it longs for a heavenly father to take the place of the earthly father. Religion is derived from this childish feeling of helplessness. Release of some of the instincts would make society impossible. So, ethics is invented to check such instincts. Conscience is the "result of instinctual renunciation."[23] For example the Golden Rule which exhorts us to love our neighbour as ourselves would be unnecessary unless we have an instinctive hate for him. Not only religion and morality, but also science and philosophy are compensations for thwarted instinctual activity. It is our basic unconscious instincts which determine what we think true and right. Even the reasoning which we undertake to prove our conclusions is a sublimation of these instincts. We try to find reasons for that which we instinctively and unconsciously believe. Natural forces such as those that guide animals guide us. Modern psychology thus justifies Aristotle's insight which classified man among the then known animals. Centuries later the Swedish naturalist, Linnaeus (CE 1735)

---

22. McDougall, *Outline of Psychology*, p. 218.
23. See Sigmund Freud, *Civilisation and Its Discontents*, p. 114.

included man among the animals. His French contemporary, Buffon also placed man in the animal kingdom, but was compelled to withdraw his statement due to the pressure of the Church.

Psychology constrains us not to take any theory that is put forward on its face-value but to analyse and see what unconscious forces, and what racial memories prompt such a theory. "Personality is largely a social fact."[24] Thus for example Freud's constant harping on the important role which a father plays in the child's life makes us wonder whether he was not a patriarchal-centric character, a typical representative of a bourgeois society demanding obedience and subjection. Also his conception of "Censor" and his assertion that the "Censor" tries to hold in check the impulses which make society impossible involves Freud's unconscious rejection of the impulses tabooed by the bourgeoisie society of which he was a member. When we study the doctrines of class-hatred and the interpretation of history as a series of class-struggles, we should remember that Karl Marx was a banished and sick man with a lot of children living in ill-ventilated quarters of crowded London. Bertrand Russell has sought to account for Dewey's philosophy in the fact that Dewey is a New Englander born and bred amidst a community governed by industrialism and collective enterprise.[25] It is to be wondered whether Gandhi would have been a "mahātmā" and preached "non-violence" if he had studied science, geo-politics and world history like Nehru and seen a little more of England, while he was there instead of confining himself to his attic. Radhakrishnan's apologetic justification of the caste-system, his infatuation with Advaita and his belief that Hinduism

---

24. See F.H. Allport, *Social Psychology*, p. 99.
25. See Bertrand Russell, *History of Western Philosophy*, p. 854.

provides the corrective to our distracted age and that "it is an outlook that satisfies the intellect"[26] may be explained on account of his birth and upbringing in an orthodox south Indian Smārta brāhmin family. His hope that Hinduism could reconcile the deep-rooted and diverse traditions and enable people to live in amity and freedom expressed in 1942 has been falsified by subsequent events. His effort to interpret Śaṅkara's theories as idealistic and to compare Śaṅkara with Bradley[27] are due to his friendship with Muirhead and Mackenzie and the great prestige which Bradley and Bosanquet were enjoying at that time in England. It is to be once again emphasized that an individual's upbringing and unconscious motives will not decide the validity of any theory. But when what is concerned is a series of value-judgements which can not be pronounced to be true or false, it helps us to know what makes that person hold such a view. Compare these lines of Shakespeare,

> Present mirth hath present laughter;
> What's to come is still unsure,
> In delay there lies no plenty.
> Then come kiss me, Sweet-and-twenty,

with those of Shelley,

> Come, trace
> The epitaph of glory fled,
> For now the Earth has changed its face
> A frown is on Heaven's brow.
>
> Away, away, from men and towns,
> To the wild wood and the downs
> To the silent wilderness
> Where the soul need not repress.

---

26. *The Cultural Problem*, Oxford Pamphlets, p. 50.

27. See S. Radhakrishnan, *Indian Philosophy*, vol. II, chap. 8.

Compare again these lines of Wordsworth,

> My heart leaps up when I behold
> A rainbow in the sky;
> So was it when my life began,
> So is it now I am a man.

with these of Shelley,

> Out of the day and night
> A joy has taken flight:
> Fresh spring, and summer, and winter hoar
> Move my faint heart with grief.

Why should life and the world appear in such different ways? And which attitude among them is the right one? None of them is the right one or the wrong one. They are merely emotive experiences expressed verbally.[28] If we wish to understand them we must go deeper and see why a particular type of emotive expression is evoked from a particular man. Thus the study of a man's character and of his habits and environment provide a clue towards understanding and appreciating his theories and beliefs. Not only is it necessary to study any theory in relation to the socio-economic structure in which it arises, but also it is necessary to pay attention to the character and personality of the man who puts it forth. Bertrand Russell's History of Western philosophy is a notable attempt to proceed on these lines.

The Nature of Thought

Some might wonder what all this has got to do with thought which is abstract and pure, because there are still many who think that there is in us a faculty, a lumen naturale, God-given, by the exercise of which we could straightaway arrive at truth;

28. For the definition of "Emotive expression," see I.A. Richards, *The Principles of Literary Criticism*.

and that such truth is not posterior to or dependent on sense-knowledge. Psychology does not support this view. Spearman has expressed this very clearly — "The first of these distinctions is a profound gulf which has from the most ancient time been declared to lie between sensory perception and abstract thinking — on behalf of the sensory perception was claimed the virtue of prior, or even of sole, genuine validity. For the thinking, the counterclaim was raised that this appertains to the lone infallible power of "intellect" or "reason." The trenchant line dividing up cognition has now been drawn elsewhere. It no longer marks off any distinct sphere of sense-perception, but one of experience-apprehension, a very different feat. As for the other or classical division, namely between perceiving and thinking — it can no longer be acknowledged to effect any sharp cut, but only a gradual transition."[29]

The belief that the human mind differs from the animal mind is based on the supposition that we can form abstract ideas which do not depend on sensory evocation. It is true we can use words having abstract meaning. But it does not prove there is a corresponding mental content.[30] When we think of a war, a famine, a nation, a melody, etc. we do not have a corresponding sense evocation. But hardly anybody would be prepared to say that wars, famines, nations and melodies are subjective experiences or pure thought. So certain objective experiences need not have correlative sense-evocation. This proves that there is no difference between pure thought and objective sensory knowledge.[31]

---

29. Spearman, *The Nature of Intelligence and the Principles of Cognition*, p. 78.
30. Bertrand Russell, *Analysis of Mind*, p. 213.
31. Hollingsworth, *The Psychology of Thought*, p. 184.

To take the excitation of certain nerve centres and the cortical centres of the brain as the criterion of objectivity is a mistake. What is the meaning when it is said that physical stimulation of nerve centres is involved in sense-perception? The neurologist can see cortical molecules dancing in my occipital lobe, when I have an experience of seeing a colour. Similarly he experiences a movement in the string that he may glue to my tympanum, when I have the experience of hearing a sound. All this is of no significance, except that certain experiences of mine are correlated with those of the neurologist. Correlations are found everywhere, between a man's weight and his height, between his income and the house rent he pays, between the rate of fall of a freely falling body and the time it has taken to fall from rest. Correlations do not indicate anything nor are they a mystery. Experience is full of them.[32] But analysing a little further we may be tempted to ask, does the neurologist experience something in my nerve centres and cortex or in his own? Unless he makes certain inferences, what the neurologist observes is only certain experiences happening within him.[33]

It is supposed that sense knowledge differs from pure thought, but the basis of the distinction is not explained. Is it pure thought when we are thinking of something without sensory excitation at all? Then as Buhler has said, "every object can be thought distinctly without help from sensuous presentation."[34] Nor is there a difference in immediacy between the two. A mental process occurs and is known when it is attended to and distinguished from other experiences. So an outer event happens and is known when it is again

32. Ibid.

33. See Bertrand Russell, *An Outline of Philosophy*, p. 140.

34. Uber Gedanken, vol. IX, p. 303.

distinguished from the others. One might stand in front of something for minutes without knowing that he is doing so. Anything either "mental" or "material" is known when it is selected from the other events. The "not self" is known as immediately as the "self."[35] "Introspection does not give us something radically and fundamentally different from external observation."[36]

A man is said to "perceive" a table, a book or some such thing. He is said to "wish" for honour or "believe" in democracy. Wherein is the difference between a perception, a wish, a belief and a thought? When somebody experiences a table almost all the fellow-men present will report the same experience. But the number of people who report the same experience when the presence of desire, belief or anger is reported is lesser. The difference noted between the two types of experiences is not a fundamental, ontological one. I say I "perceive" an object, a difference, or a relation when the majority of my fellow-men give a similar report. I say I "feel" or "judge" an object, a difference or a relation or whatever else it is when the reports of observers are likely to be frequently contradictory. When I say I "believe," the degree of confidence is taken into consideration. But these are only statistical differences, no fundamental, ontological difference is found between a perception, a belief and a thought. If however it is said that a desire differs from a joy in many ways, "so does my fountain pen differ in many ways from a whiff of smoke, an itch, an oyster, and a glass of lemonade."[37]

Rignano arrived at the conclusion that reasoning is a series of operations imagined to be performed on the subject in which

---

35. N.O. Lossky, *The Intuitive Basis of Knowledge*, p. 92.

36. Bertrand Russell, *The Analysis of Mind*, p. 40.

37. Hollingsworth, *The Psychology of Thought*, p. 178.

one is interested. The experiments are not actually performed because a series of similar experiments have been actually been performed by us in the past and their results are known to us.[38] Rignano quotes Mach and Miller in his support. Though he arrives at it from different considerations, Thurston advocates an analogous theory: "To think is to expect to act. To think is also necessarily to entertain a conflict between two or more acts."[39] The very interesting view of Newman that judgement is the result of the functioning of the illative sense, which is nevertheless a sense. He instances Napoleon's judgements, judgements on the battlefields, a peasant's judgement that rain is imminent from an observation of weather, and says that judgements in science and theology are not of a different nature.[40]

However what I am concerned to show is that while Thurston says that thought is an expectation of action, Rignano calls it imagined action. Hollingsworth and Bertrand Russell make out thought to be behaviour. Neurologists have arrived at the conclusion that mind is a manifestation of energy change, taking place in the special cells of the brain — the neurones. The various chemical processes going on in the brain condition mental processes. The materials involved in these processes, such as oxygen, the interaction of the endocrines, vitamins, state of the blood, etc. can ultimately explain all mental phenomena. Such is the hope of scientists.[41] Biochemistry and especially endocrinology have revolutionized the conception of human personality. Apart from the chromosomes, much of a man's action and thought

38. Rignano, *The Psychology of Reasoning*, p. 81.

39. Thurston, *The Nature of Intelligence*, p. 36.

40. Newman, *The Grammar of Assent*, pp. 332, 339.

41. See R.J.A. Berry, *Your Brain and its Story*.

depend upon secretions passing into the blood from the endocrine or ductless glands and the nature of the food taken.[42] "We are what we are in no small measure by virtue of our thyroid glands — a pinch too little of thyroxin spells idiocy, a pinch too much spells raving delirium."[43] "No one with blood containing slightly too low calcium content and markedly low phosphorus content has a wholesome attitude towards life."[44] Louis Berman in an illuminating book, *The Glands Regulating Personality*, explains how a person's physical, emotional and intellectual characteristics depend upon the activity of the endocrine glands. He proceeds to show that the thoughts, actions and physique of persons like Florence Nightingale, Napoleon, Shelley, and Caesar are the outward expressions of the activity of their ductless glands. Unfortunately we cannot apply this method to any of the Indian thinkers like Nāgārjuna, Śaṅkara, etc. due to the paucity of reliable and adequate biographical data. When we find the repeatedly pessimistic views voiced forth in the Post-Buddha literature and philosophy as contrasted with the *Ṛgveda* and Brāhmaṇas, it is to be remembered that a great change has taken place in the diet habits of the brāhmins who are usually the authors of post-Buddha literature and philosophy. Absence of requisite quantities of meat, milk and fresh vegetables over generations may debilitate people and might make their thought as anaemic and weak as their bodies.[45] Might this be one of the reasons for the absence of any appreciable quantity of valuable scientific and philosophical work in contemporary India and Africa?

---

42. F.H. Allport, *Social Psychology*, Chap.V; Peter Laslett, ed., *The Physical Basis of Mind.*

43. Hopkins, *Endocrinology*, p. 101.

44. Ibid., p. 115.

45. F. H. Allport, *Social Psychology*, p. 90.

It is to be emphasized that it is no more of any use to study the history of philosophy in the abstract, as psychology has conclusively established that there is no purely a priori knowledge or rational knowledge that thought is not largely different from perception and as brain chemistry has proved that thought is physico-chemically conditioned. Older psychologists like Binet also were aware that there is no decided difference between perception and reasoning.[46]

It was usual to interpret history as a chronicle of the actions of men and women, while histories of philosophy were usually a description of the ideologies that were held by men down the ages. It should now be borne in mind that actions themselves are not fundamental; they are the expressions of ideas entertained within. On the other hand ideas are not something self-contained. Actions and physical conditions are constantly mobilizing the structure of a society. Changes in social structure call for a change in the mental climate. Thus ideas, actions and physical conditions are inextricably interwoven. A history that neglects to study the guiding ideas that have shaped the socio-political structure is incomplete. A history of philosophy that fails to take into account the various social and physical factors that have given rise to and have shaped those philosophies is useless.[47] It will be clear why we should know the socio-economic, racial and geographical characteristics of the Śākya tribe and the Galilean peasantry to understand and appreciate the teachings of the Buddha and Christ.

---

46. See Rignano, *The Psychology of Reasoning*, p. 159; A. Bain, *Mental and Moral Science*, p. 2.

47. E.A. Ross, *Social Psychology*, p. 4.

Effects of Geographical Environment on Thought

Science emphatically repudiates the existence of any faculty *sui generis* which can lead us to truth independently of the senses.[48] It teaches that intelligence, the organ of thinking is made, heredity playing a part in the making. A child is not born with a readymade "reason" which will in course of time unveil the truth for him. This applies to racial or national mind. It does not mean that the racial mind or national mind goes through every step of development which an individual's mind undergoes; nor that there is such an object as the racial mind or national mind.

Recognized authorities on social psychology have concluded that the geographical characters of a country determine the occupations of people while they are in the first stages of cultural development.[49] The occupations of people determine their social and domestic organization. Giddings held that environment determines the composition of the population, which determines the mental characteristics.[50] These tend to influence the formation and growth of the racial character and mind.[51] The Marxist school does not accept that geographical factors exert any great influence. But experiments of a considerable body of sociologists establish their importance beyond doubt. Even Marxism recognizes that geographical environment "influences the development of society, accelerates or retards its development."[52]

48. R.H. Wheeler & J.P.T. Perkins, *Principles of Mental Development*, p. 3.
49. F. Thomas, *The Environmental Basis of Society*, Chap. XII.
50. Ibid., p. 143.
51. McDougall, *The Group Mind*, p. 233.
52. *History of the CPSU*, p. 186.

Geographical environment affects people in many ways.[53] A hot moist climate depresses the vitality of people and makes them indolent. People living in dry hot climate are capable of great activity but cannot sustain it for long. People living in cool climate are capable of sustained activity. The laziness of the Malays is the product of their hot moist climate. The Arabs rose to a violent spasm of great activity, but relapsed and fell into insignificance. Their dry hot climate has much to do with it. The English exhibit the effects of cool climate.[54]

The Indo-Gangetic plain runs from the foot of the Himalayas up to the Vindhya-Satpura Mountains. It stretches over a distance of 1500 miles. In the west it touches the edge of the Iran plateau and its eastern end goes up to the Patkai Range and Lushai Hills of Burma. Once this huge area was sea, but year after year through countless centuries the Indus and the Ganges and their tributaries washed sediment from the Himalayas and deposited layer upon layer. The Indo-Gangetic plain was made by these two mighty rivers. The plain is one of the greatest alluvial tracts in the world; these rivers have levelled the land. The soil is deep and at places very rich. South of the Vindhya range is the Dakṣiṇapatha, the land irrigated by the Godāvarī, the Kr̥ṣṇā and the Kāverī. This again consists of a series of small river-valleys. The climate varies greatly over this sub-continent. The season of cold weather is of brief duration in India. It falls during the months of December-January; the weather is fine, but usually cyclones visit the plains. From March 21, summer begins. Then for days work is impossible outdoors. Vegetation becomes dry and withered. Violent winds raise clouds of dust in the dry regions. Even indoors people sweat awfully and a sort of restlessness

---

53. Paschal, *The Races of Man*, p. 315.

54. E.C. Semple, *Influences of Geographic Environment*, p. 608.

and inertia seizes everybody. Most people take a nap or lie on their cots in a dazed condition. In the cities and towns the rich few and the workers in the offices are in recent times enjoying the benefits of the electric fan. In the plains in the middle of June, the heat and drought are unbearable. This helps to produce low atmospheric pressure. And then the monsoon bursts, clouds gather and heavy rains fall. Violent thunderstorms occur. The atmosphere becomes saturated with moisture.

Thus nowhere in India, unless one has money and sojourns to Darjeeling or Ooty Hills, cool climate is available. In the summer one is scorched and struck dazed by the terrible heat and in the rainy season the climate is very moist. Only between the Iran plateau and the Aravalli Range we have a region under the influence of a dry wind system at all times. The region includes Rājpūtānā, Sindh and Baluchistan. Much of this is now in Pakistan. No wonder the arid low lands have been the home of the valiant Rājpūts, and the arid highlands of the indomitable Paṭhāns. In the river valleys abundant rich crops yielded without hard labour, plus the dry moist climate discourage human endeavour to any large extent. Life becomes easy. Powers of endurance and spirit of adventure vanish. "Lands of perennial plenty have never been lands of power."[55] It may be surprising to the foreigners to know that the Indian peasant in the rice- and wheat- producing regions does nothing for months. He ploughs and sows, then for months he has nothing to do. Then comes the harvest season when he is occupied for a few days, and once the corn is securely stored or sold away, he has nothing to do for months till the monsoon breaks. He does not keep much poultry; he has no bee-keeping or sheep, he has one or two cows or buffaloes. Some peasants have a

55. J.R. Smith, *Industrial and Commercial Geography*, pp. 5-8.

pair of bullocks. If he is an agricultural labourer he has not even that. When we remember that most of the Indian population is made up of small peasants or agricultural labourers, the amount of time spent in sheer laziness by these people is amazing and if one is a brāhmin, life is still easier. In the morning in the villages from house to house he goes and collects rice, vegetables and curds. If there is a ceremony he attends to it and receives his fees. He has nothing more to do. "The undeniable fact of the leisure of the peasantry, which when it is least, is about three months in the year."[56] Statisticians and Economists have commented upon the low turnover of the Indian factory worker. Except in the barren lands of Rajasthan, the mountain districts of Maharashtra, Nepal and a few other places, where the niggardliness of nature has made the inhabitants vigorous, Indians as a rule are not resolute, self-reliant and energetic. "Asiatics lack spirit and are content to remain in subjection and slavery."[57] "Asiatics will not, under any provocation burden themselves with a sustained habit of taking trouble."[58] Surprised principals of technical and agricultural colleges told Prime Minister Nehru during his American tour that Indian students showed great aversion to physical labour.

Much has been made of the Indian scenery. The Himalayan scenery is wild and grand. Frowning crags, overlooking rock-strewn valleys, torrential streams plunging over rocky ledges and roaring through deep narrow gorges, piercing winds sweeping across the valleys, huge glaciers gliding slowly down from the ice fields of mountain crests — all this is true of the Himalayas. But who lives there? In the plains there is absolutely

---

56. J.B. Kriplani, *The Gandhian Way*, p. 20.

57. Aristotle, *Politics*, VII.7.

58. See Meredith Townsend, *Europe and Asia*.

no scenery, except the endless and monotonous rotation of crops and uncultivated tracts of wild vegetation. There is no variety of rich and pleasing scenes, for example one might travel from Chennai to Visakhapatnam or from Vijayawada to Nagpur. There are a few hills and plateaux, shrub jungles and stretches of cultivated fields. But nothing more than that is to be found unless one is a Wordsworth. Necessarily, therefore, finding little to satisfy him in the contemplation of the outer world, the Indian turns inward. His literature and philosophy are subjective. In art the outward objects are utilized to serve as symbols for the inner broodings. Unable to find any joy or worth in the world the typical Indian mind becomes indifferent to it and turns inward, imagines another world of beauty and goodness and revels therein. "Indian philosophy is pessimistic," writes S. Radhakrishnan, "if by pessimism is meant a sense of dissatisfaction with what is or exists."[59] So dissatisfied with and unable to face existence, the Indian mind occupies itself with what is non-existent or with what is super-existent. "The real, positive world disappears from the Hindu's eyes," says A.H. Guyot.[60]

The huge mountains, the great rivers and the boundless plains overwhelm the people living in countries like India. Poisonous cobras and scorpions, swarms of mosquitoes, flies and rats, the various epidemics like cholera, malaria and plague produced by these latter are everyday sights in India. The mighty rivers and their annual floods which destroy a great deal of life and crops, the erratic monsoon which produces famine often by failing to come in time and the torrential rains and thunderstorms which are common in the rainy season, are so devastating that the best efforts of man are made

59. S. Radhakrishnan, *Indian Philosophy*, vol. I, p. 50.

60. See his, *Earth and Man, Comparative Physical Geography*, p. 287.

unavailing. Then the boundless plains, the huge mountains and the irresistible rivers and epidemics overpower the minds of people. When man sees these savage forces of nature all around him he has no hope of either understanding their laws or controlling them. On the other hand he falls prostrate before them and offers worship. In India the cobras are still worshipped; there is a festival in their honour, the Nāga Pañcamī. The rivers are worshipped; the Ganges, the Yamunā and the Godāvarī are offered flowers, incense, fruits, and coins. [Many times I have thrown fruits and coins into the river Godāvarī as an offering, while crossing it in train.] Cholera and Plague deities are still worshipped under the names of Mahāmārī, etc. in every Indian village, when the epidemics are prevalent; goats and buffaloes are offered to them in sacrifices. (In some states recent legislative action has prohibited this practice). All this encourages superstition; no effort is made to discover the laws that govern these natural forces or to control them. It is to be remembered that in modern times no Indian has made even a single discovery of outstanding merit either in the field of medicine or any of the other sciences or by way of mechanical appliance. "Our contribution to the development of legal science, and jurisprudence has been almost negligible," thus remarked Justice A. Krishna Swami Aiyar.[61] Being a specialist in that field Aiyar has spoken with authority about law and jurisprudence. But his remarks equally hold well about philosophy, and I believe, the other subjects also. Sentiment and a sense of mistaken patriotism ask us to refer to Caraka and Suśruta, Bhāskara and Varāhamihira, and attribute the sorry state of affairs in modern and medieval times to Muslim and British Rules. It is worthwhile to quote Alberuni in this

---

61. Delhi University Convocation Address, November 30, 1951.

connection. "Even the so-called scientific theorems of the Hindus are in a state of utter confusion devoid of any logical order, and in the last instance always mixed up with the silly notions of the crowd. I can only compare their mathematical and astronomical lot, as far as I know it, to a mixture of pearl shells and . . . of pearls and dung."[62] The cause lies in the very atmosphere and climatic conditions of India which have gone to build up certain innate mental traits, which are averse to scientific reasoning and loves to revel the fanciful and the grotesque, the superstitious and the awesome. One may of course call this the spiritual attitude and then say that "the dominant character of the Indian mind is the spiritual tendency. . . . It is mysticism."[63] Radhakrishnan admits that the Indian mind is synthetic and speculative, while the European mind is scientific and analytic. And he adds "it is the natural conditions of India that account for the contemplative turn of the Indian mind."[64]

These are the chief traits of the Indian mind which are due to the effects of geographical environment. "Environment makes the race."[65] How has this been accomplished? Working on successive generations of men and women, geographical environment has suppressed the tendency towards free enquiry and scientific reasoning, and has stimulated imagination and superstition. It thus conditions the character of religion and philosophy, literature and art, law and habits.[66] In short it creates a particular type of social structure, which persisted over a long period and reinforced by the effect of

62. E.G. Sachau, ed., *Alberuni's India*, p. 25.

63. S. Radhakrishnan, *Indian Philosophy*, vol. I, p. 41.

64. Ibid., vol. I, p. 31.

65. J.R. Smith, *Industrial and Commercial Geography*, p. 4.

66. E. Huntington, *World Power and Evolution*.

physical environment on each new generation, moulds the innate qualities and forms the racial mind.[67] No Indian need be apologetic and explain away these facts unless he wants to be very patriotic and very Indian. Nor do I see any reason why one should use those hazy terms "spiritual" and "other worldly" instead of "the plain irrational" and "unworldly," for to be spiritual is to be not intellectual and to be other worldly is to be unworldly. It might be objected that to be spiritual is to be supra-rational. It must be remembered that whatever is not rational is irrational, whether it is supra-rational or sub-rational.

---

67. McDougall, *The Group Mind*, pp. 218-19, 233.

2

Origins of Philosophy

Emergence of Philosophy

ANTHROPOLOGISTS have studied the ideas and customs of savages. Psychologists have come to the conclusion that mythology, folk-lore and the superstitions that are found in any society are the fossils of primitive mentality. Psychoanalysis has again thrown light on the way the instincts and impulses are curbed and adapted to the needs of society and then rationalized.

Primitive man acted in accordance with emotions roused by a series of images. Systematic thought developed very late in human history. In the Palaeolithic age men lived in small groups of families and subsisted by hunting and some form of food-gathering. Social life is the resultant of the interaction between two opposing tendencies — the instinct of youth to pair off and go by themselves, and the learning of the advantages that come from staying together. Learning of course does not presuppose any high degree of thought. The rat in the maze if given mild electric shocks in one of the alleys "learns" not to go into that again. A horse if fed with oats in one particular part of the stable for some days will "know" its place and walk in. So the primitive man learns the advantages of herding and the tribe is in formation. This, as we can see, involves a certain amount of the curbing of individual egoism and the formation of what can be called the group mind. The diffusion in tool-technique over vast regions of the habitable surface of earth is due to the group mind. The Palaeolithic age is evidenced by the discoveries in south India of hand-axes of the nomadic hunting groups of those days.

Due to changing climatic conditions some animals have migrated, some of the species died out. Also the ruthless hunting of certain types of animals diminished their numbers. So the hunter instead of migrating with the animals began to accustom himself to his environment and began to try other sources of food. In the Mediterranean wheat grew wild and in south India similar must have been the case with rice. Man must have collected these seeds and eaten. Some seeds dropped by chance in moist soil which sprouted up must have set him thinking — that is to say must have forced him to connect the two events. He must have then purposely sowed them. The discovery of cultivation was a very important event, which put a stop to man's wanderings and enabled him to settle. It was an enormous revolution. By this time a kind of concept of causality — that certain things and events are connected together was formed: You put your foot on a sharp thorn, your foot is pricked, pain results; you drop a grain of rice in moist soil, it grows. The primitive man made axes from stones. Thus he was led to form the notion of causality as the making of something, and the production of something.

Primitive man tended to think of everything — stones, beasts, trees, wind and rain like him. The stone and the beast have a definite shape like himself; they also act and fight like himself, when the savage knocks himself against a stone he thinks the stone has hit him. We can see this sort of tendency in children. The wind whistles past, whispers and talks, knocks things down. Why? Naturally, just as a man might whistle and dance, whisper and kick things down. Thus the primitive people anthropomorphized every object. Just as a man may be cajoled to do a favour by nice words, gestures and presents of food and drink, the wind and the rain, the trees and the stones can also be won over.

As he stood by the grave-side and put food and utensils into the tomb for the use of the dead, primitive man felt the necessity for assuming some form of continuance even after death. The belief in a continuant something after death was probably derived from dream experience, when it was found that something left the body and wandered about freely. So believing to discover in himself a double being — the one corporeal and the other that something, he transferred this notion to every object.

The very little distinction which early man made between himself and animals, birds and reptiles led to totems or the belief that the tribal group had possibly a non-human ancestor. The remarkable similarity which children possessed to one's father or grandfather, led them to think that probably the elders were born again. And as no distinction was made between men, animals and trees, any of these could on death be born as the other.

Respect and fear for the tribal chief or the old man and the emotional reactions which a young savage felt towards his mother in his adolescence were exaggerated in dreams and were also played with by fanciful imagination. This formed a large part in the beginnings of primitive religion. The reverence for the departed and the belief that they might have gone somewhere else and become powerful, reinforced by the fact that they visited the living in dreams, led to the formation of the conception of the sacred. Objects symbolizing the ancestors are "worshipped," and in fact the objects were almost identified with them.

Anything that exceeded the usual strength of man, or the usual course of nature such as meteorites, waterfalls, lightning, eclipses, women in the menstrual period, epileptics and so on make the primitive men think of something indescribably terrible and powerful. It is mysterious and impersonal and inherent in particular or unusual objects. Certain trees, stones and springs are constantly regarded as being indwelt by great force or power. Passing on to them the conception of him as a double being, primitive man regards them as inhabited by a something imperceptible. They are supposed to be animated. The *Atharvaveda* and the *Mahābhārata* record many such animistic beliefs and practices. The *Atharvaveda* though later than the *Ṛgveda*, records the beliefs and practices which are older than those recorded in the other Vedas.[1] The *Atharvaveda* exalts many things such as grass, porridge, bulls, etc. to the rank of supreme powers.[2] Every untoward event comes to be interpreted as the work of disembodied spirits and attempts to propitiate them result in standardized ritual, worship and magic.

The man less credulous than the rest, and clever in knowing how to reap personal advantage from the beliefs of the rest, stands alone in the tribe as the sorcerer. Sorcerer and medicine-man at one time is the forerunner of the priest, philosopher and scientist. He distributes charms, drives away evil forces, causes rain to fall and cures diseases. He passes on his knowledge and his tricks usually to his sons but now and then to his favourites. Thus the sacerdotal caste arises, cleverer than the rest. The priest is disposed to reflect, tends to seek

---

1. Hopkins, *Religions of India*, Chap. XIV; T.W. Rhys Davids, *Buddhist India*, p. 213.
2. A.B. Keith, *The Religion and Philosophy of the Veda and Upaniṣads*, vol. II, p. 445.

more satisfactory explanations of nature, reduces the number of spirits, arranges them in hierarchies, and pretends to be inhabited or possessed by some of them. It is possible for some priests to believe their own inventions so forcibly that by auto-suggestion they really come to believe themselves as the possessed. By the help of fables and myths, the origins of things are explained in tangible form and conduct is guided by them. Here we see the genesis of philosophy. The consecration of a number of myths and ceremonies which makes it possible for the sacerdotal class to live as masters of the tribe gives birth to institutional religion. The existence of Neolithic settlements in which this type of culture existed has been discovered in several places in south India.

Fairly soon after the agricultural way of life is established, a second but equally revolutionary discovery was made — the discovery that certain stones can under special conditions of firing be heated to turn into substances which can be beaten into any desired shape. This recognition of the relationship between copper ore and the metal had far-reaching consequences. For a long time copper was worked only by hammering and cutting. In north India the Chalcolithic Age succeeded the Neolithic Age, while in the south there seems to have been a jump from the Neolithic to the Megalithic Age. Remnants of the Iron Age civilization have been found in Tirunelveli, Chengalpattu and Malabar districts, though they do not enable us to reconstruct the history or civilization of that age.

The earliest agricultural communities known in India were occupying regions of western India that is Baluchistan and Sindh of today. Various types of these cultures have been classified on the grounds of the technique employed in pottery-painting. In one of these, the Kulli culture — baked clay, figurines of women and cattle are an interesting and frequent feature. We know that the earliest attempt at what might be called the conception of a personal deity was the personification of fertility matter into the Great Mother. We find it among the Aurignacians of 15,000 BC (?) and among the Neolithic and Bronze Age Mediterranean people of Crete, Malta, etc. Breasts are shown on several of the figurines; one of them holds two infants in its arms. The wrists of some of them are decorated with bangles. There is no attempt at naturalism in the face; in fact the face is deliberately pinched out of clay into a fantastic aquiline shape. We cannot at this distance of time guess what idea raced through the Kulli artist as he shaped those figures. But the tendency to represent some idea rather than imitate nature which is the distinguishing characteristic of Indian art is present here. Figurines of bulls and cows are also found. These are invariably ornamented. From the contemporary worship of innumerable women deities, bulls and cows by Hindus we can conclude that the roots of this aspect of Hinduism strike back into the pre-historic past. Similar figurines, but more hideous, have been found in the Zhob Valley sites in North Baluchistan. A phallus carved in stone and the figurine of an enormously exaggerated female vulva and thighs were found at the Mogul Ghundai site. It only remained for the two to be combined to form the emblem of *liṅga* as is found today in all Śiva temples.

Excavations, carried on in the plains of Sindh and Punjab have revealed that a great civilization flourished in the Indus Valley. A complete agreement in details of material culture is found in the area stretching from Makran to Kaṭhiāwār and northwards to the Himalayan foothills. In fact, the Indus Valley culture may have been connected with south India as the gold found there is alloyed with silver and must have come from Kolar and some of the gems discovered there seem to belong to Nilgiris. Houses built of burnt bricks and wide streets with public drains, stamp seals engraved with similar scenes and uniform script and a standard system of weights have been unearthed. Wheat, barley, beef, mutton, pork, poultry and fish were eaten. Within the area above-described all products are of uniform standards, the houses, the pots, the ornaments, etc. The cities of Harappā and Mohen-jo-dāro are of common ground plan each having a defence citadel towering above the rest of the town. They may have been contemporary. All these point out a centralized, urban, complex and luxurious civilization. Wheeler assumes that priest-kings wielding absolute power and the navigable river providing the means of communication ruled the civilization. Some form of Mother-Goddess was worshipped. A sealing representing a female from whose womb a plant issues has been found. This suggests that some female vegetation god or earth-goddess was worshipped. The black goddess Kālī, the goddess Sīrī of whom Pāli literature speaks and many of the *grāma-devatā*s of contemporary Hinduism may have descended from her. A horned three-faced male god in yogic posture has also been found represented on many of the seals. He might be the precursor of Śiva, the supreme *yogī*. Evidences of phallic worship, of *pīpal* worship, of some deity reclining on the branches of the *pīpal* are found. While the two earlier still continue, we have Viṣṇu depicted as sleeping on the *vaṭa* leaf (*vaṭa-patra-śāyī*) in the Purāṇas. There are no evidences of temples. All this shows how much more Hindu society owes to Harappā and Mohen-jo-dāro, rather than to the invading Aryans for the general view of religious beliefs as found in the Purāṇas and the *Mahābhārata*, which point out that animism prevalent in Indus valley civilization was their source.[3] The

3. W.T. Elmore, *Draviḍian Gods in Modern Hinduism*.

Aryans did not exclusively contribute to these beliefs nor are all the gods and goddesses mentioned in the Purāṇas found in the Veda. In fact, the famous Vedic gods Indra, Varuṇa, Agni do not enjoy any predominant position in the popular Purāṇas such as the *Bhāgavata*, the *Devī-Bhāgavata*, *Śiva* and *Skanda Purāṇas*. Descriptions of the religious beliefs of the people found in the Pāli canon of Buddhism closely tallies with those of the Purāṇas.[4]

The religion of the Hindu Purāṇas and that described and prevalent in the Pāli literature is polytheism. It must be emphasized that it is this polytheism that has been the prevailing religion of the Hindus. In some texts it may have been asserted that the entire universe is derived from "one principle" and that therefore the soul and that "one principle" are one. But that is not monotheism. And even those who held such a view theoretically and actually worshipped and believed in the plurality of gods. Śaṅkara inculcated the worship of five gods (*pañcāyatana pūjā*) and established five differing creeds. Viṣṇu of Rāmānuja and Madhva, has a wife, lives in Vaikuṇṭha, and sleeps on a serpent. Indians writing or speaking for the benefit of Europeans have misrepresented often Hinduism as monotheism, so that it may appeal to the latter. The use of the special word "Īśvara" in some systems of philosophy grew out of the endeavour to distinguish the eternal principle or God from the popular gods, *deva*s. In spite of the philosophical systems, the average Hindu never doubted the existence of gods, demi-gods, and demons. This is too well-known to be repeated or emphasized, but for the fact that some modern writers go on distorting facts. From the fact that Śaṅkara in his *Brahma-sūtra-bhāṣya* speaks of pure-

4. See *Mahā Samaya Suttanta* and *Āṭānāṭiya Suttanta*, in Silas, *Dialogues of the Buddha*, vol. I and II.

being (*viśuddha-sattā*) as God, we cannot say that it is the representative Hindu view, just as the views of John Scotus Erigena, Abelard and Roger Bacon cannot be the representatives of Medieval Christianity. John Scotus held that the divine substance undergoes self-development, and human thought parallels this in its acquisition of knowledge. He further said that in the last analysis all our souls are a single soul and humanity a projection of the deity.[5] Abelard held that a religious truth can never be demonstrated nor can it be experimentally known. Roger Bacon asserted that revelation was made to humanity even prior to Christ, but that man due to his wickedness lost this integral knowledge though not completely, as is evidenced by divine truths, found in pagan writings.[6] Just as medieval Christians shared none of these views, the stray thoughts that we find in the Upaniṣads and the view of God as found in Śaṅkara never became popular. As Bloomfield has remarked, "On the real life of India the great philosophies are merely a thin film. Anyhow they have not as yet penetrated down to the Hindu people."[7] It is the animistic pluralism handed down by the Indus Valley culture that is and was prevalent in India. It is significant that the word Hindu religion is applied appropriately, for the "Hindu" and "Indus" are corruptions of "Sindhu." "To the present day the religious wants of the great mass of the people in India seem satisfied through the idea of the one supreme God, exalted above all other gods."[8]

---

5. De Wulf, *History of Medieval Philosophy*, vol. I, p. 137.
6. Taylor, *Medieval Mind*, vol. II, p. 536; De Wulf, op. cit., vol. II, p. 140.
7. Bloomfield, *The Religion of the Veda*, p. 10.
8. Max Müller, *The Six Systems of Indian Philosophy*, p. 47.

Polytheism or animism was the personification of some power, sometimes it was benign, sometimes it was malign but at any rate operant in real life. The conflicting, catholic experience of man points towards the existence of a plurality of conflicting powers. It is possible that some of the people regarded one of the gods as the prince or supreme magistrate of the rest, who though of the same nature may be ruled by him as earthly subjects as princes are ruled by the king.[9] There was at any rate the phenomenon of theocracies, fusion or identification of one deity with another; the *R̥gveda* (I.164.6) for instance says that the brāhmins call the one by many names. This is not a sublime idea found in the *R̥gveda* alone. Cicero has said that deity, who is different in every part of nature, appears as the earth under the name of Ceres, as the sea under that of Neptune, and so on.[10] Pluralism is the result of the diversity found on all sides. The man of those days was vaguely in search of some explanation for the various occurrences of phenomena. As the phenomena were various, he postulated various causes, though certain things are common to them all a something impersonal and vaguely mysterious hovered behind them all. As he could think of every object as analogous to himself, he invested each of them with a personality. And some of them whom he feared he courted through offerings of food and drink, sacrifice and prayer.

This was the state of the people in the Indus Valley prior to the Aryan invasion. It may be asked how the state of the people's belief in the Indus Valley was known. The figurines and the paintings on pots found in Sumeria and at Mohen-jodāro are similar and so it is thought that both the

---

9. Hume, *Natural History of Religion*, Sect. VI.

10. De Nat. Deor. XXVIII.

Mesopotamian and the Indus Valley Civilizations were parallel and might have been founded by descendents of a common stock of people. The Sumerian clay tablets have been deciphered though not the Indus Valley tablets. We know that the Mesopotamians were polytheistic. They worshipped the sun, the moon and the stars and believed that they had influences over human beings. The Mesopotamian gods were nature deities mostly, though sometimes rulers and chieftains were deified. Evil, god of the city of Nippur, presided over the earth, Iṣṭar, the great goddess at Uruk, patronized fertility and love. There was also the tendency to group and grade the gods into hierarchies and also to fuse them together, similar to the Vedic tendency to speak of gods in groups, — the Viśve Devas, the Ādityas, and the Maruts, etc. The Mesopotamian gods had huge palaces, were worshipped by sacrificial offerings of human beings, but more often of animals. In these temples, evidence of the practice of liturgical devotions, of hymns and songs of some sort of music has been found.

Fusion of Races: Formation of Indian Mind

Innate mental constitution greatly influenced by geography fundamentally determines the social organization; and through it the individuals of each generation.[11]

When once the importance of the race-mind and the permanence it possesses is recognized — as it ought to be in view of the data collected by sociologists and psychologists — another important consideration arises. F.H. Allport emphasizes the importance of "innate difference of capacity" among the different races.[12] What is the effect of the crossing of races with different physical and mental traits? The obser-

11. McDougall, *The Group Mind*, p. 118.
12. F.H. Allport, *Social Psychology*, p. 386.

vation of the blending of White, Negro, and American stocks in South America has resulted in a race inferior to all the above races. The examples of the mulattoes of North America and the West Indies, the Anglo-Indians, the blend of the Javanese and Dutch in Java, and that of the Caucasian and the Yellow race go to prove that crossing of widely different races produces an inferior race incapable of high civilization and progress. This is so because when two widely different races mingle, the number of elements that go to make up the individual will be at war with each other. Consequently the character of the cross-breeds will be made up of inharmonious elements and will be unsteady. On the physical side the cross-breed race will be lacking in vigour and resistance to diseases. Experiments in the crossing of animal breeds reinforce this view.[13]

On the other hand if the crossed races are drawn from stocks belonging to the same principal race, the resultant race is seen to be superior to both the races. In Europe almost all the nations that have been formed were of allied races. In China no cross-breeding took place on a large scale. As a result of the great purity of the race, a large variety of innate qualities was not available and so the Chinese have been unable to produce novel ideas or assimilate other ideas and they stagnated.[14]

In India we have the spectacle of all sorts of races black, white and yellow having made up the population. The result is a race of great heterogeneity which had no unity of purpose or view. From remote times this was the unfortunate fate of India. Some fifty skeletons, mostly fragments of skeletons found at Mohen-jo-dāro, Harappā and Chanhudāro have been

13. McDougall, *The Group Mind*, pp. 242, 279.

14. See Juan Comas, *Race and Myths;* M. Leiris, *Race and Culture.*

classified and reported by the anthropologists. Almost half of the classified skulls belong to the Mediterranean type, to which at the present day constitute a large number of groups of people stretching from Siberia to India. This type are medium to tall in stature, dark to light olive-brown in complexion, with a long head and face, a narrow relatively pronounced nose, black hair and large open eyes ranging from black to brown. They are of slender build. A large section of the population in north India and of the upper classes in south India is of this type. Then three skulls of the Proto-Australoid type were also found. This type is small in stature with a dark skin-colour approaching black, with curly or wavy black hair, long head, broad flat nose, and fleshy protruding lips. The main element of the south and central Indian aboriginal tribes and a large section of the *varṇa bāhyas*, "people beyond the caste system" or outcastes of Hindu society are of this type. A skull belonging to the typical Mongolian type was also found. So diverse was the difference in racial stocks in the Harappā and Mohen-jo-dāro population. To add to this confusion of stocks round about 1500 BC came the Aryans from a region lying somewhere between the Danube and the Oxus. Possibly they belonged to the agricultural tribes which were then stretched across the South Russian steppes and the lands eastwards to the Caspian Sea.

We can only imagine what must have taken place then. The fair-skinned Aryans tried to hold themselves aloof from the conquered races. But in the end they were swamped both by the numbers and the culture of the conquered. As far as possible they must have preferred to mingle with the Mediterranean type rather than with the Proto-Australoid. But through generations a good deal of crossing must have taken place. The contempt which the cross-breeds aroused amongst those who were pure or relatively pure must have given rise to the caste system.[15] These different races with their different racial memories and thoughts must have looked upon each other with suspicion and contempt. The Aryans were the conquerors. But the conquered were highly superior to them in culture and social organization. Both had points of which they could be proud. The different original races and the cross-breeds with their endless variety of custom, creed and social environment must have gone on living for some time. Then a sort of common culture must have resulted. But it was never a homogeneous and uniform culture. This is illustrated in the Vedic and Upaniṣadic literature.

There is no single dominant idea, no unity of purpose, and no evidence of any endearing bond being common to all people which is to be contrasted with the early literature of the Hebrews. There we find a common outlook and a common bond, such that all the Jews thought of themselves as one, as a nation. But in Indian literature we find the *ārya* and *dasyu* difference emphasized throughout the Veda. All the epics are full of the battles fought between these two. The caste system arose due to racial differences. It was very difficult to keep up the purity of the stocks of the original races; so a differentiation based on occupation and colour grew up.[16] Gradually the caste system developed and became rigid; and then the two upper castes began to look upon each other with hostility. The caste system became as Nehru put it "a prison for the mind of our people not only for the lower castes, who suffered most from it, but for the higher ones also. Throughout our history it was a weakening factor and one might perhaps say that along with the growth of rigidity in the caste system grew rigidity of mind, and the creative energy of the race

15. See G.S. Ghurye, *Caste and Race in India*, p. 143.

16. See E. Senart, *Caste in India*, p. 188.

faded away."[17] While the whole body of Pāli literature shows the indifference and the veiled hostility of the kṣatriyas towards the brāhmaṇas, the Brāhmanical literature asserts the superiority of the brāhmaṇas, and how even gods paid homage to them. It is interesting to note that in the Pāli books the brāhmin is so despised that sometimes he is spoken of as of "inferior birth" (*hīna jacco*).[18] Thought and action moved in terms of the duties of one's caste and naturally the rights also of one's caste. In 327 BC the expedition of Alexander took place. Then one of the great Aryan tribes, who in pre-historic times settled and became great in Europe, came into contact with another Aryan tribe settled in India. The effects of the contact are not fully known. But is it possible that Alexander's soldiers and then those of Seleukos have gone home without any contacts with Indian women? Seleukos's daughter at least became Candragupta's wife. This marriage could not have been the only Greco-Indian one. From the ninth century onwards hosts of Arabs, Persians, Turks and Afghans came and settled down as conquerors; and finally came the European races. All these have produced further cross-bred groups, as there is an extreme diversity of social environment; hence no unity of purpose and identity of interests are found among the Indians. Till recently it used to be said that Muslims and Hindus have almost become one. "As a matter of history no such synthesis of religion or culture has taken place in India."[19] Pakistan has falsified this supposition as well as the hope that India has become a well-knit nation. Only the power of foreign conquerors has at least administratively bound together the people of India. Apart from Pakistan there is a huge scattered

17. Jawaharlal Nehru, *The Discovery of India*, p. 72.
18. Jātaka, 5-257.
19. See *The Cultural Problem*, Oxford Pamphlets, p. 6.

Muslim population in India. And then among the Hindus one finds people speaking different languages, belonging to different castes and following different customs; but there is only one common bond — their polytheistic religion. In these days of decreasing influence of religion, it is uncertain whether the bond will last and grow stronger or diminish in future.[20]

To sum up, the nature of Indian thought with its lack of coherence, unity, harmony and a common purpose — what might be called the common national ideals — is due to the blending of widely heterogeneous stocks right from times immemorial. This is an objective fact which ought to be recognized as such. There is no use of getting emotional and saying as some Indians do that all this is false and that Indian thought is the best, the noblest, the most logical and the most spiritual in the world. Every impartial student has recognized the facts set forth above. "From the beginning the Indians felt that truth was many sided," so writes Radhakrishnan, "and different views contained different aspects of truth which no one could fully express." He continues that, "there are dangers . . . to such a breadth of view. Often it has led the Indian thinkers into misty vagueness, lazy acceptance and cheap eclecticism."[21]

What is Philosophy?

One great difficulty met within studies of philosophy is that there is no unanimity as to what philosophy is and what philosophical method should be.

In a way, every man may be said to have a philosophy of his own. It is constituted out of the thoughts and feelings he

---

20. See K.M. Panikkar's views in his authoritative publications.

21. S. Radhakrishnan, *Indian Philosophy*, vol. I, p. 49; Jawaharlal Nehru, *The Discovery of India*, p. 72.

entertains, which as we have seen are the outcome of his milieu. Thus for example a shepherd's philosophy is of this sort:

> I know the more one sickens, the worse at ease he is;
> and that he that wants money, means, and content is without three good friends:
> That the property of rain is to wet, and fire to burn;
> That good pasture makes fat sheep;
> and that a great cause of the night is lack of the sun;
> That he, that hath learned no wit by nature nor art, may complain of good breeding, or comes of a very dull kindred."[22]

But when we are concerned with philosophy as a science it means a set of thoughts put into a system, such that one of them does not contradict another in the set and the entire set as a whole is coherent.[23] This description tries to differentiate philosophy from poetry, theology and science. In poetry what is sought is an expression of what is felt within such that the same complex of feeling is aroused in the reader or hearer. As Longinus has indicated, poetry "which immediately sinks deep, and makes such impression on the mind as cannot easily be worn out or effaced" serves its purpose.[24] Poetry is intended to evoke a certain response, a state of mind in the hearer or reader. "When words are selected and arranged in such a way that their meaning either arouses, or is obviously intended to arouse, aesthetic imagination, the result may be described as "poetic diction."[25] Poetic statements express a certain

---

22. William Shakespeare, *As you like It*, Act III.
23. See W.E. Hocking, *Types of Philosophy*, Chap. I; Bertrand Russell, *History of Western Philosophy*. pp. 11-12.
24. Longinus, *On the Sublime*, sect. 7.
25. Owen Barfield, *Poetic Diction: A Study in Meaning*, p. 13.

attitude. They are neither true nor false; indeed poetry need not refer to facts nor be based on facts. On the other hand philosophy does not aim at producing any particular kind of emotional response. It must be based on facts, and it must consist of propositions; it must be such that a person must be able either to contradict it or accept it as true. It is different from theology because theology claims to have in its possession certain facts which are not and will never be observable or verifiable in the ordinary way. It differs from science in the sense that science consists of knowledge, which is precise, undoubtedly established and verifiable by ordinary experience. Some of the sets of ideas which have been called philosophies fail to fulfil these requirements strictly. Bergson's philosophy, for example, is more akin to poetry than to science. The entire Indian philosophy except that of the Cārvāka and early Sāṁkhya consists of dogmas and that knowledge which is claimed to have been got in an extraordinary way and which is and will never be verifiable in the ordinary way. "Philosophy in India has not as a rule completely freed itself from the fascinations of religious speculation."[26] Very little in Hindu thought could strictly be called philosophy. There are of course those who believe that philosophy must be based on dogma and that only then can it fulfil its task successfully. Some of the medieval thinkers and those two famous scholars of modern India — Aurobindo and Radhakrishnan are of this view. They say that there are sources of knowledge other than those open to ordinary experience. No outstanding philosopher in the West accepts this position. Even the neo-scholastic thinkers do not say that philosophy should be based on revelation. Philosophy, they emphasize, should be based on reason and experience; they only insist

26. S. Radhakrishnan, *Indian Philosophy*, vol. I, p. 26.

that philosophy leads up to theology. This is the position of the great neo-scholastics like, Maritain, D'Arcy, and Gilson among others. It must be very clearly noted that this is not the view of Radhakrishnan and Aurobindo. Radhakrishnan justifies the basing of philosophy on what he calls "soul sense" and "the experience of the pure in heart."[27] Whatever these vague intriguing terms may mean, Aurobindo seeks to have a philosophy based on the integral vision obtained through Yoga. This involves a confusion of philosophy with theology and a certain type of special experience, explained by some psychologists as pathological. Professor Leonard Woolf calls this sort of philosophy "metaphysical quackery."[28]

If philosophy is not as precise and verifiable as science, and on the other hand, if it is as indefinite and unascertainable as theology, one might justifiably wonder what it exactly is.[29] We have a variety of facts — facts which have been discovered by ordinary observation, then again facts gathered in the course of the progress of sciences like physics and chemistry, psychology and biology, mathematical logic and mathematics. Taken in it as self-complete any one of these rigid systems of ideas develops parochialism and assumes it to be of universal application.

Philosophy ought to take into account the totality of experience and survey it as a whole, so that thought may not be vitiated by abstraction and partial over-emphasis and lack of balance. At the bottom of these various aspects of experience there ought to be certain common general ideas. Philosophy should discover them and try to form a coherent system out

---

27. S. Radhakrishnan, *Indian Philosophy*, vol. I, pp. 31, 51.

28. Leonard Wolf, *Quack Quack!*, p. 160.

29. A.N. Whitehead, *Adventures of Ideas*, Chaps. IX and XV.

of them. Sometimes in this effort it will be found that the general ideas presupposed by one of the sciences or one kind of experience contradict the general ideas presupposed by another science or another kind of experience. It is the business of philosophy to bring into the open such inconsistencies in thought, if they are there. For instance it is worthwhile to examine how far the ideas of "survival of the fittest" and "natural selection" are consistent with the ideas of "equal rights of all men" and "equality of races." Again could the conception of "order" and "simplicity" employed by science be consistent with the facts revealed by quantum phenomena and interpreted by Heisenberg's principle? To cite one more instance, can the quantum theory and the theory of relativity be simultaneously applied to matter? Both the theories are independently proved true; but when applied to dimensionless point particles, they were continually stymied by a recurrence of infinite terms in the answers which should have contained finite terms only. The correct solution to this puzzle has a large bearing upon conceptions of the infinite and finite. Also there is another important consideration: if two theories are both true but mutually contradictory does it mean that they are only apparently contradictory or does it mean that we have to give up the principle of non-contradiction? Further if we give up the principle of non-contradiction and hence of identity, as Marxism urges us to do, could we have discovered those two theories on which we are basing our discussion?

Philosophy therefore consists in finding the principles implied in human thought of a particular age and then forming them into a coherent system. But how could anybody take stock of the entire thought of even a particular age and then extract the general principles involved in it? Clearly it is impossible but that should be the guiding ideal. It happens that one inevitably selects certain aspects of experience or some of the sciences which interest him and then tries to build up a system of ideas. Obviously therefore no philosophy can be final, none can be complete. Nor a system of philosophy valid in and for one age will be of value for another age. A philosopher should be careful to indicate the facts on which he bases his system, and the range of experience within which he thinks his system will be applicable. No Philosophy can be all-comprehensive. The fate of the Aristotelian and of the Hegelian systems emphasizes this. The validity of a philosophy is to be judged by the degree of systematization it has been able to impose on a variety of facts and the aspects of experience which it is able to interpret by means of a few general ideas, while not contradicted by other aspects of experience. Philosophy is therefore the "science of sciences, the criticism and systematization or organization of all knowledge."[30]

We should be thoroughly conversant with the old systems of philosophy, not because they are still valid in any large degree but because to understand the past ages we must understand the past philosophies and because it is the past ages which have led to or have become the present. History in every age is constituted by the reactions of men and women towards the basic problems of that age. Human reactions depend upon the beliefs and hopes entertained in a particular age, which are again the products of the circumstances of that age. Philosophy while coordinating the various ideas of an age clarifies the issues and exhibits the relative values of things.

Russell has written, "Science tells us what we can know, but what we can know is little. . . . Uncertainty, in the presence of vivid hopes and fears is painful, but must be endured; if we

30. D.D. Runes, ed., *The Dictionary of Philosophy*, p. 235.

wish to live without the support of comforting fairy tales. . . . To teach how to live without certainty . . . is perhaps the chief thing that philosophy in our age can still do for those who study it." It also provides us with new ideas, new possible ways of looking at things and also a way as to how to evaluate these possibilities. We have, therefore, a constant need for new philosophies. A stagnant philosophy spells the doom of the people that hold it. The bygone civilizations of Greece and Rome and the withering civilizations of China and India are illustrations of this truth.

It is clear from all this that to construct a system of philosophy is not a joke. A jumble of beliefs inconsistent with each other but held together is not philosophy. If a man has certain ideals which are held to be high or sentiments which are "noble" it does not mean that he has a philosophical outlook; neither will all his ideals nor sentiments put together constitute a philosophy, nor will an ethical life be philosophical. If this criterion is applied the judgement upon certain sets of beliefs which are claimed to be philosophic would be so drastic that it will greatly upset their champions. Phrases like the "Śākta philosophy," "Gandhian philosophy," are misnomers. Cults and creeds are not philosophy.

General Features of Indian Philosophy

There are some books claiming to be histories of Indian philosophy. Some of them are mere handy compilations of old texts with their traditional interpretation. Others again are attempts to interpret or explain, usually in the light of modern Western systems of thought. Interpretation or explanation presumes that a proposition is true and tries to make it manifest. Usually histories of Indian philosophy have ignored criticism. To interpret is not to appreciate rationally. Criticism which tests the consistency of the logic of a particular system of philosophy is to appreciate it rationally. It is also very important to notice the first principles assumed by every system and how they have been derived. Much depends on whether they are self-evident taken from some source like a book believed to be revealed or some special science or a particular type of human experience like mysticism. If they are claimed to be self-evident, it is necessary to examine the criterion of self-evidence employed by a system of thought.

Lastly it is necessary to see whether a system of philosophy is in harmony with known facts. Unfortunately no history of Indian philosophy proceeds in this way. Another defect with them is that they confuse religion with philosophy, though the two are not identified. Pūrva Mīmāṁsā is scriptural exegesis of the ritualistic portion. This is a fact recognized by the traditional interpreters as well as the modern. "There is little room for real philosophy in Pūrva Mīmāṁsā." "Jaimini's treatment of the sacrificial system of the Vedas would hardly seem to us to deserve the name of a system of philosophy."[31] So Paul Deussen writes: "But the six orthodox schools are not philosophical systems in the strict sense of the term. The Mīmāṁsā is only a methodical handbook treating the various questions arising out of the complicated Vedic ritual. The Yoga is a systematic exposition of the method of attaining union with the *ātman* by means of concentration in oneself."[32] "Mīmāṁsā is probably counted among the philosophic systems only because of its forms and its connexion with Vedānta doctrine, for it is concerned with the interpretation of the Vedas, classifying its component parts and treating the rules

---

31. Max Müller, *The Six Systems of Indian Philosophy*, pp. 199, 213.

32. Paul Deussen, *Outlines of Indian Philosophy*, Cf. *Indian Antiquary*, vol. XXIX of 1900, p. 397.

for the performance of the ceremonies as also the rewards which singly follow upon the latter."[33]

The Yoga, as Patañjali himself defines, is a discipline which is meant to still the *citta* (mind). The object of Yoga is to put an end to all thoughts: *yoga citta vṛtti nirodhaḥ*. Radhakrishnan has also written that the main interest of Patañjali is the practical motive of indicating how salvation can be attained through disciplined activity.[34] He explains it further, "Yoga discipline is nothing more than the purification of them — body, mind and soul, and preparing them for the beatific vision."[35] "Yoga is indeed, as the brāhmins say, Sāṁkhya, only modified, particularly in one point namely in its attempt to develop and systematize an ascetic discipline by which concentration of thought could be attained, and by admitting devotion to God as part of that discipline."[36] Yet it is surprising to find Yoga classed as a system of philosophy. In a history of British philosophy nobody would include an exposition of celestial rituals and a discussion on the dogmas of a religion. An exposition of the theories that lay behind the Osmophoria and the Omophagia of the Dionysian rites is not included in any history of Greek philosophy, yet strange as it may seem a detailed exposition of the theories about the Vedic sacrifices — the Pūrva Mīmāṁsā — is included in all the histories of Indian philosophy. Max Müller gives a curious reason as to why he included Pūrva Mīmāṁsā in his *The Six Systems of Indian Philosophy*: "In allowing a place to the Pūrva Mīmāṁsā among The six systems of Indian philosophy, I was chiefly influenced

33. See R. Garbe, *The Philosophy of Ancient India*, p. 16.

34. S. Radhakrishnan, *Indian Philosophy*, vol. II, p. 338.

35. Ibid., p. 372.

36. Max Müller, *The Six Systems of Indian Philosophy*, p. 318.

by the fact that from an Indian point of view it always held such a place."[37]

The ancient Hindus had no conception of philosophy as it is now understood; the word *darśana* cannot be translated as philosophy. Moreover Indian writers on the six systems are not unanimous as to what the six are. Haribhadra, Jinadatta and Rājaśekhara mention the Bauddha, the Naiyāyika, the Sāṁkhya, the Jaina, the Vaiśeṣika and the Pūrva Mīmāṁsā. Haribhadra mentions and deals with the Cārvāka system also. Thus the Vedānta school is significant by its omission. The early Jaina literature mentioned five systems besides itself — the Vaiśeṣika, the Bauddha, Sāṁkhya, Lokāyata, Śakti-Tantra.[38] Here the Vedānta system is again omitted. When Max Müller says that Indians regarded the Pūrva Mīmāṁsā as a system of philosophy, he leaves two questions unanswered — which Indians, and what was their conception of philosophy? Does he mean by the six systems only the Brāhmanical or the *āstika* ones? Here again there is no unanimity among the Indian writers. Kumārila regards Sāṁkhya, Yoga, Pañcarātra and Pāśupata as "*a-vaidika*" like Bauddha.[39] Bhīmācārya in his *Nyāya-kośa* classes Sāṁkhya and the Advaita Vedānta among the *nāstika* or "*a-vaidika*." Śaṅkara regards Sāṁkhya as "*a-vaidika*." In these circumstances the phrase "six Brāhmanical systems" is misleading. If the claim of each system to follow the Veda is the criterion of its being Brāhmanical, there will not be six but many more, the Śākta, the Pāśupata, the Śaiva, etc. Nor are they less popular than the others. While nobody in India is a Patañjalite or a Mīmāṁsāka, there are many Śāktas and Śaivas. Simply because two different things have been confused in

37. Ibid., p. 213.

38. Weber, *Sanskrit Literature*, pp. 236, 249.

39. *Tantra-vārttika*, 1.3.4.

the dim past, we need not still maintain the confusion. Astrology and astronomy, chemistry and alchemy were confused by all nations in the past, but there is no reason why we should do so. The Pūrva Mīmāṁsā and the Yoga have no right to be classed as systems of philosophy though ancient Hindus may have done so. In the earlier stages of intellectual development, systematic thought and belief overlap. The point of departure for a history of philosophy is the distinction between the two. No history of Indian philosophy has done this so far.

Stretches of Indian philosophy have been often compared with those of modern philosophy of the West. No doubt there are some points of similarity between any two things. Both the emerald and the leaves of a tree are green. There have been writers who have argued that the Copernican theory is to be found in the Vedas because the *Aitareya Brāhmaṇa* (III.44) and the *Chāndogya Upaniṣad* (3.2.1-3) speak of the sun as never rising and setting, but only changing about after reaching the end of the day and making night below and then again changing about after reaching the end of the night. We have only to remember A.N. Whitehead's famous saying that "everything of importance has been said before by somebody who did not discover it."[40]

It is true that we find anticipations of some modern standpoints in Śaṅkara, Śrī Harṣa, Vedānta Deśika and others. (Ajantā painters have anticipated some of the latest fashions in hair dressing). I have myself indulged in a study of such parallelisms, in one of my earlier books.[41] I have shown there the striking similarities between the philosophies of Śaṅkara and Thomas Aquinas, between the conceptions of existence

40. *Proceedings of Aristotelian Society*, N.S., XVII, p. 72.

41. See my *Rhythm of the Real.*

as found in Vedānta Deśika and in Bertrand Russell and Moore. I have again shown how the theory of the indemonstrability of God's existence is found in Rāmānuja, Madhusūdana Sarasvatī and William of Occam. The close similarity between Śaṅkara's Advaita and the position of St. John of the Cross has also been pointed. The conception of history as found in *Śrīmad Bhāgavata* is very similar to that found in the Bible and St. Augustine. The Upaniṣadic account of creation has points of similarity with that as set forth by Aquinas in his Summas and by Karl Barth. No previous writer had noted these similarities, but I am afraid that all this does not establish anything of much significance, except that parallel thoughts are found in different countries and times. Just because something like what has been put forward by Bertrand Russell or Bradley is found in some ancient Indian thinker, it does not make either the former or the latter more logical. A philosophy is a unity, it has to stand or fall as a whole. Part of it cannot remain and part of it cannot be demolished. Its validity is to be judged by the complete consistency of all its parts with each other.

It must be distinctly remembered that if Indian philosophy is to be compared with anything as a whole, it is Medieval Scholasticism which it resembles most. Many in India think low of Scholasticism, because their ignorance of it is shocking. Scholastic philosophy is a great structure, great both in its scope and the vigour of its a priori method. Unfortunately in Indian universities its study is sadly neglected. However that be, my point for the present is that Scholastic philosophy and Indian philosophy resemble each other a great deal, while there is no resemblance between Indian philosophy and modern philosophy of the West. I am speaking of the resemblance in methodology and in scope, not of a few parallel thoughts here and there. Indian philosophy like Scholasticism assumes a certain subject-matter as unquestionably and absolutely true. "Indian philosophy is closed all around by four walls of unproved dogmas."[42] In India the exceptions are the Lokāyata and the early Sāṁkhya; Buddhism and Jainism are not rationalistic. The Buddha bases his teaching not on reason, but on a peculiar experience of his which he claimed as *bodhi*. The Buddha's teaching is the word for all the Buddhists, anything in contradiction of it cannot be true.[43] Similarly Jainism is based on *kevala jñāna* or omniscience of Mahāvīra, which he obtained after twelve years of wandering and penance and which is full, unimpeded, infinite and supreme.[44] For all the Jainas, Mahāvīra's teaching is the last word and complete truth, he who truly believes the true teaching possesses righteousness.[45] Still a certain work was left for the intellect. Granting that dogma is an established fact, it may be possible to show that these doctrines are not obnoxious to reason and are acceptable to it. As some Vedāntists have put it reason can remove the implausibility of dogma (*asambhāvanā*) and demolish that which is contradictory to dogma (*viparīta-bhāvanā*).

The characteristic of both Scholasticism and Indian philosophy is to systematize and rationalize religious dogma. There was another point which determined the peculiar character of both. The scholastics had at hand a large mass of knowledge about history, geography and the natural sciences — collected by the Greeks and Arabs. But the Schoolmen never cared to acquaint themselves with it. Similarly in India, there were a lot of facts collected by astronomers, mathematicians

42. S.N. Dasgupta, *Contemporary Indian Philosophy*, p. 177.
43. A.B. Keith, *Buddhist Philosophy*, p. 33.
44. Sinclair Stevenson, *The Heart of Jainism*, pp. 38-39.
45. *The Uttarādhyayana*, Sacred Books of the East, XIV, p. 154.

and travellers. In CE 499 Āryabhaṭa's great work was available, in which he stated that the earth is a sphere diurnally revolving on its axis, that the eclipses are caused by the shadow of the earth or moon. Varāhamihira lived in the sixth century. Brahmagupta composed his books in the seventh century. In the twelfth century Bhāskara wrote his *Siddhānta Śiromaṇi*, where he enunciates the principle of differential calculus and applies it to astronomical problems and computations. Indians travelled to Sumatra, Java, Bali, Borneo, Cambodia, Annam and Ceylon. But Indian philosophers like Śaṅkara, Rāmānuja, Madhusūdana Sarasvatī, Vyāsatīrtha and others are entirely ignorant of the rich fruits of all this experience and knowledge. Uncritically they go on assuming the existence of the seven worlds (*loka*s) above, the seven below, the oceans of milk and honey, the Meru Mountain of gold, etc. They go on discussing in their exposition of the *Brahma-sūtra*, how the soul goes by "the path of gods" or "the path of fathers," how it reaches the moon, etc. Similarly the work of Caraka and Suśruta does not influence them to modify their conception of soul, or the interaction of body and mind, and other allied problems.

None of the scientific advances impel the Indian philosophers to make some creative efforts towards new cosmologies. The only reason for this is that the astronomers and physicians of India, whenever they hit upon new facts, did not advocate them too openly, being afraid the popular opinion may discountenance them and ostracise the authors of such theories. To be branded an *a-vaidika* was almost tantamount to being branded heretical in Medieval Europe. The great scholar-critic Alberuni in his *Tārikh-ī-Hind* gives the same reason: "The religious books of the Hindus and their codes of tradition, the Purāṇas, contain sentences about the shape of the world which stand in direct opposition to scientific truth as known to their astronomers. By these books people are guided in fulfilling the rites of their religion, and by means of them the great mass of the nation have been wheedled into a predilection for astronomical calculation and astrological predictions and warnings. The consequence is that they show much affection to their astronomers, declaring that they are excellent men, that it is a good for men to meet them, and firmly believing that all of them come into paradise and none into hell. For this the astronomers require them by accepting their popular notions as truth, by conforming themselves to them, however far from truth most of them may be, and by presenting them with such spiritual stuff as they stand in need of. This is the reason why the two theories, the vulgar and the scientific, have become intermingled in the course of time, why the doctrines of astronomers have been disturbed and confused."[46] Speaking at another place of Varāhamihira and Brahmagupta who knew the real cause of the eclipses and based their calculations on the correct theory, but who nevertheless still talked of Rāhu and his swallowing the sun and such nonsense, Alberuni writes, "Varāhamihira seems sometimes to side with the brāhmins, to whom he belonged; and from whom he could not separate himself. Still he does not deserve to be blamed, as, on the whole, his foot stands firmly on the basis of the truth, and he clearly speaks out the truth."[47] Of Brahmagupta, Alberuni comments that "he shirks the truth and lends his support to imposture."[48] It is remarked that "that which made Brahmagupta to speak the above-mentioned words (which involve a sin against conscience) was something of a calamitous fate like that of Socrates."[49] Alberuni

46. E.G. Sachau, ed., *Alberuni's India*, vol. I, p. 265.
47. Ibid., vol. II, p. 110.
48. Ibid., p. 110.
49. Ibid., p. 112.

adds these significant words which speak of the inquisition of the brāhmins: "As for the above-mentioned people, the Hindu theologians, from whom you must take care not to differ, how should they be able to understand the astronomical theory regarding the moon's eclipsing the sun, as they, in their Purāṇas, place the moon above the sun and that which is higher cannot cover that which is lower in the sight of those who stand lower than both. Therefore they required some being which devours moon and sun, as the fish devours the bait. However in each nation there are ignorant people, and leaders still more ignorant than they themselves . . . and who think they can increase the light of their minds; the fact being that the masters are as ignorant as the pupils."[50] Of Alberuni's impartiality, objectivity and critical acumen there could be no question.[51] So, such was the state of medieval India, priest-ridden and superstitious, not much different from medieval Europe. It is no wonder therefore that Indian philosophers like the Schoolmen were unacquainted with the contemporary trends in science and restricted themselves to an endless effort of interpretation and systematization of old texts.

Finally in the later medieval philosophers such as Madhusūdana Sarasvatī, Rāmācārya, Vyāsatīrtha, Brahmānanda, we find a spinning out of fine distinctions and implications with surprising acuteness, from statements which are in a large measure empty of any vital significance. Bacon's description of the Schoolmen is equally applicable to them: "Surely like as many substances in nature which are solid do putrefy and convert into worms, so it is the property of good and sound knowledge to putrefy and dissolve into a number of subtle, idle, unwholesome, and as I may term them,

50. Ibid., vol. 11, pp. 112-13.

51. P. Sykes, *A History of Persia*, vol. II, p. 60.

vermiculate questions, which have indeed a kind of quickness and life of spirit, but no soundness of matter or goodness of quality. This kind of degenerate learning did chiefly reign among the Schoolmen, who having sharp and strong wits, and abundance of leisure, and small variety of reading, but their wits being shut up in the cells of a few authors as their persons were shut up in the cells of monasteries and colleges; and knowing little history either of nature or time did out of no great quantity of matter, and infinite agitation of wit, spin out unto us those laborious webs of learning which are extant in their books." This is a fine appreciation of the great logical acumen but complete barrenness of medieval philosophy, whether of India or Europe.

While in Europe modern philosophy with its new outlook and methodology arose, in India its genesis has not yet taken place. A Bruno and a Descartes are yet to be born in India. The conclusion therefore is barring the Lokāyata, and early Sāṁkhya, we do not have any Indian philosophy exclusively based on reason. In spite of this we have splendid efforts at construction of systems of thought on the basis of scriptural texts or words of their master. We do not find any clear distinction between philosophy and theology, reason and faith as found in Thomas Aquinas. On the other hand there are systems like classical Sāṁkhya, which though they rely on tradition (*āpta vacana*) are atheistic. In the case of all the systems it is possible to some extent to extract their philosophy from their concomitant theological and mythological trappings, and assess the value of such philosophy. But Pūrva Mīmāṁsā and Yoga must be put aside while we are concerned with philosophy. Only then can a history of Indian philosophy be accomplished, which it can be asserted, is no light task.

3

The Vedas and Upaniṣads

Philosophy in the Vedas

Some time before 1500 BC, people belonging to the pastoral tribes who were living in South Russian steppes and lands eastwards to the Caspian Sea — barbarians who never knew what a city was — broke loose upon the peaceful urban civilization of the Indus Valley. They were people of the forest clearings and parklands. They raised wheat crops; and as soon as they reaped, they moved on. They had some sort of ox-wagons in which they huddled their things and wandered about. They achieved something of great significance — they tamed the horse and learnt how to use iron, from which they made mail.

"The warrior's look is like a thunderous rain-cloud, when armed with mail, he seeks the lap of battle."[1] They were vigorous, tall and largely built. It was the horse-chariot and the coat of mail that enabled the Aryans to conquer the Indus Valley people and settle down in their midst.

The Aryans were barbarians who invaded and settled down in an empire of literate urban culture. But in the *Ṛgveda* we see the conquest described from the Aryan point of view. Scant respect is paid to the defeated people, who were more skilled in the arts of peace than of warfare. The Indus Valley

---

1. Griffith, tr., *Ṛgveda*, VI.75.

people are spoken of as *dasyus* or *dāsas*. They have black complexions, without noses (*anāsa*) and language; they neither worship the Aryan gods nor offer sacrifice in the Aryan way. They live in forts, formed into groups and are rich. But the god, Indra is powerful, he will rent their forts (*purandara*), burn their weapons and will make himself "rich with wine and carts and horses." Indra is the apotheosis of the Aryan warrior-leader; he is the "ideal of an ever-fighting, never conquered hero, and therefore, the favourite of the race fighting for new homes and rich herds." "In him the Aryan has found an ally able to contend with the barbarians." "He is no friend or companion of the man who provides no *soma*, and has no favour for the rich miser who grudges gifts."[2] The Indra is "strong, young, immortal and ancient." He is strong-armed, colossal and tawny-bearded. He drinks a lot of *soma* and is pot-bellied; he devours enormous quantities of beef, porridge and cakes. His drunkenness and its after-effects are faithfully described in the *Ṛgveda*: "Indra, a blustering, braggart god, who has to befuddle himself with soma, in order to get the necessary courage to slay demons."[3] He is a cattle-raider, breaker of the forts of *dasyus* in association with Rudra and his faithful band of Maruts. The Ṛgvedic pantheon consists of many such gods, but Indra is the most popular, for to him about a quarter of its hymns are addressed. Indra and Varuṇa fight for supremacy.[4] We have fights of gods also as in the Iliad. None of these gods are those of the conquered people. Sometimes one god is praised as the greatest, at other times another. As such the gods enjoyed equal status, though each of them was exalted above the rest, on different occasions by

2. Adolf Kaegi, *Life in Ancient India*, p. 51.
3. Bloomfield, *The Religion of the Veda*, pp. 37-38.
4. *Ṛgveda*, IV.42; X.124.

different persons.[5] The present Hindu custom of choosing the beloved god (*Iṣṭa-devatā*) from among a lot is foreshadowed.

We might see how these Ṛgvedic gods were made: Indu is rain, Indra the spirit or force which rains, the rainer. When once it was believed that rain was due to a rainer, the rainer was invested with all the qualities — mental and physical found in a leading Aryan warrior. Varuṇa is the coverer or compasser, the dark sky covers or compasses everything, so the principle behind it is Varuṇa. He covers the starry expanse of heaven "as with a robe, with all the creatures thereof and their dwellings."[6]

The previous account explains why and how this sort of making of gods takes place. A question is raised in one of the hymns as to whom oblations should be offered and the answer is given, "he who among the gods was the first god" and it is added that the oblation should be offered to Prajāpati. In that solitary hymn we find a sort of monotheistic view. But it is not clear whether the Hiraṇyagarbha mentioned in the *Ṛgveda* (X.121.1) is the same as Prajāpati. No explicit identification of the two is made. Possibly the hymn like the *Ṛgveda*, IV.42 discusses the relative supremacy of the two and establishes the supremacy of Prajāpati, just as that of Indra over Varuṇa. Hiraṇyagarbha may be translated as "gold-bosomed" or "the gold foetus" or "he whose interior is gold." Nowhere is it stated that Prajāpati conceives the golden foetus or that Prajāpati is the golden germ or gold-bosomed. It might be stated so later. But that does not mean we should read the later thoughts into the previous ones and then credit them with the former. Max Müller considered the mention of

5. Z.A. Ragozin, *Vedic India*, p. 429; F.H.D. Griswold, *The Religion of Ṛgveda*, p. 342.

6. *Ṛgveda*, VIII.41.

Prajāpati here as an interpolation.[7] However the name Prajāpati marks an advance over the other names for it means "Lord of the people," unless we think that it was a chief who was deified or translated as "Lord of the offspring." It may have been a male fertility God which was probably worshipped as a phallic god by the people of those times. The hymn which states that the one is called by *vipra*s in many ways — Agni, Yama, and Mātarisvan has already been mentioned.[8] It does not mean much except that there was a tendency towards theocracies, which was present in Mesopotamia also. It is interesting to see that the author of this hymn is reputed to be Dīrghatamas, Long darkness; in fact the hymn is very obscure.

There is another hymn which deserves attention, the hymn of non-being, as it is called.[9] It starts with the assertion that in the beginning there was neither being nor non-being, nor the sky nor heavens. Then it is asked, what covered? Obviously the primitive mind is here struggling to think. It is striving to conceive what could have existed before everything. Nothing also could have existed, for, how could nothing exist? But the hymn-maker is unable to keep up the thought. So he again begins step by step — he says there was neither sky nor heavens. Immediately it flashes across his mind if there was neither sky nor heavens, what could have covered or enveloped everything? He is unable to remember that there was nothing to be covered, and so there arises no question of covering. However the hymn ends with two significant sentences, the gods came later than creation, and they cannot know anything about it. Did creation take place by itself or did somebody create it, probably the highest seer in the highest

7. Max Müller, The *Six Systems of Indian Philosophy*, p. 47.

8. *Ṛgveda*, I.164.6.

9. *Ṛgveda*, X.129.

heaven knows it, or does he also not know? And there ends the hymn. It is genuinely philosophical in spirit; in fact the hymn-maker tries to think, but breaks under its strain for lack of suitable concepts.

Though even the remotest solution is not offered it registers a significant advance that such a problem should have been raised and grappled with. It is highly unwarranted to read into the hymn a discrimination on the part of the hymn-maker between *natura naturans* and *natura naturata,* equally so to interpret it in terms of the absolute, the ego and non-ego, and the "I" confronting the "not-I."[10] Bloomfield goes to the other extreme. Since in the hymn it is stated that through *tapas* living-force enveloped in a shell developed, Bloomfield understands it as meaning that the priests claimed that the world was created through their *tapas*.[11] Whitney's remarks on the hymn are just:

> It is of the highest historical interest as the earliest known beginning of such speculation in India, or probably anywhere among Indo-European races. The attitude of its author and the audacity of his attempt are exceedingly noteworthy. But nothing can be said in absolute commendation of the success of the attempt. On the contrary it exhibits the characteristic weaknesses of all Hindu theosophy, a disposition to deal with words as if they were things, to put forth paradox and insoluble contradiction as profundity.[12]

There is another hymn where this philosophic spirit is displayed.[13] There the question is asked, how and with what

10. S. Radhakrishnan, *Indian Philosophy,* vol. 1, p. 101.
11. Bloomfield, *Religion of the Veda,* p. 237.
12. *Proceedings of the American Oriental Society,* vol. XL, p. CXI.
13. *Ṛgveda,* X.81.

did Viśvakarmā produce heaven and earth? Another most interesting is the hymn where the question is raised, who saw the gods and if nobody saw them as is the fact, then who is the God? Is it he who supports the six skies?[14] We are also told that there were people who asked, who is Indra, who saw him?[15] Naturally enough there were some who denied Indra.[16] The priests of course promptly rebuked such and emphasized that Indra was real.[17] Many other such interesting speculations must have been made by the people of those times; but all those containing sceptical elements inimical to religion must have been destroyed. Thus we find in the *Ṛgveda* important questions, the answers to which would constitute philosophy. But no answers worth the name are found, such efforts as made are rudimentary.

A long account has been given here to put *Ṛgveda* into its proper setting with reference to how religion arose and philosophy slowly emerged. There are some who like to take *Ṛgveda* as the last book in wisdom, while there are iconoclasts ready to declare it as complete nonsense. Either way to regard *Ṛgveda* is not scientific. It is a book which was composed at least 3000 years ago by cattlemen and cultivators. It is as improper to expect to find therein developed philosophy as to find nuclear physics. On the other hand to read into it a latter view is to say the least unscholarly.

Madhva made a great effort to interpret the first forty hymns of the *Ṛgveda* to mean that they have their entire purport in Nārāyaṇa, the supreme spirit and supreme God. His argument is that as the Upaniṣads have said that *puruṣa* is the

---

14. *Ṛgveda*, I.167.5, 6.
15. *Ṛgveda*, II.12.5.
16. *Ṛgveda*, VIII.103.3.
17. *Ṛgveda*, II.15.1.

meaning of all words, and as the *ṛk*s are words, the purport of all the *ṛk*s is Nārāyaṇa.[18] His disciple Rāghavendra gives two reasons why they should be so interpreted: the souls (*jīva*s) are in ceaseless sorrow and suffering: the *parama sṛṭi* says that its aim is to remove such sorrow by removing their bondage. Bondage can be removed only by His grace, so says *Nārāyaṇa Śruti*. The *Bhagavad-Gītā* says that the grace of God can be had only by the wise. Wisdom about *puruṣa* can be attained by Vedic study alone; so the meaning of Vedas is Viṣṇu. Rāghavendra then puts it in syllogistic form: All the Vedas are engenderers of Viṣṇu-jñāna, for their existence is for the sake of *mokṣa* to be achieved by Viṣṇu-jñāna, like the words "pot," etc. whose existence is for the sake of the experience of pot, etc. to be achieved by the knowledge of pot, etc.[19] As the Vedas are meant to give us knowledge of Viṣṇu, they are so intended; the Upaniṣads, the *Bhagavad-Gītā* and the Purāṇas declare: *vedaiśca sarvaiḥ aham eva vedyo*. The *Harivaṁśa* records: *vede adavante ca madhye ca viṣṇuḥ sarvatra gīyate*. The *Bhāgavatam* states: *vāsudeva parāveda vāsudeva parātmakhaḥ*.

All words, popularly established, have a meaning as well as their etymologically proper meaning. So Madhva and following him Rāghavendra take the proper meaning of a word wherever the established one does not give the requisite sense. In short the meaning of the first line of the *Bṛhadāraṇyaka Upaniṣad* (5.1.3) would be, "I praise the most Supreme, who is favourable to all living beings, who being the controller of the *ṛtvik* is the *ṛtvik*, who is praiseworthy and sports and

---

18. *sa eva sarva śabdārtha ityaḥopaniṣat para, tava eta ṛcaiti viśeṣeṇapi ṛgārth atām* — Madhva, *Ṛgveda-bhāṣya*, p. 1.

19. *sarve veda viṣṇujñānajanakaḥ, tat sādhya mokṣārtham pravṛtta tvat, yathā ghaṭādi jñānasādhya ghaṭādi vyava-harārtham pravṛtto ghaṭādi śabdaḥ — Mantrārtha-mañjarī*, p. 2.

conquers and who being the controller of the *hotā* is the *hotā* and who is an abundant giver of happiness." How different this meaning is from that usually given can be seen by comparing it with the usual one, "I magnify Agni, the domestic priest, the divine ministrant of the sacrifice, the invoker, best bestower of treasure." This has been accomplished by the astonishing erudition and ingenuity of Madhva and Rāghavendra. All this is done because the Vedas are assumed to have their purport in the one Supreme God, Nārāyaṇa, so they must be shown to have it. And it is so assumed, because the Upaniṣads and the later literature say so.

Sri Aurobindo has interpreted the *Ṛgveda* as mystical literature, which for unknown reasons sought to hide real knowledge behind symbols: thus Sūrya is an intelligence, Agni will and Soma feeling, etc. Sri Aurobindo has taken care to say that this is a hypothesis. His disciple Kapāli Sastri has written an erudite commentary on these lines. This is not something novel, for we have such interpretations of the *Rāmāyaṇa* and the *Mahābhārata* and the *Bhāgavatam*. We have the *Adhyātma Rāmāyaṇa*, seeking to interpret the *Rāmāyaṇa* spiritually. Allegorical interpretations are not something to be found only in India; the *Bible* has been allegorically interpreted many times. Some like Vicar of St. Hugo have given greater prominence to that kind of interpretation. But usually allegorical interpretation is resorted to when the ordinary one is not satisfactory. Thus the "Song of Songs" in the *Bible* has three different interpretations. We have such interpretations of *Kṛṣṇa-līlā*. I think I can allegorize any of the folk tales in Australian folk tales by Mrs. Langloh Parker.

The history of the Second World War can be allegorized, it can be maintained that Hitler, Himmler, Goring, Stalin among others are symbols of psychological functions or spiritual forces or hobgoblins. All that will lead us nowhere.

From the Hymns to the Upaniṣads

The *Atharvaveda* is a latter work than the *Ṛgveda,* but in it an effort is made by the Aryan priests to incorporate the deities and religious practices of the people whom they conquered. Before the discovery of the Indus Valley civilization, the Aryans were supposed to have come and conquered barbarian tribes and so the *Atharvaveda* was thought to contain the barbaric and religious practices of the conquered peoples. This has now been falsified. The *Atharvaveda* is an evidence of how the conquerors were conquered by the beliefs and practices of the non-Aryans. In it we find the Aryan and non-Aryan beliefs and customs amalgamating together by giving birth to what is at present called Hinduism. The *Atharvaveda* was not for a long time regarded as a Veda. Neither early Buddhist canonical works nor the early Upaniṣads mention it as a Veda. The pride of the Aryan priests and their belief that their gods were superior to the non-Aryan gods made its acceptance difficult for a long time; but at last the mere force of the greater numbers of people who believed in the non-Aryan gods compelled the Aryan priests to recognize them, because "outside the schools of the priests the curious and interesting beliefs recorded in the *Ṛgveda* had practically little effect."[20] "It is quite certain that the beliefs and practices to which *Atharvaveda* is devoted are as old, if not older than those which the three other Vedas refer to, and that they were commonly held and followed by the Aryans in India."[21] The only difference between the theology of the *Ṛgveda* and that of *Atharvaveda* is that the gods

20. T.W. Rhys Davids, *Buddhist India*, p. 211.

21. Ibid., p. 213.

of the former are strong, manly and robust like the Nordics, while those of the latter are strange, eerie and terrible.

The prayer or hymn of the *Ṛgveda* is called *Brahman*, because "Bṛh" is "to grow" or "to spread"; and *Brahman* means that which breaks forth or spreads — speech or prayer.[22] The great value which the early people attached to incantations, lead them to think of a great power inhering in them and gradually the word was extended to cover holy power in general. Thus the gods are said to discuss *Brahman*; and *Brahman* is put as against the three Vedas as a power of equal force. The two divinities Bṛhaspati and Brahmanaspati are closely connected with this idea of *Brahman*. In the *Aitareya Brāhmaṇa* (I.19.1; I.30.6) and *Śatapatha Brāhmaṇa* (III.9.1.11; XIII.5.4.25), Bṛhaspati is identified with *Brahman*. He is further identified with *ṛta*, the inescapable order which pervades the universe.[23] He is identified with Sun, the first born of the day and possibly first born of the creation.[24] While earlier, Prajāpati is mentioned as the creator of *Brahman*, later it is identified with *Brahman*. Finally, the *Taittirīya* and *Śatapatha Brāhmaṇa*s are able to think of *Brahman* as Svayambhū or self-existent that was the ground of the universe and into which all things finally return. In *Taittirīya Brāhmaṇa* (II.8.9.3-7) he takes the place of the highest god Viśvakarman. The *Atharvaveda* (X.2; XI.5) recognizes the same idea. In the Upaniṣads, *Brahman* comes to mean the ultimate reality, though hints of its original meaning of prayer or sacred hymn are not absent.[25]

22. *va ghi bṛhati, tasya esa patiḥ . . . . yovakam brahmā iti upasate — Chāndogya Upaniṣad*, 1.2.11; 7.2.2.

23. *Śatapatha Brāhmaṇa*, II.1.4.10; IV.1.4.11.

24. Ibid., VII.4.1.14; VIII.5.3.7.

25. *Taittirīya Upaniṣad*, 1.8.

In the *Ṛgveda* (X.16.3), *ātman* meant breath, *vatam ātmā* from which the meaning "self" as found in the sentences, "putting strength into oneself" came. Again Sūrya is spoken of as the self of that which stands and moves. Then gradually the self was distinguished from breath and blood. In the *Atharvaveda* it is clearly distinguished from breath and body. In the *Śatapatha Brāhmaṇa*, we find it distinguished from breath and also an attempt made to identify it with consciousness, *vijñāna*. In the *Ṛgveda* the creator is mentioned as entering into his creation with his spirit and the *Taittirīya Āraṇyaka* speaks of his entering with the self into the self. Finally in *Śatapatha* and *Taittirīya Brāhmaṇa*, *ātman* is identified with *Brahman*; and this line of speculation culminates when it is declared that *ātman* is the lord of all beings and king of all beings.[26] But these texts are almost contemporaneous with the Upaniṣads. There are also attempts to arrive at a conception of being and not-being. Being is that from which the world came, if so from where did it come? Probably from not-being or is it from something beyond being and not-being? This something higher than both that is and is not is identified with mind. Again not-being is at one place spoken of as the desire to become being.

Epistemologically another significant point occurs in this literature. A distinction is made between what is perceived (*pratyakṣa*) and what is not perceived (*parokṣa*); and then it is argued that what is perceived by men, the gods may not perceive; while what is perceived by gods may not be perceived by men. So the real must not be identified with the perceived. One must achieve special insight to penetrate reality, which can be obtained only by *tapas*. Thus though we find flashes of philosophical insight and though we may be able to

---

26. *sa va ayam ātma sarveṣām bhūtānām adhipatiḥ, sarveṣām bhūtānām rājā.*

trace the development of the conceptions of *Brahman* and *ātman* and empirical knowledge and real knowledge, the Brāhmaṇas as a whole are concerned with sacrificial worship of various gods. Yet we cannot fail to notice an improvement in the clearness and subtlety of modes and categories of thought.

Unfortunately the morals of the priests did not keep pace with these developments in thought. They in fact became worse. Sylvain Levi wrote that it is difficult to imagine anything more brutal and more material than the theology of the brāhmins. A notion whose usage was afterwards gradually refined and clothed with a garb of morality takes us aback by their savage realism. "Morality finds no place in this system. Sacrifice which regulates the relation of man to the divinities, is a mechanical act, operating by its own spontaneous energy, and that hidden in the bottom of nature is only brought out by the magic art of the priest."[27] "As to the fees, the rules are precise, and the profounder of them are unblushing. The priest performs the sacrifice for the fee alone, and it must consist of valuable garments, horses, or gold — when each is to be given is carefully stated. Gold is coveted most, for this is immortality, the seed of Agni and therefore peculiarly agreeable to the priest."[28]

A.B. Keith has described brutal morality at length.[29] Sin is automatically removed by sacrifice; even a sinner can sacrifice and become great; things wrongly accumulated can be made thus fit and proper. Water or application of sacred *darbha* grass can wash away lies and impurity. By means of gifts to the brāhmins one can go to heaven; the gift of a cow protects

---

27. Cited from T.W. Rhys Davids, *Buddhist India*, p. 241.
28. Hopkins, *Religions of India*, p. 192.
29. A.B. Keith, *The Religion and Philosophy of the Veda and Upaniṣads*, vol. II, p. 475.

one's life, and the gift of a garment prolongs it. Adultery can be washed away by acknowledging it to a priest at the time of sacrifice.[30] In fact, sexual laxity of the brāhmins went to such an extent that he is told not to commit adultery while at any sacred ceremony. But if he is not able to control himself he can absolve himself from the sin by offering curdled milk to Varuṇa and Mitra. With shocking coolness the texts say that the murder of any one, except a brāhmin, is not really murder; and a "judge must always decide in favour of a brāhmin as against his adversary who is not a brāhmin."[31] The brāhmin may regard the śūdra as his slave and take away his property, for whatever a slave has got belongs to the master. To top this all, the Brāhmaṇa records, finally, that there are two sorts of gods, the real gods and the brāhmins, who repeat the Veda; the brāhmin represents all the divinities, he, in fact, is the God of gods.[32] Garbe remarks that this is "a unique case of its kind where clerical presumption has gone to the point of making such claims."[33] Koppen in the introductory chapter of *Buddhism*, R. Garbe in *The Philosophy of Ancient India* (p. 58) and Rhys Davids in *Buddhist India* have gathered a mass of incontrovertible facts of priestly claims, doctrines and atrocities, which will shock any sensible person.

It was inevitable that a reaction against these claims and teachings of brāhmins should start among the nobles and warriors, the kṣatriyas, though the vaiśyas and śūdras could not resist them. Added to this the brāhmins had no organization, and were divided among themselves. "They vied

---

30. *Śatapatha Brāhmaṇa*, II.5.2.20; III.1.2.10.
31. R. Garbe, *The Philosophy of Ancient India*, p. 62.
32. *Śatapatha Brāhmaṇa*, II.2.2.6; II.4.3.14.
33. Cited from S. Radhakrishnan, *Indian Philosophy*, vol. I, pp. 59, 125-26.

with each another for sacrificial fees. The demand for their services was insufficient to maintain them all. Brāhmins followed therefore all sorts of other occupations; and those of them not continually busied about the sacrifice were often inclined to views of life, and of religion, different from the views of those who were."[34] These brāhmins began to rank *tapas* or asceticism above sacrifice. For instance the *Aitareya Brāhmaṇa* (XI.6.4) says at one place that on *tapas* are established heaven, air, earth, waters and truth. In the *Śatapatha Brāhmaṇa* (XI.3.3.5) we hear of students living by begging. The same book mentions of Uddālaka Āruṇi wandering about in search of wisdom. So, two tendencies manifested themselves in those days. The growing brāhmin class could not entirely subsist on priestly duties because sacrifices performed in the Aryan way lost their significance due to the gradual ascendance of the beliefs and practices of the majority of the people — those inherited from the Indus Valley culture. Moreover the cost of Vedic sacrifices was enormous. Few people therefore were ready to incur so much expense, "and preferred, if they wanted magic, magic of other and cheaper kinds."[35] Therefore a section of the brāhmins who could not get their livelihood from priestly duties, and the majority of people, who were dissatisfied with the sacrificial religion enough and naturally the nobles, took a leading part in this reaction.

The Upaniṣads contain the views of this class of people, brāhmins, dissatisfied with sacrificial religion, and kṣatriyas. Of course, it is to exaggerate facts, to say that there was a conscious class-struggle between the kṣatriyas and brāhmaṇas; because caste regulations did not yet become very rigid, though usually the son of a noble was a noble. Intermarriages

---

34. T.W. Rhys Davids, *Buddhist India*, p. 249.

35. Ibid.

were allowed, though as far as possible marriages were made within the same class. There was probably no bitter antagonism, except that the Brāhmanical religion with its rituals, and immorality failed to satisfy the needs of reflective minds among both the classes. So there resulted an emphasis on austerity and asceticism (*tapas*), meditation and contemplation (*dhyāna* or *upāsanā*) of sacred syllables like *oṁ* or sentences like "He who is in the sun is in the eye." Also an impetus was given to bold speculations about the nature of the soul, *Brahman*, etc. But in all this the kṣatriyas took a predominant part. Many distinguished Indologists, Deussen, Garbe and Hertel among others are of the opinion that the philosophy of the Upaniṣads is almost exclusively of kṣatriya origin. A.B. Keith on the other hand is dogmatic that the Upaniṣads are not the work of warriors; and that even if the kṣatriyas originated them it was the brāhmins who developed and handed them down. Both these views suffer from exaggeration. The empty dry formalistic sacrificial religion of the brāhmins and the exaggerated claims of the brāhmins and their increasing arrogance must have vexed the nobles. There can be no denying of that. Also some among the brāhmins were dissatisfied with ritualistic religion, due to both its emptiness, as well as their inability to live on it. These two together must have given rise to the theories we find in the Upaniṣads. They clarified the conceptions of *Brahman* and *ātman*, enlarged their scope and finally came to certain conclusions. But in every case it was the kṣatriyas together with the declassed brāhmins that did it. The internal evidence of the Upaniṣads itself suggests this. The theory of *ātman-Brahman* is no doubt a logical development of the views contained in the Brāhmaṇas, but these developments were made because ritualistic religion produced a revolt in the minds of people. The *Chāndogya Upaniṣad* (5.11-24) narrates how King

Aśvapati Kaikeya taught Uddālaka Āruṇi and five other brāhmins about the nature of *ātman* — Vaiśvānara. The same Upaniṣad mentions that Sanatkumāra, the god of warriors taught Nārada, a brāhmin. The *Bṛhadāraṇyaka Upaniṣad* (2.4) contains the story of Bālāki, a brāhmin, becoming the pupil of a king, Ajātaśatru. The *Kauśitakī Upaniṣad* also mentions this. Three Upaniṣads — *Chāndogya, Bṛhadāraṇyaka* and *Kauśitakī* contain the story of King Pravāhana Jaivāli instructing brāhmins. In the *Śatapatha Brāhmaṇa* (XI.6.2), Janaka is said to have instructed Yājñavalkya on the nature of Agnihotra. In the *Bṛhadāraṇyaka* and *Kauśitakī Upaniṣads* we also read of King Janaka promoting philosophical discussions and presiding over them. On the other hand the *Chāndogya* mentions King Janaśruti going to brāhmin Raikva for instruction. In the *Maitrī Upaniṣad,* King Bṛhadratha sought instruction from brāhmin Śakayana. Again Satyakāma, the son of a whore, is taken as a pupil by Haridramata and attains complete knowledge.[36] All this indicates that the Upaniṣadic speculations were neither the exclusive products of the priestly class, brāhmins nor of the kṣatriyas. Both together shared in the intellectual developments recorded in the Upaniṣads, though the kṣatriyas seem to have taken the leading part but not without the help of the thoughtful brāhmins like Uddālaka.

According to many scholars, Draviḍian elements have exerted a great deal of influence over the Aryans. They have put forward the hypothesis that changes in the language of the Upaniṣads are due to Draviḍian influence, and Draviḍian contributions to Hindu pantheon are immense. I have suggested long before I came to know of the hypotheses of these distinguished scholars that "The Aryan and Draviḍian worked together and there emerged from this conjoint

36. The *Chāndogya Upaniṣad*, 4.4.

endeavour, a distinct cultural pattern of life and thought, Hinduism."[37] Though the *Ṛgveda* to a large extent retains the beliefs and customs of Aryans as they were before they came into contact with the Dravidians, the *Atharvaveda* shows how an Aryo-Draviḍian thought-pattern was being evolved. This is traceable in the Brāhmaṇas also. It is to be noted that the *Atharvaveda* and the Brāhmaṇas register an advance in thought over the *Ṛgveda*. It is inconceivable that Draviḍian elements should have exerted no influence at all in thought and practice. But in the end they fused with each other so much that both became unrecognizable, though looking at contemporary Hindu customs, religious beliefs and deities, it must be commented that the Indus Valley influence is more discernible than that of the blue-eyed and fair skinned Nordic invaders. The unsystematic nature of the Upaniṣads and the absence of any single idea being worked out to its logical conclusion are probably due to the mixed blood of the people.

The Upaniṣads cannot be dated with precision. The only point that enables us to allot some date is that since they are presupposed by the Buddha's teaching they are prior to the Buddha. So the earlier Upaniṣads may be prior to 500 BC. But then the date of the Buddha rests on the Buddhist canon, while the date of the latter is mere tradition. Then again the Upaniṣadic language is similar to that of Pāṇini, so even the oldest Upaniṣads cannot be dated beyond 600 BC.[38]

In these days of revivalist tendencies in India, it is sane to recollect what the other peoples were doing at that time, so that one may not think too much of "glorious and unrivalled past" of India. In 538 BC, Cyrus conquered Babylon and united

---

37. See my *Hinduism and its Development*, p. 79.

38. R.E. Hume, *The Thirteen Principal Upaniṣads*, p. 6; Farquhar, *An Outline of the Religious Literature of India*, p. 35.

the Babylonian and Median Empires. His son subjugated Egypt, but met with an accident early. So Darius I one of the councillors of Cyrus succeeded him. His was a great empire, stretching over Asia Minor, Syria, the old Assyrian and Babylonian empires, Egypt, the Caucasus and Caspian regions, Media and Persia, the empire extended up to the Indus. It had great arterial roads, post-horses carried administrators and travellers to and fro, coined money was used; and trade and commerce were on the increase. It is significant that Balthazar, who was conquered by Cyrus, was hated by the priests of Babylon who did not like his attempts to reform their religion by trying to unify various local gods. Then again in Egypt and Mesopotamia, between 1600 and 600 BC a great civilization flourished. Life was highly cultured, people were comfortable, they lived in beautiful highly furnished houses, wore richly decorated clothing and lovely jewels. Already it was three thousand years since the Pyramids were built. The great temples of Karnak and Luxor, the monuments of Nineveh, the winged bulls, were all works of this time. Writing was already developed there. Great advance in geometry and mathematics was made.

In the seventh century BC, the Semitic people were the greatest people on earth. They ruled Assyria, and conquered Egypt. Babylon and Syria were also Semitic. World-trade was in their hands. The colonies of Tyre and Sidon, and those in Spain, Sicily and Africa were of great proportion. Carthage had a population of over a million. It was for a time the greatest city. Its ships went to Britain, out into the Atlantic and reached Madeira even. By 538 BC, at least the Pentateuch of the *Bible* existed. At least in outline the Hebrew conception of God was clear by that time. Their God was remote and invisible, he was one Jehovah, he had no other names, he was in heaven;

and he was far above priests and sacrifices. He was the "Lord of Righteousness" throughout the earth. All other gods were national gods who lived in images and temples; once the image and temple are destroyed those gods are put an end to. But Jehovah is not like that; he is eternal, created heaven and earth, and none can see him. I need not compare this conception with that of Varuṇa, for the similarities and differences between the two are obvious.

It is necessary to have a glimpse of Indian life of sixth and seventh centuries. There were a number of clans and tribes. Kośala and Magadha were the leading kingdoms; interminable feuds existed between the various princes. Nothing is known of what was happening south of the Vindhya. The houses were all together and separated by narrow lines. All around were forest clearings and cultivated land. Cattle were owned severally, but wasteland and wood was common to all villagers. There was no proprietary right in land; each family was allotted a plot. Lands could not be sold or mortgaged except in extraordinary circumstances and then too with the permission of the village council. The village headman represented the government; he was either hereditary or elected by the village council. People were secure, nobody starved. There was little crime. Of course, there were frequent famines, then people suffered intolerably and there were robbers and despots.[39] The towns were noisy and dirty. There were few big houses.[40] Till the seventh century there was no writing in India, Vedic literature was handed down orally. Writing first became known to Indians when the Draviḍian merchants in the course of their trade with Babylon became acquainted with the alphabet of the Akkadians. The script

---

39. See T.W. Rhys Davids, *Buddhist India*, Chap. III.
40. Ibid., Chap. IV.

was brought to India, adapted to Indian needs and a thousand years later it was known as Brāhmī script.[41]

The agricultural states of north India at that time were peaceful and quite civilized but not at all on a par with those of Egypt and Mesopotamia or Assyria; while they cannot be compared at all with the Persian empire of Darius I. People were not at all adventurous and vigorous as the Semites. India was probably on the level of the Maya civilization then. In material culture and physical amenities there was nothing superior to any of the existing civilizations. As for philosophy we have the Upaniṣads and it must be said that none of the ancient peoples of that period have left any evidence of such fertile thoughts.

Many of the Upaniṣadic passages are in a dialogue form, the disciple or the son is allowed a large number of guesses, then the teacher or father states the truth. Usually no reason is given as to why it is the truth and the other views false. Sometimes similes are substituted for reasoning. The comparison of something with another is supposed to establish the truth of the former. In this the method of the Saṁhitā still haunts the Upaniṣads. The tendency to substitute the citation of examples in the place of reasoning is evidenced everywhere in Indian philosophy. Usually the examples cited are irrelevant. Some instances from Śaṅkara may be given. How can God create and sustain the world without himself undergoing any change? Śaṅkara gives the example of a person who in his dreams creates all sorts of forms in himself without undergoing any change.[42] How can this world of inanimate and animate objects with its great diversity arise from undifferentiated

41. Ibid., Chap. V & VI; Adolf Kaegi, *Life in Ancient India,* p. 23.

42. *Brahma-sūtra-bhāṣya,* 2.1.23.

pure being? Śaṅkara replies that it is possible just as it is possible for diverse objects like diamonds and ordinary stones to be the effects of one common thing, the earth. Why does God create the world, has he a purpose to achieve? If he has no purpose to achieve how can he act? Śaṅkara says that creation has no purpose, it is natural and like sport.[43] It is, he adds, spontaneous like inhalation and exhalation.[44]

This is a great defect of Indian philosophy. For example, a famous contemporary Indian writer says, "Truth is like a gem which has many facets. So there can be many and different versions of the same truth." Another, more famous, author says that "Hinduism is a movement, a process" and continues, "it cannot stop still, it must move, it must develop, from glory to glory." Loose and unconnected thinking, in terms of metaphors and similes, are found often in Indian philosophy. "Indian teaching is steeped in parable and simile" is due to a defective logical method.[45] "It has often been said that the Vedānta deals too much in metaphors, and that most of them, though fascinating at first sight, leave us in the end unsatisfied, because they can only illustrate but cannot prove. This is true, no doubt."[46]

The Upaniṣads do not give either a unanimous or a cogently argued answer to the question, what is *Brahman* (ultimate reality). We have seen how the *Brahman* came to be applied in this sense. In the *Bṛhadāraṇyaka Upaniṣad* (2.1), King Ajātaśatru says that ultimate reality is that from whence breaths emerge, on which men, gods and the world depends.

---

43. *svabhāvadeva kevalam līlārūpa.*

44. *Brahma-sūtra-bhāṣya*, 2.1.33.

45. C.A.F. Rhys Davids, *A Manual of Buddhism*, p. 99.

46. Max Müller, *The Six Systems of Indian Philosophy*, p. 195.

In the same Upaniṣad, Yājñavalkya says that unless we go behind the attributes and their manifestation, the oneness of the ultimate reality cannot be recognized and that can be done only by identifying our own self with it. In the *Chāndogya Upaniṣad,* Aśvapati teaches that *ātman* cannot be found anywhere outside but only within. In the same Upaniṣad, Sanatkumāra takes Nārada through a series of conceptions like *Brahman* as speech, mind, force, food, etc. and the breath which is the soul, and finally declares that the real is the great or the immense, which comprehends everything and is identical with the ego (*ahaṁkāra*) and the self (*ātman*). A kind of argument is also found here. Truth depends on knowledge, knowledge on thought, this on faith, which depends on concentration (*niṣṭhā*) and this on productive food, which again on pleasure. As pleasure can exist only in the unlimited, the unlimited is the ultimate real. In the *Chāndogya Upaniṣad* (8.7), there is a passage of interest: what is *ātman*? That is the question raised. Prajāpati says that the *ātman* is that which is free from sin, from hunger, thirst and old age, which desires what it ought to desire and imagines what it ought to. Indra finds that the body as it suffers from hunger, thirst, youth, old age and death cannot be the *ātman*. Then he finds that the self which dreams also cannot be the *ātman,* for in dreams it is liable to pain, and sometimes also experiences itself as struck or as lame or deceased. The self which sleeps at perfect rest untroubled, cannot also be the *ātman,* for then what is left of the self? It indeed, becomes destroyed.[47] But Prajāpati insisted that though it is so, the *ātman* is not different from this.[48] Prajāpati goes on to say that it is not the annihilation of the self, that the *ātman* as is found in dreamless sleep is one with the ultimate reality, untouched by pain, pleasure, and change.

---

47. *vināśā mevāpito bhavati.*

48. *evaṁ eva eṣaḥ — na eva anyatra etasmāt.*

Prajāpati then goes on to say that it is the same self which knows and perceives and is also conscious of its knowledge and perception.[49] *Ātman* then is the changeless self-conscious subject underlying the states of waking and dreaming experiences, but which is in its own undisturbed condition in sleep.

In the *Taittirīya Upaniṣad* (3.4.1) again we read the story of Bhṛgu going to his father, Varuṇa and asking, "Teach me *Brahman*." Varuṇa replies that food, breath, the eye, the ear, mind and word, and that from which beings are born, born by which they subsist, and in which they merge at the end is known to be *Brahman*. Then Bhṛgu practises *tapas* and came to know that food is *Brahman*, breath is *Brahman*, mind is *Brahman*, bliss is *Brahman* respectively. We are not told anywhere that only one of these is the final view. In fact, many sections follow extolling the greatness of food, how good it is, that sustains everything, how it should be worshipped and how finally one will realize that he is food and the eater of food.[50]

Like those of the early Greek philosophers the Upaniṣads at several places conceive the ultimate reality in terms of physical things. For example both the *Bṛhadāraṇyaka* (3.3; 3.7) and the *Chāndogya* (4.3.1) *Upaniṣad* have passages which say that air is the ultimate reality. So again space, water, the *udgītha* (a sacrificial chant) and light are stated to be the ultimate reality at various places. In view of all this it is distortion of facts to say that the Upaniṣads contain any one view regarding ultimate reality. "The teaching of the Upaniṣads is not a homogeneous, self-contained system, but lacks unity and completeness."[51]

---

49. *yoveda idaṁ manvanīti sa ātma.*

50. *ahaṁ annam, ahaṁ annadaḥ.*

51. See A. Schweitzer, *Indian Thought & Its Development*, p. 55.

But finding one of these ideas alone as fruitful and deserving of attention, the later commentators have chosen it and then have tried to explain away all the other texts, either by citing grammatical rules and etymology or by interpreting it allegorically. This fruitful conception which suited later interpreters occurs in the *Taittirīya Upaniṣad* (2.1.1), where it is said *Brahman* is being, knowledge and eternity.[52] In the *Bṛhadāraṇyaka Upaniṣad* (3.9.28), it is said consciousness and bliss is *Brahman*: *vijñānam ānandam brahma.*

In the *Bṛhadāraṇyaka Upaniṣad* Yājñavalkya tells Janaka, *ātman* is that which persists in all the states of experience and also beyond death. But it is unaffected because it is incapable of being affected. It is like a lump of salt, which has no inner or outer aspects. It is a single unit, consciousness has no differentiation; it is one unity. The absolute cannot be described by any of the definitions in terms of the things we know. So it can be only described as "not this," "not this."[53]

The universe proceeds from the eternal (*akṣara*) like the threads from the spider and the plants from earth.[54] The *Kaṭha Upaniṣad* (2.2.9-11) compares the self to the all-penetrating light, air and sun, which adapt themselves to all forms. The *Chāndogya Upaniṣad* (6.2.1) says: "In the beginning there was only the existent which is called by some the non-existent. So from the non-existent the existent is born. But how can this become? So there was only the existent at the beginning. It wished, "may I become many, may I be born manifold." So it created energy (*teja*). Energy wished "may I become many"; it created water. That is why whenever anybody is excited or is sorrowful, he sweats. Then from energy (*teja*) only waters are born. The

52. *satyam jñānam anandam brahmā.*

53. *Bṛhadāraṇyaka Upaniṣad*, 4.3.4; 4.2.4.

54. *Muṇḍaka Upaniṣad*, 1.1.7.

waters wished, "may we become many, may we be born in multiple ways." They created food. That is why wherever there is rain, there a lot of food. That food, etc. is born from water only. This is an accurate rendering of the second section of the sixth chapter of *Chāndogya Upaniṣad*. Unless we make a fetish of it, one can see its value immediately. Of course, by painstaking *vyākhyāna* it can be made to mean anything we like.

It is in the *Chāndogya Upaniṣad* (6.10.1-3) that the great sentence (*mahāvākya*), *tat tvam asi* occurs: The rivers are flowing eastward and westward; they form the ocean, go into the ocean and become the ocean. As they do not know then, "I am this"; so all the beings (*prajāḥ*) having come from the real, do not know "we are coming (*āgacchamaha*) from the real." Here whatever they become — tiger, lion, pig, locusts, bird, bug or mosquito, they come from that. That is the truth, which is *ātman*. That "being" became tiger, lion, pig, man, etc. which are again becoming "being." This form occurs at many places in the Upaniṣads, and leaves us conjecturing whether they conceived *Brahman* or the real as process or static being. The Buddha's conception of the real as process may have its origin in these Upaniṣadic speculations.

Speculations regarding the nature of the human soul are found. The soul dwells in the cavity of the heart.[55] It is of the size of a barley or rice grain.[56] Sometimes it is spoken of as of the size of the thumb.[57] Its shape is that of a man.[58] It resembles a flame, a flash of lightning, a light without smoke and the

55. *Chāndogya Upaniṣad*, 8.3.3; *Taittirīya Upaniṣad*, 1.6.1.

56. *Chāndogya Upaniṣad*, 3.14.3.

57. *Kaṭha Upaniṣad*, 4.12.13.

58. *Bṛhadāraṇyaka Upaniṣad*, 1.41; *Taittirīya Upaniṣad*, 2.

smoke-coloured wool. In dreams the soul leaves the body; wanders about like a falcon and at last tired it returns to the body.[59] A passage suggests that the soul might have existed before birth in some other body.[60] After death some souls go to the moon, become food to the gods there, and live in the gods. After the efficacy of their good deeds is worn out they pass to the space from the gods, and then to the air. From it they go into rain and then to the earth, from earth they go to the plants, which become food to the males. There they become the semen, pass into the females and are reborn.[61] In the same Upaniṣad, Yājñavalkya tells Ārtabhāga that after death a man's speech departs to the fire, his breath to the wind, his eye to the sun, his mind to the moon, his ear to the pole, his body to the earth, his *ātman* to the ether, his hair to the plants and trees, his blood and seed to the waters, and there remains only his *karma* to migrate.[62] It is significant that the Upaniṣad mentions here the annihilation of the *ātman* and puts it on par with hair, blood and water. Again in another passage Yājñavalkya hints to Maitreyī that there is no more consciousness after death: *pretya saṁjñā nāsti*.[63] Similarly the *Chāndogya Upaniṣad* (6.9.2) says, having attained the real, i.e. after death, they do not know.[64] It may be said that such ideas led to the no-soul theory of the Buddha and the Cārvāka schools. On the other hand in some passages the soul is to proceed to another body after death, as a caterpillar proceeds

---

59. *Bṛhadāraṇyaka Upaniṣad*, 4.3; *Chāndogya Upaniṣad*, 8.12.3.
60. *Bṛhadāraṇyaka Upaniṣad*, 3.2.13; 4.4.6.
61. *Bṛhadāraṇyaka Upaniṣad*, 6.2.16; 6.3.13.
62. *Bṛhadāraṇyaka Upaniṣad*, 3.2.13.
63. *Bṛhadāraṇyaka Upaniṣad*, 2.4.12; 4.5.13.
64. *sati sampādya na vidaḥ*.

from one leaf to another,[65] or as a goldsmith chisels out a new and fairer form, so the soul fashions for itself another form on death.[66] We have earlier noticed how the belief in transmigration arises.

The position of the Upaniṣads is refreshing in contrast to that of Brāhmaṇas. The Upaniṣads emphasize meditation and knowledge as the means of salvation; *tapas* (penance) is praised at various places. The man who knows that he is the *Brahman* becomes the *Brahman* forthwith.[67] Immediately all his sins and virtues are washed away.[68] But sometimes the souls of even those who have knowledge migrate and after a long process reach *Brahman*.[69] The *Kauśitakī Upaniṣad* gives a detailed description of "Brahmā's world" (*brahma-loka*) with its Aparājita palace, and Śalajya city. The *Chāndogya Upaniṣad* (8.12.3) speaks of the person who attains his own form after death and having attained the supreme *jyoti*, laughs, plays and enjoys with women or his relatives and travels by vehicles.[70] The *Taittirīya Upaniṣad* (3.8.10) says that he who knows that the ultimate reality is food, becomes a possessor of food and eater of food, he becomes great by having many children, cattle, and *Brahman* also. Similarly in the same book it is said that he who knows, after death, goes to various worlds and assumes desired forms, eats desired food and goes on singing: "I am food, I

65. *Bṛhadāraṇyaka Upaniṣad*, 4.4.2-6.

66. Ibid., 4.3.33.

67. *Muṇḍaka Upaniṣad*, 3.2.9.

68. *Bṛhadāraṇyaka Upaniṣad*, 4.4.22.

69. *Kauśitakī Upaniṣad*, 1.2.; *Bṛhadāraṇyaka Upaniṣad*, 6.2.

70. *asmāt śarīrāt samuthāya param jyoti rūpasampādya; sa uttama puruṣah sa tatra paryeti jakṣaṇ krīḍān ramamanaḥ strībhirvayanaisva jñātibhirva.*

am eater of food, I am the maker of this song."[71] The Upaniṣadic idea of *summum bonum* may be compared with similar ideas entertained by Jesus Christ and Mohammad. Jesus' teaching is full of hints about a triumphant banquet in the coming Kingdom of God. A sumptuous feast with a lot of eating and drinking was very prominent in Christ's conception of the kingdom of God and for him it formed the climax of the vista of victory.[72] The Islamic conception of heaven, peopled with houris and sumptuous food and wine, is well known.

We do not find any ethical theory worked out in the Upaniṣads. Of course, common maxims like speak the truth, respect your father, mother, brother and preceptor are not lacking.[73] But once it is accepted that it is the absolute that resides in everything as the inner controller, it follows that it is that which makes men do good and evil deeds.[74] One who has real knowledge is not bound by moral laws. Indra tells Pratardana that he who has knowledge can slay an embryo, can murder father or mother and still be not bound;[75] of course, Indra does not say that he who has knowledge should do these things nor does these things. The result of pushing this view to its logical end occurs in the *Jaiminīya Brāhmaṇa* (1.5). There it is told that a deity obstructed a soul from going to the sun and beyond saying that only those who have done good can pass through, and since the soul did only evil, he cannot be allowed. The soul replied, "You saw whatever I was doing, you would not have made me do it (if it were

71. *ya evam yit, asmāllokān pretya, imāllokan kāmanni kāmarūpyanur-sañcaran, etat sama gayannāste.*

72. C.J. Cadoux, *The Life of Jesus*, p. 174.

73. See *Taittirīya Upaniṣad.*

74. *Kauśitakī Upaniṣad*, 3.8.

75. Ibid., 3.1.

evil); so you are the doer in fact." The deity satisfied with the answer allowed him to pass. Such are the Upaniṣads.

It can be concluded that there is no philosophy in the Upaniṣads, because they are the works of numerous authors at numerous periods. As Max Müller wrote, such "utterances as I have here quoted from the Upaniṣads will hardly seem worthy of the name philosophy. . . . What we find here are philosophic rhapsodies rather than consecutive treatises. But that is the very reason why the Upaniṣads are so interesting to the historical student."[76] A.B. Keith, probably the greatest Vedic scholar of modern times, says the same: "Those theories are of historic interest; as philosophy they are unworthy of a moment's consideration."[77] Radhakrishnan says the same, "The aim of the Upaniṣads is not so much to reach philosophical truth. . . . They contain much that is inconsistent and unscientific." He again says, "The Upaniṣads had no set theory of philosophy. . . . They hint at the truth in life but not as yet in science or philosophy."[78] Dasgupta reminds us that the Upaniṣads are not a systematic treatise "but a depository of diverse currents of thought."[79] Bloomfield writes "The Upaniṣads contain in fact no system of thought, though they did unquestionably inspire later Hindu systematic philosophy We are often vexed with their unstable, contradictory, and partly foolish statements."[80]

To have a balanced view it is to be observed that the ideas expressed in the Upaniṣads are not peculiar to India. Such

76. Max Müller, *The Six Systems of Indian Philosophy*, p. 139.

77. A.B. Keith, *The Religion and Philosophy of the Veda and Upaniṣads*, vol. II, p. 593.

78. S. Radhakrishnan, *Indian Philosophy*, vol. I, pp. 138, 140.

79. S.N. Dasgupta, *History of Indian Philosophy*, vol. 1, p. 42.

80. Bloomfield, *The Religion of the Veda*, p. 57.

ideas have been expressed in Greece roughly at about the same time. The Upaniṣads, we may remember, are to be placed in the sixth century BC. Heraclitus (536-470 BC) conceived process or movement as the ultimate truth. Xenophiles (570-480 BC) maintained that there is only one God and that this God cannot at all be anthropomorphically conceived and that he is the reality of the universe. Parmenides (about 470 BC) defined the doctrine clearly: Only the One exists and the One is eternal, immutable and immovable. Change and multiplicity are reduced to illusion. He distinguishes between opinion and knowledge. It is to be noted that the Upaniṣads do not state that the world is an illusion explicitly anywhere, except in a late Upaniṣad, the *Śvetāsvatara*. As contrasted with the Indian theories, those of Greece are definite, free from mythology and allegories. Also the Greek theories sharply eschew religion and belief in any sort of authority. They base themselves on thought, not on *tapas* or the teaching of some seer or scripture. The Greek thinkers are not obsessed with salvation, heaven and after-life. Some Orientalists such as Roth, Gladisch, C.B. Schluter, B. Saint-Hillarie, L. Scherman, Schroeder, Lassen and Garbe have put forward the view that Greece owed much to India. Though there are resemblances, the whole approach and method is different — that of Greece being, logical, virile and manly, that of the Upaniṣads being imaginative, fanciful and erratic. There is also no evidence that there were any contacts between Greece and India, though it is probable that travellers and merchants might have met each other in the lands held by Darius I.

4

The Bhagavad-Gītā

The Bhāgavatas

PROBABLY in the third century BC, a religion with Vāsudeva as deity and with its followers known as Bhāgavatas seem to have been prevalent in and around Mathura on the banks of Yamunā, among some tribes of kṣatriyas known as Śūrasenas. This was noted by Megasthenes,[1] the Greek ambassador to the court of Candragupta Maurya who ruled in the last quarter of fourth century BC. It must have taken at least a hundred years to become a well-developed religion, called the Bhāgavatas.

From the Nārāyaṇīya section of the *Mahābhārata* (Śānti-parva) we learn that some sages known as Citra-śikhaṇḍins founded a religion in which Hari is the supreme God; and he is to be attained neither through sacrifices nor austerities, but through devotion. It is also mentioned that Nārāyaṇa told Nārada about the religion, which consists in being devoted to Vāsudeva with one's heart. The religion is called Bhāgavata Dharma and Śāsvata Dharma; and is identified as the same that is found in the *Bhagavad-Gītā*. The religion is also described as *ekāntika* or monotheistic.[2]

---

1. J.W. McCrindle, *Indika of Megasthenes and Arrian*, Fragment VIII.
2. See H. Raychaudhuri, *Early History of the Vaiṣṇava Sect*.

At that time, about the third century BC, a tribe called Yādavas occupied a part of the country from Mathura to Gujarat. Some of the Yādavas were known as Vṛṣṇis and Sāttvatas. Vāsudeva was the name under which they worshipped God. The *Mahābhārata* gives the meaning of Vāsudeva as he who covers the whole world and is the abode (*adhivāsa*) of it. It is likely that Kṛṣṇa, a hero of the Satiate tribe was identified with this God; and later both of them with Viṣṇu, the Vedic God.[3] What is important is that it is this Bhāgavata sect that has produced the *Bhagavad-Gītā*, one of the finest religious books. Von Humboldt has called it the only true philosophical song existing in any known tongue.[4]

The importance of the *Bhagavad-Gītā* is that it conceives God as personal, entirely spiritual and transcendental entity, who is immanent in the world and beings, creator and lord of all beings. The *Bhagavad-Gītā* is monotheistic, but it is surprisingly catholic that it declares that whatever path a man may take he reaches God only. Further it says that it is the one God who is worshipped in diverse forms as different gods, because the principle in all of them is the same one God. The *Bhagavad-Gītā* further says that the only way of attaining the *summum bonum*, the grace of God is to surrender oneself to God, for which man does not need to practise austerities, leave the world and become an anchorite, neither resort to sacrifices nor other methods. One should perform the duties that devolve upon one to his social position disinterestedly as worship offered to the Divine. The *Bhagavad-Gītā* seems to make no discrimination between castes and sexes. Everyone is entitled to worship God and receive grace. It even makes

---

3. Charles Eliot, *Hinduism and Buddhism*, vol. II, p. 194; R.G. Bhandarkar, *Vaiṣṇavism, Śaivism and Minor Religious Systems*, pp. 9, 11, 33.

4. Letter to Fr. Von Geutz, 1827.

the remarkable declaration that castes have been created by God not according to one's birth, but according to one's nature and occupation.

The *Bhagavad-Gītā* borrows largely the Sāṁkhya scheme of *prakṛti* and evolutes. In addition to souls, the *Bhagavad-Gītā* assumes the *Uttama Puruṣa*, the supreme Spirit. It is not clear from the *Bhagavad-Gītā* whether it regards the *prakṛti* as eternally coexistent with God or as a creation of God or as God's nature. Sometimes the *prakṛti* is spoken of as the uterus (*yoni*) in which God places his seed. It is not also clear whether the *Bhagavad-Gītā* holds the difference between the souls and God as to be real or only apparent. However, the *Bhagavad-Gītā* as a scripture *par excellence* of the Bhāgavatas, teaches by synthesizing the purport of the other scriptures of this sect. He is the personal God and the first emanation of the ineffable godhead: from Vāsudeva proceeds Saṁkarsana, from him Pradyumna, from him Aniruddha, and subsequently twelve other emanations (*vyūhas*). But none of these are within the cosmic egg (*brahmāṇḍas*) or universe. Next begins the creation of souls and matter, of space and time and then the elements, a process being somewhat akin to the Sāṁkhya. The *summum bonum* of souls is to attain "likeness" unto God, *sādharmya*.[5]

From this it may be deduced that the views of the *Bhagavad-Gītā* are also the same as both these books belong to the same religious sect and cannot obviously hold contradictory theories. The *Bhagavad-Gītā* may therefore be described as monotheistic, teaching that God is the sole creator, preserver and destroyer of the world including *prakṛti* and *jīvas*; and the highest goal of the souls is to become like God.[6] The souls

5. See Schrader's Introduction to the Pañcarātra.

6. *paramam saṁyam upaiti* — *Muṇḍaka Upaniṣad*, 3.1.3.

have been created by God — this was the view of the Bhāgavatas. Śaṅkara describes this view and criticizes them by saying that since the Bhāgavatas say that the souls originate from Vāsudeva they must have also an end, as what originates must come to an end.[7] It is thus clear that the Bhāgavata religion is highly monotheistic and the *Bhagavad-Gītā* being their scripture should not be interpreted in any other way, unless it is explicitly required to state otherwise, which however, is not the case. Aurobindo has interpreted the *Bhagavad-Gītā* on such lines also.

Though the *Bhagavad-Gītā* took over the Sāṁkhya philosophy and tried to adapt it to monotheism, it did not succeed; and betrayed its eclecticism. This is the inevitable characteristic of some of the best theological works of Europe and India. We know how Pauline theology tries to harmonize Christianity with Greek philosophy, how Augustine interprets Christianity in terms of Neo-Platonism. Anyway since the *Bhagavad-Gītā* does not claim to be philosophy but something more, it is foolish for us to pronounce that is not philosophical.

Patañjali mentions that there was a sect known as Śiva-Bhāgavatas. The *Mahābhārata* (XII.349) mentions Pāśupatam as a religion. In the *Vāyu Purāṇa* it is said that Śiva will incarnate as Lakulīśa; certain inscriptions have been found which mention that a Lakulīśa was actually born and lived and that it was Śiva who was thus incarnated. It has therefore been argued that one Lakulīśa or Nakulīśa was the founder of Pāśupata.[8] Whatever this may be, it is certain that by the second century BC, there was a sect of Śaivas, for Patañjali mentions them. It is

7. *Brahma-sūtra-bhāṣya*, 2.2.42.

8. R.G. Bhandarkar, *Vaiṣṇavism, Śaivism and Minor Religious Systems*, p. 116; Charles Eliot, *Hinduism and Buddhism*, vol. II, p. 202.

also possible that Śiva was a tribal deity of Niṣādas and Vrātyas. As Patañjali styles them Śiva-Bhāgavatas it is probable they imitated Bhāgavatas. In the *Mahābhārata*, Śiva tells Dakṣa that Pāśupata has been established by him and that it partly contradicts *varṇāśrama*, the system of caste and stage.

Monotheism

The terrible god who howls and rushes past in the thunderstorms, Rudra, the howler of *Ṛgveda* is believed to bestow blessings on those who pray to him; he protects the cattle, saves children from diseases and confers health.[9] In the *Taittirīya Saṁhitā* (IV.5.1), he is conceived as possessing two forms — the benign and the terrible. In the *Atharvaveda* (VII.87.1), Rudra is conceived as the creator of all beings and also immanent in them. Finally in the *Śvetāsvatara Upaniṣad*, Rudra-Śiva appears as the Supreme Lord, creator and destroyer of the universe. Deussen has called the *Śvetāsvatara Upaniṣad* a monument of theism, according to which Rudra is the great Lord-creator and preserver of all men; he is present everywhere and knows everything.[10] Śiva existed before everything, none can see him with the physical eye; he may be intuited as dwelling in the heart.[11] He is the only God, all-pervading, present in all beings by presiding over all activities and supporting all beings; yet without any qualities, he is the Absolute.[12] He is to be understood through Sāṁkhya-Yoga.[13] Those who know Śiva, become immortal.[14] One should know

9. *Ṛgveda*, I.114; 1.8.9.
10. *Śvetāsvatara Upaniṣad*, 3.1.3.
11. Ibid., 4.18, 20.
12. Ibid., 6.2.
13. Ibid., 6.13.
14. Ibid., 2.1; 4.16; 4.2.

Śiva as he is; pray and dedicate oneself to him.[15] Śiva is the possessor of *māyā*, the great power and *prakṛti* through which the world is created. Śiva is the lord of *māyā*, and his great power *māyā* is indestructible and endless.[16] Reality (*Brahman*) is of three kinds, the enjoyer, enjoyed and the dispenser.[17] Śiva rules over the changeable *prakṛti* and the soul.[18] Śiva, the supreme, is without form, it is he who creates the multiplicity of forms with a certain purpose.[19]

In the *Śvetāsvatara Upaniṣad* (4.6), God and the souls are compared to two birds one occupying the higher branch of the tree, the other the lower. The former does not eat the fruits of the tree, the latter lives on them. This bird which eats enjoys and suffers according to the fruits — whether sweet or sour. When there are no fruits to eat, then again it suffers. The other first bird which just looks on to God, is untouched even by pleasure and pain, abiding always in blessed condition. The second bird is *jīva*, subject to pain, pleasure and other conditions and vicissitudes of life.

The *Bhagavad-Gītā*, similar to the *Śvetāsvatara Upaniṣad* also borrows the phraseology of Sāṁkhya and tries to adapt it to monotheism. We cannot with definiteness fix the date of this Upaniṣad. Some scholars have opined it to be post-Buddhist, while A.B. Keith regarded it not to be so late. We cannot also be sure whether this Upaniṣad propagated the Śiva cult or whether it is the Śaiva sect which gave rise to its theology. Whatever it be, in the *Bhagavad-Gītā* and in the *Śvetāsvatara*

---

15. Ibid., 6.18-19.
16. Ibid., 4.10; 5.I.
17. Ibid., 1.12.
18. Ibid., 1.10.
19. Ibid., 4.1.

Upaniṣad, India touches the highest pinnacle of monotheism, for once abandoning absolutistic pantheism and polytheism. It is sad to comment that the Vaiṣṇava and Śaiva sects have not stuck to them.

Senart, Barth and Schweitzer regard the cult of Vāsudeva to be pre-Buddhist and pre-Jaina. Senart regards that but for it "Buddhism would not have come to birth at all."[20] Barth believes it to be "anterior to the rise of Jains in the eighth century BC."[21] Seal has put forward the hypothesis that the Nārāyaṇīya section of the *Mahābhārata* indicates that some Vaiṣṇavas travelled to Egypt and Asia Minor and learnt of Christianity.[22] On the other hand some scholars have suggested that the stories of Christ's mission, birth and his teachings show great influences on the Kṛṣṇa cult and Buddhism.[23] It is however certain that the Bhāgavata religion owes nothing to Christianity, for archaeological evidence goes to prove that Heliodara, a Greek ambassador to Bhāgabhadra was a Bhāgavata and erected a "Garuḍa stambha"[24] in honour of Vāsudeva during second century BC. Tendencies towards monotheism are visible in the Vedas and Upaniṣads. They have been developed by the Bhāgavatas and Śaivas and monotheism at its best is found in the *Bhagavad-Gītā* and the *Śvetāsvatara Upaniṣad*.

Abhorrence of animal sacrifices and austerities are common to these religions and Buddhism. The difference is that the

---

20. *Indian Interpreter*, 1910, pp. 177-78.
21. *Indian Antiquary*, 1894, p. 248; cited from Albert Schweitzer, *Indian Thought and Its Development*, p. 181.
22. Seal, *Vaiṣṇavism and Christianity*, p. 30.
23. Bunsen, Angel Messiah and J.M. Robertson, *Christianity and Mythology*, part II, p. 50.
24. Eagle pillar or Pillar of Praise.

God of the former religions is a personal and transcendent deity, creator, preserver and destroyer of this universe; while the God of Buddhism is an immanent deity, who is being realized. In contrast with the Upaniṣads, the conception of God in Bhāgavata and Śaiva religions is personal and the way to salvation is adoration and devotion to him.

5

The Cārvākas

Indian Materialism

CONTEMPORANEOUS with the Upaniṣads there seem to have been many currents of thought — atheistic, agnostic and materialistic, etc. The Upaniṣads contain certain of them. All these various thoughts appear to have had their own growth, but after some centuries when the scholastic writers wanted to systematize them they perhaps looked back to the Vedas and sought to reinforce their views by quoting the Vedas in support. Unfortunately enough the process of the various doctrines as they were slowly evolving themselves is not preserved to us in any of the books now extant.

In the early Upaniṣads the accounts of creation assume that besides the creator there was something — some material or matter — out of which creation has proceeded. The creator is then described to have actually entered into the creation.[1] Even as far back as in the *Ṛgveda* (X. 121.1) Hiraṇyagarbha is said to have entered into creation after *Brahman* has created. On the one hand there is *Brahman* outside all creation, and on the other the creation. *Brahman* merely affords the end, and the goal is to be attained by the annihilation of everything empirical — the world of thought and action. According to

---

1. *Aitareya*, 1.11.12; *Taittirīya*, 2.6; *Chāndogya*, 6.33.

this view liberation becomes meaningless, for there is really only one *ātman* which became connected with *prakṛti* and produced many separate *ātmans*. The connection of *Brahman* and *prakṛti* is inexplicable and liberation has no meaning at all, since all the souls are nothing but *Brahman* conditioned by *buddhi* and *ahaṁkāra*. The point to be noticed is that *Brahman* is robbed of all empirical reality, while *prakṛti* is that out of which all empirical reality has come forth. Naturally enough the point was raised — if the entire world is an evolute of *prakṛti*, why should *Brahman* be posited? *Prakṛti* itself can be conceived as evolving itself into the world, by sheer chance or by principles inherent in itself. Thus we have the first system of philosophy based on reason in the Lokāyata.

It has been already pointed out how in the *Ṛgveda* itself, we find keen minds questioning, "who is Indra, who has seen him?" and some denies that there is an Indra. We are also told in the *Ṛgveda* (X.71, 72) that there was a Bṛhaspati Laukya and a Bṛhaspati Aṅgīrasa. The materialistic philosophy of India is said to be based on the aphorisms (*sūtras*) of Bṛhaspati. However it is doubtful whether Bṛhaspati himself wrote those *sūtras* or somebody else composed them and ascribed them to Bṛhaspati. Undoubtedly, Bṛhaspati Laukya must have held sceptical views and must have been a critic of the religion and priests. Otherwise he would not have been mentioned as the author of this school of Lokāyata philosophy. The term Lokāyata may be due to its being founded by Laukya or it may mean the "doctrine accepted throughout the world" or "the doctrine directed to the world of senses." From the great space devoted to the criticism of this school of philosophy it may de inferred that it was very popular.

Materialism is very old in India; it existed prior to the Buddha and Mahāvīra. The *Sūtrakṛtāṅga* and the *Dīgha-Nikāya* mention

Ajīta Keśakaṁbalin who held that perception was the only source of knowledge; that man reduces into the four elements after death; and that consciousness will not remain any more.[2] We also read of people like Pūraṇakāśyapa who refused to acknowledge moral distinctions and advocated the fortuitous, origin of things and Payasi, who experimentally established that the soul did not survive death.[3]

While writing the *History of Materialism*, Lange says that materialism is as old as philosophy, but not older. From the pre-historic days people have tended to believe that something survives after death. But the conception of that something is as vague and hazy today as it was then. It is no wonder, therefore, that the denial of it was found to be the simplest way of getting rid of a belief, which had no justification in experience. Even Yājñavalkya remarked that there is no consciousness after death.[4] Together with this, if the belief in the *Brahman* as something beyond material world is rejected materialism arises.

The Lokāyatas

Unfortunately we do not have any of the works of the Lokāyata school preserved. We find caricatures of their doctrines in other books. Haribhadra and Madhava give brief descriptions of their views: Knowledge is solely dependent on sense-experience. What is called inference is nothing but the recollection of a past perception from present perception, through association. The body is evolute.[5] Consciousness arises

2. *Sūtrakṛtāṅga*, Sacred Books of the East, XLV, p. 341; B.M. Barua, *Pre-Buddhistic Indian Philosophy*, p. 289.
3. *Dīgha-Nikāya*, *Sāmaññaphala-sutta*, *Pāyāsi Suttanta*.
4. *Bṛhadāraṇyaka Upaniṣad*, 2.4.13; 4.5.13.
5. *samudāya mātram* — *Ṣaḍ-Darśana Samuccaya*, 82.

out of the four elements — earth, water, fire and air, just as the red colour is produced by a combination of betel, arecanut and lime.[6] Life is only a configuration of matter.[7] As such all those objects of religious faith such as heaven and soul, gods and sacrifices are fictions invented for the sake of livelihood by priests.[8] Therefore man should try to live happily as long as he can without being obsessed by heaven, sacrifice, fears of demons and gods, etc. The ethics of the Lokāyata is: "While life is yours, live joyously."[9]

The Cārvāka School is remarkably similar to that of Epicurus. The greatness of the Cārvāka School is that it discovered that men torture themselves unnecessarily with fear. They are afraid of gods and goblins, of what Indra and Varuṇa, Yama and Garuḍa might do to them. The Cārvākas tell us that there are no such beings; they are either the projections of our own fears and morbid fancies or the creations of wily priests. Men again are afraid of what might befall them after death. The Cārvākas assure that death need not be feared, death being only a loss of consciousness like sleep. Of course, there are much hardship and misery encountered in life; but it should be remembered that life has also its joys. Who will throw away rice grain because it is covered with husk or the egg-yolk because it is enclosed in a useless shell? So it is man's duty to derive as much pleasure as he can, bearing the hardships of life, bravely and without fear of anything. The Cārvākas therefore explain that there is no soul; for consciousness is the resultant of the combination of material elements. There is no God; the order and design

6. *Sarva-Siddhānta-Sāra Saṁgraha*, II.7.

7. *Prabodha-Candrodaya*, II.

8. *Sarva-Darśana Saṁgraha*, I.

9. *Sarva-Darśana Saṁgraha*, p. 2.

evident in the world being natural. They ask: "who colours wonderfully the peacocks, or who makes the cuckoos coo so well? There is, in respect of these, no cause other than nature."[10] What Lucretius said of Epicurus, as stated below, is equally applicable to Bṛhaspati, founder of the Lokāyata School:

> "When Man's life upon earth in base dismay
> Crushed by the burden of religion, lay,
> Whose face, from all the regions of the sky,
> Hung, glaring hate upon mortality,
> First one — man against her dared to rise.
> His eyes, against her strive through all his days;
> Him noise of gods nor lightnings nor the roar
> Of raging heaven subdued, but pricked the more
> His spirit's valiance, till he longed the Gate
> To burst of this low prison of man's fate.
> And thus the living ardour of his mind—
> Conquered, and clove its way—
> he returned to make Man see
> At last what can, what cannot, come to be;
> By what law to each thing its power hath been
> Assigned, and what deep boundary set between
> Till under foot is tamed religion trod." (I.62, 78)

And the Lokāyata can be summed up in the very words in which Gilbert Murray summed up Epicurean philosophy: "thus the great system is built, simple, intelligible, dogmatic, and as such systems go, remarkably water-tight. It enables man to be un-afraid, and it helps him to be happy. . . ."[11] It is remarkable that such views as those of Lokāyata should have been held in those hoary old days. Possibly materialist philosophy was very powerful in India at one time. Elaborate

10. *Sarva-Siddhānta-Sāra Saṁgraha* II.5.

11. Gilbert Murray, *Five Stages of Greek Religion*, p. 106.

attempts are made to disprove the Lokāyata views in many books and "their very eagerness to discredit it shows how important it was in their eyes. Possibly much of the literature of materialism in India was destroyed by the priests and other believers in the orthodox religion."[12] It is to be remarked in this connection that the Lokāyata School is the only rationalistic philosophy that has been formulated in India barring early Sāṁkhya; no other school is purely and exclusively based on reason.

12. Jawaharlal Nehru, *The Discovery of India*, p. 73.

6

Jainism

Historical Background

THE sixth century BC was a period of great intellectual ferment throughout the world. Jainism and Buddhism arose in that century, Jainism preceding the other. At Ephesus, Heraclitus was carrying on his speculative inquiries; in Babylon, Isaiah was laying the foundations of a firm monotheism; and in China, Confucius and Lao Tzu were propagating their moral teachings. As we have seen, it was at this time that the views collected in the Upaniṣads were given rise to. It is of course certain that the older Upaniṣads preceded Mahāvīra and the Buddha, but others are post-Buddhistic. It was a century of criticism and bold enquiry. It questioned the authority of priests, the validity of magic and religion, the value of blood sacrifices and worship of gods and goddesses. Materialism, Jainism, and Buddhism are the results of this tendency.

India at that time was divided into numerous principalities constantly vying with each other. Kings oppressed the common people, the priests tabooed this and that; famines and epidemics were frequent; houses were not safe due to robbers and fire. No wonder, the common man was bewildered by the misery all around him. The *Ācārāṅga-sūtra* described the insecurity of the citizen: "At one time, his manifold savings are a large treasure. Then at another time, his heirs divide it, or those who are without a living steal it, or the king takes it away, or it is ruined in some way or other, or it is consumed by the conflagration of the house."[1] Again a passage in *Uttarādhyayana* shows us that those who could think were critical of sacrifices: "the binding of animals (to the sacrificial pole), all the Vedas, and sacrifices, being causes of sin, cannot save the sinner."[2] Though in every land and age, it is the nobles that are the highest class, the brāhmins began to claim supremacy over every other caste. Caste distinctions also ossified by this time. As has been shown, the Upaniṣads themselves are due in a great degree to the kṣatriyas. Throughout Jaina and Buddhist works the kṣatriya caste was mentioned as the first and highest and the brāhmin as the second.[3] Traces of antagonism between the brāhmins and kṣatriyas are found in Jaina and Buddhist works.[4] The brāhmins are sometimes referred to as *hīna-jacco*, low-born, compared to the kṣatriyas.[5] The kṣatriyas began to take notice of the preposterous claims of the brāhmins, as the exclusive mediators between gods and men, in fact their claim to be gods on earth.

Mahāvīra was the son of the chief of a kṣatriya clan of Vaiśālī, corresponding to the present Besarh near Patna of present-day India.[6] In those days there were wandering ascetics who practised austerities, denounced sacrifices and ceremonies, and emphasized meditation and renunciation as the ways for salvation. One such sect of wandering monks of the order of Pārśvanātha was living in a park near Vaiśālī.

1. Sacred Books of the East, vol. XXII, p. 20.
2. Ibid., vol. XIV, p. 140.
3. T.W. Rhys Davids, *Buddhist India*, p. 61.
4. Sacred Books of the East, vol. XIV, pp. 136, 294, 366.
5. *Jātaka*, 5.257.
6. Sinclair Stevenson, *The Heart of Jainism*, p. 22.

They were supported by Mahāvīra's clan. In his thirtieth year Mahāvīra joined this order. He practised many kinds of austerities and penance. But after a year, dissatisfied with that order, he left them and wandered alone in a state of absolute nudity.[7] At the end of twelve years of wandering and penance, Mahāvīra gained *kevala jñāna* or omniscience. Thenceforward he began to teach. At first petty chieftains and rulers were attracted to his teachings. The Jaina books mention king Cetaka of Videha, king Kuśika of Aṅga, king Śatānīka of Kauśāmbī, king Śreṇika of Magadha, and king Hastipāla of Pāpā as the disciples of Mahāvīra. The kings of Campā, Vaiśālī, and Mithilā were also his followers.

Brief Sketch of Jainism

Mahāvīra's message to mankind is that caste and birth are nothing, while it is the *karma* which is the cause of all misery. Therefore for the sake of happiness, *karma* should be annihilated, which can be done only by austerities.[8]

Jaina philosophy classifies things into nine categories, *jīva, ajīva, puṇya, pāpa, āśrava, saṁvara, bandha, nirjarā* and *mokṣa*. *Jīva* is the conscious substance, capable of development, imperceptible to the senses, an active agent, and as big as the body it animates. Everything, such as clay, stones, diamonds, men, animals and plants are *jīva*s. The only difference is the number of senses which they possess; so even stone and clay can suffer, and they are animated (*prāṇī*). Only an omniscient *kevalī* like Mahāvīra can perceive this. *Ajīva* or "not-*jīva*" is of two kinds, that which has no form and that which has form. Motion, non-motion, space and time are formless "not-*jīva*": *arūpī ajīva*. Matter (*pudgala*) is that which possesses qualities

7. Ibid., p. 35.
8. Sinclair Stevenson, *The Heart of Jainism*, pp. 39-40.

and decays or alters its form and gets destroyed; it is the *ajīva* with form. The third category is *puṇya* or actions (*karmas*) that involve giving food or water or clothes to the needy and poor. The fourth category is sin or *pāpa*, which consists of killing of any *jīva*. Even to wish harm or death of another being is sin, it being "idea of killing" (*bhāva-hiṁsā*) as distinguished from "actual killing" (*dravya-hiṁsā*). Though killing is the cardinal sin; Jainism enumerates other sins like lying, dishonesty, unchastity, etc.

Āśrava or the way through which *karma* enters into a soul is the fifth category. The five senses; the four emotions — anger, conceit, deceit and avarice; failure to take the five great vows; the three *yogas* of mind, speech and body — are the seventeen major *āśravas*. That by which the inflow of *karma* can be arrested is the *saṁvara* — the sixth category. To walk without injuring any living-being, to speak kind and truthful words, to be regulated in food and drink, to control one's emotions and desires, etc. are *saṁvara*.

Bandha or bondage is the union of soul with *pudgala*. As a heated iron ball takes up water-particles in which it is immersed, so the soul takes up *pudgala* or matter-particles, when it indulges in passions like anger and love, etc. This constitutes the *bandha* or bondage of the soul. *Nirjarā* is that which wears away or destroys accumulated *karma*. External austerities like fasting, pulling out the hairs by their roots (*loca*), etc. and internal austerities like confession and penance, study of Jaina scriptures, meditation, etc. are *nirjarā*. The most effective and best way of annihilating one's *karma* is to mount up some sacred hill like Girnār or Pārśvanātha and stay still without doing anything till one dies. This of course, only ascetics in their final stage of development practise.[9] Freedom

---

9. *padopa-gamana santhāro*.

from all *karmas* and possibility of rebirth is *mokṣa*. While some Jains believe *mokṣa* to be the attainment of some kind of heaven, others hold it to be a state of freedom. He who attains *mokṣa* is a *siddha*. According to some Jains the eunuchs cannot attain *mokṣa*, while the Digambara sect of Jains holds that a woman cannot attain *mokṣa*.

From this brief sketch of Jainism, its value as philosophy can be judged. It is not rationalistic; it claims to be based on the omniscience or *Kevala-jñāna* of *siddhas*, attained through austerities and penance. Nor is it based on the principle of equality and brotherhood of all men. It started, no doubt, partly as a reaction of the kṣatriya against the sacrificial religious practices and their protagonists, brāhmins. But it never took into account the lower castes nor did it regard men and women to be equal. The Jaina temple erected by Seth Hatthi Siṁha in 1848 at Ahmedabad contains a notice that dogs and low caste servants should not enter the temple. The Jains believe in many worlds and gods, but not in God. They worship *Jinas* and the *Arhats*. While early Jainism had no God, Haribhadra states that Mahāvīra, the *Jina par excellence* is the God, worshipped by all gods and demons.[10] And *Jinas* are worshipped in all Jaina temples almost in the same way in which the Hindu gods are worshipped. In short Jainism took over the conceptions of *karma* and rebirth prevalent at the time, made austerities — physical and mental, as the way to escape *karma*; and *ahiṁsā* (non-violence) became the principal duty. There is of course that famous doctrine of *sapta-bhaṅgī-naya*, which teaches that while the existence of a thing can be affirmed from one point of view, it can be denied from another point of view. Thus when an agnostic denies the soul, the Jaina can argue that the soul being a substance exists. But it

---

10. *jinendro devatā . . . surasurendra sampūjyaḥ* — Haribhadra.

does not exist in matter, nor does matter exist in it. Also sometimes it exists, at other times it does not. So from this point of view a soul does not exist. But if all knowledge is relative to the point of view adopted and if there are several points of view, why should one believe the Jaina philosophy only to be the true one? Why cannot one have a different philosophy arrived at from a different point of view? The Jaina's reply is that the knowledge of the *kevalin*, the *siddha*, is integral and complete and that the Jaina philosophy is such. One is not permitted to ask why the *sapta-bhaṅgī-naya* is not applicable to the *kevala jñāna* also, nor can one ask how and why we should believe that Mahāvīra had omniscience and that his doctrines are infallible. That is so because Jainism is a religion not a philosophy. To the Jains the crucial point is how may a *jīva* free itself from its transitory imprisonment, and, following the upward path, attain deliverance at last?[11] Radhakrishnan remarks, "Jainism is the product of an age of immature philosophizing."[12]

11. Sinclair Stevenson, *The Heart of Jainism*, p. 93.

12. S. Radhakrishnan, *Indian Philosophy*, vol. I, p. 335.

7

Buddhism

Life and Message of the Buddha

THE Buddha came from the tribe of Śākyas, one of the many tribes then inhabiting north India. What now corresponds to south of Bihar, west of Bengal and the south of the Ganges was the country of Magadhas with the capital at Rājagṛha. West of the Magadhas were the Kāśīs with their chief city as Benaras; to the north of them as far as the Himalayas extended were the Kośalas with their capital at Śrāvastī. The northern borders of the Kośalas were inhabited by the Śākyas and Koliyas; and all these are nothing but tribal names.[1] The Buddhist books speak of the Śākyas as the exiled sons and daughters, who intermarried and gave rise to the Śākya tribe. The Śākyas were so named because they resided in a Śaka grove.[2] As in the other tribes of Vattis, Koliyas, etc. the upper stratum of the Śākya tribe were also warriors and nobles; each of them was considered a *rājā*; and the Buddha was the son of one such *rājā*. In the *Majjhima-nikāya* (II.124), king Pasenadi calls himself and the Buddha as Kośalas. In the *Sutta-nipāta* (422.3), the Buddha speaks of his birth and renunciation to Bimbisāra thus: "There is, O king, a country on the slope of the Himalayas, rich in wealth and heroes who dwell among the Kośalas. They are descendents of the sun by clan, Śākyas

1. E.J. Thomas, *The Life of the Buddha*, p. 13.
2. *Dīgha-Nikāya*, I.109; *Mahāvastu*, I.351.

by birth. From that family I have gone out, O king, having no longing for sensual desires." The *Dīgha-Nikāya* (1.115) merely speaks of the Buddha as a kṣatriya and his family being rich and great. His birth-place Kapilavastu was about the south-east of Nepal and some 150 miles north of Benaras.[3] The Buddha had neither kingdom nor palace, but belonged to an agricultural society, where the leaders were all *rājās*, possibly with an elected *mahārājā*. It is only the later legends that made the Buddha a prince and his father, a powerful monarch of vast dominions.[4]

From his childhood the Buddha was prone to trances. In the *Majjhima-Nikāya* (I.246), the Buddha says that at the time when his father the Śākyan was working, he was seated beneath a rose-apple tree and fell into a trance. The father must evidently have been ploughing. The Buddha was of the brooding meditative type. At the age of twenty-nine, he became an ascetic. Why? To put it in his own words, he was "troubled, ashamed, and disgusted" that he should become old and sick and then die.[5] How to escape from these and "seek out the unborn, supreme peace of *nirvāṇa*"? (*nir* or *nis* = intensive; *va* = to blow; *nirvāṇa* = complete extinction). Later legends created the term, *mahā-niṣkramaṇa* or the "great renunciation." But the Pāli scriptures know nothing of this "great-renunciation."[6] So the Buddha set out to seek a way out of old age, sickness and death, a way to *nirvāṇa*; and he thought he could best find it as an ascetic. "Now before my enlightenment, while yet a *bodhisattva* and not yet fully enlightened, I thought, oppressive is life in a house, a place of

3. C.A.F. Rhys Davids, *A Manual of Buddhism*, p. 42.
4. Ibid., p. 42.
5. *Majjhima-Nikāya* I.163; *Aṅguttara-Nikāya* I.145.
6. E.J. Thomas, op. cit., pp. 51-52; Rhys Davids, op. cit., p. 53.

dust. In the free air is abandonment of the world. Not easy is it for him who dwells in a house to practice a completely full, completely pure, and perfect religious life."[7] The Buddha must have observed the social degradation of the tradesman, the labourer and the slave, the castes below the kṣatriya and the brāhmin, and the pitiable position of the woman. The Pāli scriptures are conscious of these social ills; and the Buddha also must have noted them. But the scriptures do not mention or even suggest the Buddha to have uttered anything which could justify us in so thinking.[8] After becoming an ascetic, the Buddha was for some time a disciple of Alara Kalama and Uddaka Rāmaputta whose doctrines were aimed at the attainment of the state of nothingness. The Buddha soon understood and left them thinking that this doctrine "does not conduce to aversion (*nibbidā*) absence of passion, stopping (*nirodha*), rest (*upāsama*), higher knowledge (*nirvāṇa*)."[9]

Then in the company of five disciples he practised austerities for six years, which was stated as: He pressed his tongue to his palate, restrained and crushed it. Sweat flowed from his armpits, his body remained unquiet and uncalmed, though the pain overwhelmed him, his mind was not overpowered. Then he practised restraint of breathing in and out from mouth and nose. The result was that violent winds disturbed his head and the sounds of those winds rang in his ears. Then he began to take food in very small quantities. He took a palmful of the juice of beans, vetches, chickpeas or pulses. As a result his body became extremely lean. His ribs stuck out, his eyes sunk in and the skin of his head withered. The skin of his stomach clung to his body; his decayed hair

7. *Majjhima-Nikāya*, I.240.

8. Rhys Davids, op. cit., p. 49.

9. *Majjhima-Nikāya*, I.240.

began to fall off. Then he thought "those ascetics and brāhmins in the past, who have suffered sudden, sharp, keen, severe pains, at the most have not suffered more than this. But by this severe mortification I do not attain superhuman, truly noble knowledge and insight. Perhaps there is another way to enlightenment."[10] Then he recollected how at home he fell into a trance of joy and pleasure, without evil desires and combined with reasoning and investigation. The Buddha thought that it was the way to enlightenment, but impossible to gain that happy state while he was so lean. So he took solid food, rice and sour milk. "Now having taken solid food and gained strength without sensual desires, without evil ideas I attained the abode in the first trance of joy and pleasure, arising from seclusion and combined with reasoning and investigation."[11] Then gradually he passed through successive trances, abandoning reasoning and investigation, joy and aversion, pleasure and pain. Then with this mind concentrated, purified, cleansed, spotless with the defilements gone; he directed his mind to the knowledge of his past births, then to the knowledge of the death and rebirth of beings and then finally to the knowledge of the destruction of *āsava*s (instincts or impulses). "As I thus knew and thus perceived, my mind was emancipated from the *āsava* of sensual desire, from the *āsava* of desire for existence and from the *āsava* of ignorance. And in me emancipated arose the knowledge of my emancipation. I realized that destroyed is rebirth, the religious life has been led, done is what was to be done, there is nothing beyond this world."[12] The five ascetics who were with the Buddha left him as soon as they saw him abandoning austerities

10. E.J. Thomas, *The Life of the Buddha*, pp. 64-68.

11. Ibid.

12. Ibid.

and taking food. As soon as enlightenment came to the Buddha, he was wandering whether he should teach the truth he has discovered or whether men will be able to understand it. It is said that Brahmā, God came to him and prayed him to impart the doctrine to others. Accordingly the Buddha set out to teach his doctrine. Finding Alara Kalama and Uddaka Rāmaputta were dead, the Buddha thought of the five ascetics who left him and who were then in Benaras. So he went to them, preached his doctrine and converted them.

The message of the Buddha was recorded in the *Dhamma-cakka-pavattana-sutta* and the *Anatta-lakkhana-sutta*.[13] Rhys Davids always proceeds on the assumption that the teaching of the Buddha must have been something different from that we find and ascribed to him.[14] Buddhism is a world religion. The founder of a world religion must have such and such a view, so the Buddha must have held such and such a view. That roughly seems to be her reasoning. With her wonderfully intimate knowledge of Pāli scriptures, Rhys Davids has successfully managed to read into them what the Buddha must have taught. But as E.J. Thomas has pointed out, "there is no rivalry between the Pāli and other schools in their canonical sources. They developed new problems, but all accepted the same scriptural utterances as their authority. We can see . . . nothing to indicate that Buddhism ever lost hold of the doctrines once delivered to the disciples."[15] With this, of course, we must be careful to remember that Rhys Davids' profound scholarship and years of unremitting study make her translations more accurate and her interpretations more truthful than those of the others.

---

13. *Saṁyutta-Nikāya*, V.420; III.66.
14. C.A.F. Rhys Davids, *A Manual of Buddhism*, pp. 51-53.
15. E.J. Thomas, op. cit., p. 209.

The first sermon of the Buddha teaches how the two extremes — "that conjoined with the passions, low, vulgar, common, ignoble and useless, and that conjoined with self-torture, painful, ignoble, and useless" should be avoided. Man is often in trouble and is ill; birth and old age, sickness and dying are full of sorrow. How to escape these, how to get a thorough knowledge and understanding, to blowing-out (*nirvāṇa*)? Not of course by resorting to either of the two extremes, that of self-indulgence and worldliness and that of becoming a slave to meaningless body-tortures and rules. One must follow the middle way, the way following by which one becomes better, for there is a better state and there is a way of becoming better. And this middle way, the way to become better, lies in practising right views, right intention, right speech, right action, right livelihood, right effort, right mindfulness and right concentration.[16] The importance and sanity of the Buddha's teaching cannot be exaggerated in an age when on the one hand was prevalent the commercial sacrificial religion of the brāhmins with its gross superstitious animism, and on the other hand a reaction against it, wherein some people begin to follow severe austerities and all sorts of esoteric practices. Therefore the Buddha came and taught that *paramattha*, the highest good, did not lie in following either way.

Further in the famous *Anattalakkhana-sutta* the Buddha teaches that the form or that which is seen (*rūpa*) is not the self (*anatta*); when the Buddha said that the "body is not the self," he did not mean to say the "the body is soul-less." Similarly feeling, perception and the aggregates (*khandha*s) are not the self, because they cannot become for us. They are

---

16. E.J. Thomas, *The Life of the Buddha*, p. 62; C.A.F. Rhys Davids, *A Manual of Buddhism*, p. 109.

hindrances; moreover the form, that which is seen (the body), is impermanent and painful. Is it fitting to consider what is impermanent, painful, and subject to changes, this is mine, this is I, this is myself? Therefore in truth monks, whatever seen — things, feeling, perception, activities, mind, whether it be past, future, present, internal or external, gross or subtle, low or eminent, near or far — is to be looked on by him who duly and rightly understands as, "all this is not mine, not this am I, this is not myself." Later Buddhist books derived the conclusion that there is no self at all, because the Buddha denied both body and mind are "self" and what else remains? The Upaniṣads say that the *ātman* is neither mind nor the body, it is the doer behind the doing; and it is the knower behind the mind. The Man, the *puruṣa* or the "spirit" is separate from the mind and the body. What that cannot be described or defined, "this self, should be searched for," says the *Chāndogya Upaniṣad* (8.1.1). Was this the Buddha's teaching also? In the *Mahāvagga* we have an interesting story, where the kṣatriya youth asked the Buddha, who was sitting on the road-side, whether he had seen a woman passing by. The Buddha replied, "What have you to do with a woman? Were it not better that you seek the self, *attam*," to which they agreed. The Buddha said. "Sit down, I will teach you *dharma*."[17] It is significant that the Buddha uses the word *attam*; and does not use the plural "selves" nor does he prefix the adjective "your."

Another word often used in Buddhist literature is *dharma*. Its meaning is as significant and allusive as that of *Brahman* in the Upaniṣads. In the *Saṁyutta-Nikāya* (VI Book) we are told that the Buddha, just after enlightenment, decided to honour and worship *dharma* alone and nothing else. And it is explained that he who desires the self and longs for the great self

---

17. *Mahāvagga*, I.14.

(*mahāttam*) must revere the very *dharma*. Sogen has written, "Buddhism loves to acknowledge the presence in this world of a reality which transcends the bounds of phenomena, which is imminent everywhere and in which we live and move and have our being."[18] And again "God, according to the proclamation of the Buddha, is immanent in the universe."[19] And the last words of the Buddha to his disciple, Ānanda are, "Live as they who have the self, who have *dharma* as a lamp, as refuge." In the Upaniṣads, *dharma* is used to mean standard or norm, law, right or truth and conduct or duty.[20] The Upaniṣads enjoin that one should walk on the path of *dharma*; and the Buddha tells Śuddhodana and Rāhula: "One should practise well the *dharma*; who practises the *dharma* rests in bliss." Also when the first five disciples after attaining knowledge (*annasi*) ask for being granted *pabbaja* and ordained for consummation (*upasaṁpadā*), the Buddha admits them with these words: "Come, monk, well proclaimed is the *dharma*; move in *Brahman* (*brahmacarya*) for making a complete end of suffering." In the *Dīgha-Nikāya* (III.25), the Buddha is asked, "What is this *dharma* which your disciples, when trained therein and finding comfort, confess as the base of Brahmā-living which they prefer." This should be compared with such passages in the Upaniṣads, "what is here in this Brahmā-citadel that should be searched out, that one should want to understand?" The *Bṛhadāraṇyaka Upaniṣad* (1.4.14) tells: "*Brahman* creates *dharma* than which nothing is higher." *Mahānārāyaṇa Upaniṣad* (XXI.6) says that the whole universe is encircled by *dharma*.[21]

---

18. Y. Sogen, *Systems of Buddhist Thought*, p. 64.
19. Y. Sogen, *Systems of Buddhist Thought*, p. 301; H.S. Gour, *The Spirit of Buddhism*, p. 281.
20. *Kauśitakī Upaniṣad*, 2.1; *Bṛhadāraṇyaka Upaniṣad*, 1.4.14; 1.11.1.
21. See Geiger, *Dharma and Brahman*.

Considerable space is given to the Buddha's original doctrine and how he arrived at, because there are many who say that Buddhism is an original and rationalistic doctrine. It is remarked that his appeal was to logic, reason and experience; and his method was one of psychological analysis, a psychology without a soul. But it is nothing of the kind; he did not gain truths by reasoning and logic. "It is an illusion to suppose that we can prove that the Buddha taught the doctrine of non-self."[22] He gained them by falling into a kind of trance, a mystic trance, by going through what may be called a kind of inner spiritual development. In fact, the second trance begins when reasoning and investigation cease.[23] This is not, of course, the place to discuss the validity and value of mystic experience. Suffice it to say that the Buddha arrives at what he believes to be the truths not through reasoning and logic, but through a supernormal experience.[24] He is the *tathāgata*, the *arahat*, whose teaching is indubitable, true and beyond logic. His conception of *dharma* and the soul are not entirely original; we find them in the Upaniṣads: "It is certain that Buddhism has acquired as an inheritance from Brāhmaṇism not merely a series of its most important dogmas, but what is not less significant to the historian, the bent of its religious thought and feeling, which is more easily comprehended than expressed in words."[25] "Buddhism grew and flourished within the fold of orthodox belief."[26] Nor do we find the Buddha preaching the doctrine of no-soul.[27] Buddhism not only acknowledges the permanence

22. E.J. Thomas, *History of Buddhist Thought*, p. 99.
23. Ibid., p. 66.
24. A.B. Keith, *Buddhist Philosophy*, p. 33.
25. H. Oldenberg, *Buddha*, p. 53.
26. C.A.F. Rhys Davids, *A Manual of Buddhism*, p. 85.
27. H.S. Gour, *The Spirit of Buddhism*, p. 351.

of the noumenal ego, but actually enjoins its adherents to train people in such a manner as to be able to attain union with the great Soul of the universe, the technical term for which is *mahātman*.[28] "The conception of the soul which is abhorrent to Buddhism is that of the *hīnātman* or the individual soul, regarded as a concrete agent enshrined in the body and even acting, thinking and feeling."[29] Y. Sogen makes an illuminating remark: "*Hīnātman* which is here condemned resembles in many respects the *ahaṁkāra* or egotism of Sāṁkhya philosophy."[30] The Buddha is said to have taught that "he who holds that there is no soul is a man with false notions."[31]

The greatness of the Buddha lies in another direction. He rose above the animistic and polytheistic beliefs of his age, which could not be got rid of, even by the Upaniṣadic authors. Buddhism admitted gods as a higher species of beings subject to birth and death. Secondly in an age when there were only two alternatives — the sacrificial religion of the brāhmins and the foolish asceticism of the *parivrājaka*s, the Buddha boldly struck a sane middle path. The state of the times is described by the *Lalitavistara* thus: "People are crowded by *tīrthaṅkara*s or revealers of the truth, with diverse wishes and at a time when their faculties are wriggling in the grasp of the crocodile of their carnal wants. Stupid men, who seek to purify their persons by diverse modes of austerity and penance, inculcate the same. Some of them cannot make out their *mantra*s; some lick their hands; some are unclean, some have no *mantra*s; some wander after different sources; some adore cows, deer, horses, dogs, monkeys, or elephants. Seated at one place in silence

28. Y. Sogen, op. cit., p. 23.

29. Ibid., p. 20.

30. Ibid., p. 24.

31. Warren, *Buddhism in Translations*, p. 161.

with their legs bent under them, some attempt greatness. Some attempt to accomplish their penance by inhaling smoke or fire, by gazing at the sun, by performing the five fires, resting on one foot or with an arm perpetually uplifted or moving about the knees. . . . Some pride themselves on their saluting Brahmā, Indra, Rudra, Viṣṇu, Devī, Kumāra." The Buddha came and taught that all this was nonsense. To seek the *summum bonum* man need not fast or practise foolish austerities. He can eat and drink well; and the Buddha himself lived well, he ate meat and rich nourishing food,[32] and lived in a scented chamber.[33] In fact, he was accused by the first disciples that he was addicted to *bahula* (muchness) or luxury.[34] And when he went to Benaras and proclaimed himself a *tathāgata* to them, they asked in bewilderment: "Will you, when you now live in abundance, have given up exertion, and have turned to a life of abundance, gain that supernatural truly noble knowledge?" It was the Buddha's greatness that he practised, and taught like Aristotle the "golden mean" between the two extremes, in an age when extremes were attracting the attention of people.

The other great contribution of the Buddha is his conception of reality as becoming — not only the whole world is becoming, but even the very self of man is becoming. As he pointed out in the *Anattalakkahana-sutta*, the self is that which can become for us as the body, the senses and the mind cannot so become; they are not the self. Now what does the self become? It can become the *Brahman* (*Brahma-bhūtva*). While in the Upaniṣads the emphasis seems to be that man should know that he is *Brahman*, in the teaching of the Buddha it is said that man should become *Brahman*. In the Upaniṣads we find the

---

32. *Majjhima-Nikāya*, I.368.
33. *Dīgha-Nikāya*, II.6; *Udāna-Nikāya*, VIII.7.
34. *Majjhima-Nikāya*, 26.

supreme reality becoming the world. As Mrs Rhys Davids has explained, "becoming is here no longer a state of progress from a more imperfect to a less imperfect; it is raised to the higher level which we tend to see in the work of such a man as we call a genius. Becoming is in such to be rather described as a becoming — other, a becoming a new manifold."[35] His message was "that man has it in his nature, by becoming more, to become ultimately that supreme Godhead who he potentially is."[36] And whereas the Upaniṣads emphasized that man knows what he really is, and the Buddha emphasized that the life of man is such that he may become what he may be. What that is *saṁsāra* is *nirvāṇa*; and what that is *nirvāṇa* is *saṁsāra*.[37] Nāgārjuna has clearly expressed that, whatever is being itself of God (*tathāgata*) is itself being itself of the world (*jagat*).[38] The Japanese scholar Gyonen has explained that, "All beings are the Buddhas (gods) in their fundamental nature; and all beings in the six *gati*s namely — hell, *preta*, beast, demon or *asura*, man and heaven — without any exception attain to *nirvāṇa*."[39]

The doctrine of *paticca-samuppāda* has been often called a philosophy. No doubt the doctrine proceeds on the presumption that everything has a cause. "When that exists, this exists; with the arising of that this arises; when that does not exist, this does not exist; with the cessation of that this ceases."[40] In an age of animism and polytheism it is a big achievement to arrive at the conception of everything being

35. C.A.F. Rhys Davids, *A Manual of Buddhism*, p. 96.
36. Ibid., p. 93.
37. Nāgārjuna's *Mādhyamika-Śāstra*, 25.9, 19, 20.
38. Nāgārjuana's *Mādhyamika-Śāstra*, 22.16.
39. Y. Sogen, op. cit., p. 205.
40. *Majjhima-Nikāya*, 11.32.

caused naturally, deities and spirits having no hand in the matter. But this principle was never applied to the universe as a whole. The world is full of suffering, it must have a cause; he who comes to know the cause of suffering can escape suffering. As for that wearisome "chain of causation" which says that ignorance causes the aggregates, the aggregates cause the consciousness, from consciousness arises mind and body and so on, several such chains are mentioned differing both in the order of links and number.[41] Scholars like Senart and E.J. Thomas have come to the conclusion that there is no real logical connection in the sequence; it has merely been assembled from various sources.[42] It must however be remembered that the Buddhist scriptures themselves do not claim that it is based on logic. It is a truth which they believe was arrived at by insight (*paññā*) the result of long and deep meditation (*dhyāna*) and concentration (*samādhi*). It is possible that the Buddha himself had nothing to do with this formulation of the twelve-linked chain of causation or dependent origination. In the *Mahānidāna-sutta*,[43] the Buddha is said to mention only nine links. And Sogen writes, "This period division of the "Twelve-linked chain of causation" is, so far as I know, not explicitly stated in any of the works contained in the Pāli *Piṭaka*."[44]

Some modern scholars have attempted to show that the Buddha tried to remove caste barriers and preached equality. There is no evidence in the Buddhist scriptures to show that he tried to abolish caste as a social institution. The Pāli scriptures mention the saying of the Buddha that the kṣatriya

---

41. C.A.F. Rhys Davids, op. cit., p. 78; E.J. Thomas, op. cit., p. 193.

42. E.J. Thomas, op. cit., pp. 194, 198.

43. *Dīgha-Nikāya* II.55.

44. Y. Sogen, *Systems of Buddhist Thought*, p. 81.

caste is the highest, "the best among gods and men."[45] Again the Buddha is said to have put forward another view, namely that the true brāhmin is he who is virtuous and learned and not he who is born in the brāhmin caste.[46] The brāhmins were ridiculed at several places; thus for example the Buddha is said to have asked two brāhmins — Vasettha and Bhāradvāja, whether any brāhmin has ever seen Brahmā and other gods face to face. They admitted that no brāhmin saw them. Then the brāhmins were ridiculed for being like the man who is in love, but cannot say who the lady is or the man who builds a staircase without knowing, where a palace is.[47] The *Madhura-sutta* deliberately rejects the view that the brāhmin came from the mouth of Brahmā. In the *Aggañña-sutta*,[48] the Buddha mentions that the kṣatriyas were the first caste and that the other three castes were subsequently differentiated. The Pāli scriptures describe the Buddha as simply ignoring the other castes, their troubles and degradation. Likewise Plato or St. Paul never raised their voice against slavery. He was only concerned with asserting kṣatriya supremacy over the brāhmins by criticizing and rejecting brāhmin's claims. It appears as though these claims and counter-claims of both the castes were being just then voiced in the sixth century BC; and we have no records to show that the Buddha rose above these wrangles and tried to abolish caste. On the other hand he is said to have eagerly and with warmth championed the claims of kṣatriyas to be the best among men. The Buddhist legends say that the Buddhas can arise only in one of the two highest castes. The Buddha, of course, did not accept any caste

45. *Madhura-sutta, Majjhima-Nikāya*, II.84.

46. *Sonadaṇḍa-sutta, Dīgha-Nikāya*, I.III.

47. *Tevijja-sutta, Dīgha-Nikāya*, I.235.

48. *Dīgha-Nikāya*, III.4.

distinctions among Buddhist monks. Buddhist monks of the four castes, "when they have gone forth in the doctrine and discipline taught by the *tathāgata* from a house to a houseless life, lose their former names and *gotras*, and are known as ascetics, sons of the Śākyan."[49] But among those who did not become monks, caste distinctions based on birth were to continue. When an accomplished young man Ambattha came to the Buddha and complained of the rudeness of the Śākyans to him in an assembly, the Buddha justified it and admonished Ambaṭṭha: "But Ambaṭṭa, if you remember your name and clan on your mother's and father's side, the Śākyas are nobly born, and you are the son of a slave-girl of the Śākyas."[50]

The Buddha's views about women were also very narrow. He laid down eight great rules (*guru-dharma*), which a nun should accept. Four of them indicate his attitude towards women:

(1) a nun even of a hundred years standing shall first salute a monk and rise up before him, even if he is only just ordained;

(2) a nun shall not spend Retreat in a place where there is no monk;

(3) a nun is not to rebuke or abuse a monk on any pretext;

(4) from this day forth utterance of nuns to monks is forbidden, of monks to nuns is not forbidden.[51]

The Buddha agreed to admit women into the Buddhist order with great reluctance and agreed because the first women who asked for admission were Mahāpajāpati, who

---

49. Udāna, V.5, cited from E.J. Thomas, *History of Buddhist Thought*, pp. 110, 198.

50. *Ambaṭṭha-sutta, Dīgha-Nikāya*, I.3.

51. *Aṅguttara-Nikāya*, IV.274.

was his aunt, nurse and foster-mother, and some other women of his own Śākya tribe. Even after admission the Buddha confidently spoke to Ānanda that a religious doctrine, discipline and system in which a woman goes forth will not last long; and he predicted that as women were now admitted, his system would not last long. A dialogue between the Buddha and Ānanda throws further light on the Buddha's attitude to women: "How are we to act, Lord, with regard to women?" "Not seeing them, Ānanda." "If we see them how are we to act?" "Not speaking, Ānanda." "What must be done by one who speaks?" "Mindfulness must be exercised, Ānanda."[52] Whatever else the Buddha was, he was not a social reformer, not a preacher of the equality of all men and women irrespective of birth and sex. Nor was he a rationalist, he was one of those several "who have gone forth" wandering about in the India of that day, seeking an escape from birth, old age, sickness and death. His greatness lies in discovering that ascetic practices are useless and meaningless, that healthy and sane living is necessary to attain truth. He also arrived at a dynamic conception of reality. It is not certain whether he owed it to the Upaniṣads or whether he arrived at it independently. He no doubt developed it in a remarkable way. He never had an idea that he was the bearer of a universal message. The fact that as soon as he was enlightened he turned to his former friends, the five ascetics, his wife, father and tribe go to prove this. As Rhys Davids wrote, his effort "was in consequence of an ardent will to bring light to his kith and kin on the things that most mattered." We have no warrant for assuming he was at this time aware of a call to a wider mission." "The 'world' will not have meant for him what it meant for us."[53]

---

52. *Mahā-parinibbāna-sutta, Dīgha-Nikāya,* II.3.

53. C.A.F. Rhys Davids, *A Manual of Buddhism,* p. 53.

And this is no drawback in the Buddha alone. Christ's message was for the Jews, more especially to the Galilean peasantry only. It was St. Paul who extended it to the Gentiles. We do not find any great advance in ethical theory in Buddhism. Virtues such as truth, honesty, filial piety, etc. are enjoined at many places in the Vedas and Upaniṣads. Also in the Upaniṣads we find at a few places the idea that all men are entitled to be dealt within the same way in which one would like others to deal with him, because in all the same *ātman* resides. The *Silakkhanda-vagga* enumerates in each *sutta* a list of virtues, but the difference noticeable is that the Buddhist scriptures are very earnest about their implementation. Another notable feature of Buddhism was it preached against the performance of sacrifices, though it did not prohibit meat eating. Buddhism also banned such arts and practices as the interpretation of dreams, portents, marks on the body, prophecies about wars, epidemics, etc., astrology and magical practices such as the curing of diseases through charms, driving of devils, etc.[54] All this registers a great progress over the Vedic and the more prevalent animistic religions.

Progress of Buddhism

While the Buddha was living and later for years, Buddhism was limited to Magadha and Kośala. Magadha extended from the confluence of river Son-kosi with the Ganges, around 150 miles east of Bhagalpur. North of the Ganges lived the tribes of Vajjis and further north the Kolas and Mallas. West of these between the Ganges and the Himalayas was the Kośala kingdom with its capital at Śrāvastī and later at Sāketa.[55] At the time the Buddha was leading a wandering life, Cyrus overthrew Babylon and became the autocrat of an empire,

54. *Samaññaphala-sutta, Dīgha-Nikāya*, I.47.

55. E.J. Thomas, *History of Buddhist Thought*, p. 4.

comprising all the Aryan lands south of the Himalayas. At this time in the porticoes of Ionian temples, Heraclitus (536-470 BC) was discoursing on the soul and elemental matter. Like the Buddha, Heraclitus came from an aristocratic family, but he was against democratic tendencies. Like the Buddha, his philosophy was for dynamism; there are no static beings, and no unchanging substratum. Change, movement is the law of the universe; and everything is in a state of becoming. Heraclitus proclaimed that "one cannot step into the same river twice." Man too is not an exception to this; he is "kindled and put out like a light in the night-time." Similarly there was a simile of candle flame in *Milindapañha* to explain the nature of self. Long before that, Pythagoras (580-500 BC) founded a brotherhood with ascetic, social and ethical ideals. Prohibition of animal sacrifices, practice of celibacy and ascetic practices, meditation and devotion were some among the requirements of Pythagorean brotherhood. Some have alleged that Pythagoras borrowed these ideas from India and that he was probably influenced by Jainism and Buddhism. Pythagoras was born before the Buddha was born in 563 BC, according to Theravāda tradition. Many of the ideas and practices of Pythagorean brotherhood are nothing but survivals of primitive savagery, based on the notion of taboo, and similar customs and superstitions. All the ascetic practices of assertions and negations evolve ultimately from them. Neither Greece need borrow them from India nor India from Greece; they are there embodied in every race.

Zoroaster also lived about this time, and had protested against sacerdotal corruption and obscurantism. Zoroaster built up a dualism with Ormazd, the good principle, and Ahriman, the evil principle. They are locked in combat at all levels of thought and existence. But ultimately Zoroastrianism is monistic because the two principles are believed to be reciprocal and dialectically necessary to each other; but in the end Ormazd wins over Ahriman. Man must choose between good or evil, between truth and falsehood; and thus gain either eternal bliss or agony. Some writers believe that this ethical dualism influenced Christian theology. Hall has suggested that it is the spiritual enthusiasm roused by Zoroastrianism which inflamed Cyrus, Cambyses and Darius to a desire for world conquest.[56] The Magis, the brāhmins of Persia have successfully resisted Zoroastrianism.

After Cyrus' death, Egypt also was added to the Persian Empire. Darius I added an Indian province to it. The free cities of Hellas constantly rebelled against Darius. Two centuries later when Macedonian autocracy became supreme in Hellas, it was quite natural that Alexander should seek to destroy Persian power and also annex the Indian provinces. But as soon as he reached the Bias River, his exhausted Greek soldiers refused to go further. He made some sort of administrative arrangements with his vassals and went back. Within a year he died and a year after the Indian provinces threw off the Greek yoke; and the Greek garrisons he left behind, were annihilated.

Candragupta who was connected with the Nanda dynasty of Magadha was banished for having conspired to overthrow the king. When the Macedonians were conquering and occupying, he was in Takṣaśilā. He studied the methods of warfare and the arm-organization of the Greeks. Phillippos, one of the Greek governors, was murdered and there was discontent against the Greeks. Candragupta put himself at the head of this discontent, roused the clans of Punjab and annihilated Alexander's garrisons, then marched to Magadha,

56. H.R. Hall, *Ancient History of the Near East*, p. 555.

threw off the Nandas and proclaimed himself the King. He was assisted by an extraordinarily clever brāhmin diplomat, Cāṇakya. In 321 BC, Mauryans became lords of Magadha and compelled all the small states of north India to accept their suzerainty; and the government was guided by the able Prime Minister, Cāṇakya. He was so strong that in 305 BC, when Seleukos attempted another Greek invasion, his army was crushed. He presented his daughter to Candragupta's harem and made over all the districts west of Indus as dowry to his daughter. He even stationed an envoy, Megasthenes at Candragupta's court.

Ajātaśatru, founder of Pāṭaliputra, was an admirer of the Buddha, patronized Buddhists, and built a *stūpa* over the Buddha's relics. Even before him Bimbisāra was a friend and patron of the Buddha. Royal patronage, the simplicity of the teaching and the helpful life which the Buddhist *bhikhu*s led must have had a great appeal; and a substantial number of people became Buddhists. From the principles of polity as outlined in Cāṇakya's *Arthaśāstra,* a king should be generous and tolerant towards all religions. Candragupta practised this principle. The unification of north India under him had facilitated the spread of Buddhism. Along the trade routes of the Ganges and the Jamunā Buddhism must have spread to the north-west of Kashmir and south of the Ganges along the Vindhyas, and turning south to the west coast. Vedic religion with its worship of personified natural forces and animal sacrifices was by now almost extinct. The great religions were those of Viṣṇu and Śiva and next after them came Buddhism, which was not yet a religion, because it had not yet developed an intelligible conception of God.

In 269 BC Aśoka ascended the throne. In his youth he was governor of both the north-western province, with its capital at Takṣaśilā and of eastern India with its capital at Ujjain. The first was the zone of influence with the Vedic religion and the birth land of Upaniṣadic speculations. The second was the land where Bhāgavata religion prevailed, for the Vṛṣṇi-Sātvata tribes of Yādava clan were spread over from Saurāṣṭra to Mathurā. In his youth Aśoka must have acquired an acquaintance with all these religions and schools of thought. Thirteen years after he ascended the throne, Aśoka successfully invaded Kaliṅga. The large-scale havoc and slaughter of that war produced a profound psychological change in Aśoka. Moreover Buddhism with its teaching of love for all beings, prohibition of animal sacrifices, and the quiet conduct of its monks appealed to Aśoka. Added to this, the persuasion of the monk Upagupta, who was his friend and who also must have been an able preacher and a good man, brought Aśoka into the Buddhist fold. Aśoka could have found equal refuge in Bhāgavata or Śaiva, but they had no propaganda, no brotherhood of monks leading exemplary lives, engaged in acts of benevolence and charity. So to Aśoka's emotional temperament Buddhism seemed the panacea for all ills.

It was Aśoka who made Buddhism a religion in the proper sense of the term. In his edicts Aśoka refers to the blessed life in *svarga* or heaven as the goal to which the pious should strive to reach. "His majesty thinks nothing of much importance . . . that which concerns the next world," so says one edict. *Nirvāṇa* is nowhere mentioned in the edicts as the *summum bonum*. Animal sacrifices were prohibited. Aśoka went further and gave up meat-eating; and in his palace all were vegetarians. In the twenty-seventh year of his reign by a special edict he proclaimed rules for the preservation of birds, beasts and fish. Slaughter of some animals and birds was prohibited under any circumstances. Pregnant animals, including goats and cows were made immune from butchery. Catching of fish on certain days was forbidden. Horses and cattle should not be branded or castrated. Often the edicts cite the Buddha, the Blessed one, as the authority for all the ethical precepts. Thus reverence for scriptural authority and for the sayings of the Master spread over. Aśoka was responsible for the growth of ritual in Buddhism. Ceremonial worship of the Buddha's relics with a lot of fan-fare, pageantry and processions was evolved. One of the edicts says, "The sound of the drum of *dharma* is heard, while heavenly spectacles of processional cars, elephants, illuminations and the like, are displayed to the people." Pilgrimages to the holy places associated with the Buddha were instituted. The custom of distributing alms and gifts to the mendicants and the poor at those holy places was also begun by Aśoka. At all those places Aśoka built *dhvaja-stambha*s (Pillars of Victory) or shrines. Many of these still exist. All the resources of his vast dominions were used for the spread and propagation of *dharma*. Mostly he used his authority in an autocratic manner and a large section of his people must have disliked it. But there was no manifest discontent because there was no persecution of any sect.

Aśoka's missionary zeal has extended beyond the limits of his empire. "Where the Greek king named Antiochus dwells, and beyond that Antiochus, to where dwell the four kings named — Ptolemy, Antigonos, Magas and Alexander, and in the south the kings of the Coḷas and the Pāṇḍyas, and of Ceylon . . . everywhere men follow the *dharma* as proclaimed by His Majesty."[57] The Kings referred to in this edict were kings of Syria, Egypt, Macedonia, Epirus and Cyrene. Archaeological evidence in Egypt reveals that Aśoka's claim that the *dharma* spread to all these foreign countries was not

57. Aśoka's Edict XIII.

exaggerated. Buddhist missions established by Aśoka in these countries may have influenced the growth and development of Christianity and Islam.[58] The powerful influence of the strong centralized government of Aśoka which placed restrictions on meat-eating and intoxicants did much to change the dietic habits of people and lead to inculcate a tradition of vegetarianism. Aśoka's ascetic life and the legend of the Great Renunciation of the Buddha attracted people to the monasteries.

The teaching of the Buddha as a kṣatriya leader won for him the personal devotion of all the kṣatriya chieftains and princelings throughout north India. The legend of the Great Renunciation, the miracles and the noble lives led by many of the early *bhikkus* together with the patronage and propaganda of Aśoka created a mass enthusiasm for the Buddha. Art, folklore and tradition ramified and strengthened in Buddhism. The sentiment of hero-worship began to venerate the Buddha as the Blessed One, the Saviour and the Supreme Teacher. Aśoka's institution of pilgrimages and ceremonial worship of relics built up a Buddhist cult. For instance on the Bharhut *stūpa*, the gods of Vedic religion stand guard at the four gateways of the *stūpa*; popular divinities like the snake-gods, goddesses and denizens of the forest, lake and river are carved with intense realism on all sides, showing them in an act of homage to the *stūpa* and its significance. The suggestion is that the Buddha is the God of gods, the Devatideva, as he is reverenced even by these mighty divinities. The "Palace of the Gods" at Bharhut *stūpa* devoted to the worship of Buddhist emblems is planned as a Hindu temple with a *garbhagṛha*, an *antarāla*, a *maṇḍapam* and is roofed with a *śikhara*.

---

58. Charles Eliot, *Hinduism and Buddhism*, vol. III, pp. 441, 443; J.E. Carpenter, *Nineteenth Century*, p. 975.

In Aśoka's time this symbol i.e. *stūpa* was appropriated by Buddhists. It began to be constructed in the apse at the end of the chapter house and was profusely sculptured or painted in fresco over a layer of white plaster. The Jains and Buddhists took it over and used as a reliquary. This ancient funeral symbol probably recalled to their minds the concept of *pari-nirvāṇa*. Previously *stūpas* were built of timber; in Aśoka's time it was replaced by stone. Legends of the Buddha's life were carved in iconic symbols or hieroglyphs, for as yet the Buddha was not openly worshipped as God in the assembly halls of the *vihāras*, though he was already added to the existing pantheon by the common folk.

Fifty years after Aśoka's death his heirs lost their power; one of the commanders, Puṣyamitra killed the Mauryan king in 183 BC; and usurped the throne. Thus the Śuṅga dynasty came to power. Puṣyamitra was a great champion of Vedic religion, and performed many sacrifices including the Aśvamedha. From Tibetan and Chinese records Puṣyamitra is known to have persecuted Buddhists ruthlessly.[59] His successors, however, were not so very bigoted, for the gateway of the Bharhut *stūpa* was erected during the Śuṅga rule. In 72 BC the heir of the Śuṅga dynasty was killed and another dynasty that of Kaṇva came to power. In his time Puṣyamitra repulsed the invasions of Milinda and the King of Kaliṅga. Provinces beyond the Indus and probably even the Punjab were not in his jurisdiction. Kaliṅga and the territory, north of Narmadā overthrew Magadha sovereignty in his time. The fourth of the Kaṇva dynasty was defeated and killed by an Āndhra King in 27 BC. With that Magadha had its downfall. It must however be noted that the partiality of the Śuṅga and Kaṇva dynasties did not very much affect the Buddha

---

59. R. Kimura, *Origin of Mahāyāna Buddhism*, p. 21.

adversely, as is made out by some writers.[60] From the second century BC to the end of the fourth century CE, there are left no traces of a building or sculpture devoted to Brāhmanical religion. It does not mean that Brāhmaṇism died, but only that it was followed by a minority.[61]

Even in Puṣyamitra's reign a Bactrian named Milinda established himself strongly in Kabul, which was formerly in Aśoka's realm. He held sway over the Indus Valley, Sindh and Rajasthan. In 170 BC the nomadic tribes of Turkey began their trek into India. Thirty to forty years later they overran the Parthian and Bactrian kingdoms and were later followed by Kuṣāṇa, another nomadic tribe. Gradually they established themselves in Punjab, Rajasthan and Gujarat. By this time western Asia was acquainted with Buddhism. Milinda was a follower of the Buddha. The nomadic tribes, who already knew about the Buddha and India, in a vague way, threw off their nomadic habits and settled down as Indians. In the middle of the first century BC, Kuṣāṇa established their supremacy over the border states of India. Khaḍphises the First and Second were the founders of the Kuṣāṇa empire. Khaḍphises II was a Śaiva, his successors Kaniṣka and Vāsudeva were Buddhist and Śaivaite respectively.

Aśoka's interpretation of Buddhism made it a religion with a dogma and a cult. Even before Aśoka there must have been people who hailed Buddhism as the Message of the Master, the vision of the Seer and the Revelation of the Divine. The zealous monks who went from village to village, from country to country and spread the message among the masses must have further popularized it. The cravings of the people for

60. Vincent Smith, *Early History of India*, 2nd edn., p. 190.

61. Bhandarkar, *Religions of India*, p. 548.

the miraculous and the superhuman could not be satisfied without investing the Buddha with divinity. The Vedic gods were personifications of natural forces and gradually they were conceived more and more anthropomorphically. The burning theological question in the Vedas was which among these gods was the greatest. By the Buddha's time the Bhāgavatas evolved the idea of the Supreme Person, creator and controller of the universe, who manifests himself in many forms as Brahmā, Śiva and Viṣṇu, etc. The Buddhists took over this idea. The *Avatāra-vāda* of the *Bhagavad-Gītā* that God manifests himself in every age to establish the *dharma* and save the good was incorporated into Buddhism: *paritrāṇāya sādhūnām . . . dharma saṁsthāpanārthāya sambhāvami yuge yuge*. Thus the Buddhist theology was developed: There is the self-created Ādi-Buddha, creator of the universe. Directly from him the Buddhas make their appearance in every age and every part of the universe. Amitābha is one such Buddha; he is the protector of the present world. He dwells in Sukhāvatī, the Paradise. Gautama, the Buddha is another heavenly being who has manifested himself in the world to redeem it. The path of devotion (*bhakti-mārga*) to God also was taken over by Buddhism from Bhāgavata cult. Anyone who prays to Amitābha or one of the other Buddhas goes to Paradise.[62]

Until the advent of Buddhism there was no image worship in India. Only symbols and emblems were worshipped. The artists in the courts of the Buddhist kings of Bactria began to manufacture the Buddha idols and statues. Hellenistic sculptors who began to represent the Buddha as the deity took over the features of the Sun god, Apollo and depicted him either seated in the Yogic pose or standing as the *guru* proclaiming

62. R. Kimura, op. cit., p. 405; E.J. Thomas, *History of Buddhist Thought*, pp. 179, 199.

the *dharma*. Hellenistic sculptors only translated into stone what the Buddhists in general thought of the Buddha, the God of gods. The spiritual inspirer of Buddhism was Bhāgavata cult and the Indian Mind, not Greece. Hellenic art served only as a vehicle for the Indian conceptions.

Some writers describe Kaniṣka as the cause for the formation of Mahāyāna school of Buddhism and for propagation in China. Buddhism began to reach China during the time of the Christian era.[63] After Kaniṣka came to power, the Mongolian connections of his dynasty and the large extent of his empire may have given an impetus to Buddhist propaganda in China. Similarly through Hellenistic sources Buddhism might have influenced the Christian thought, ritual and folklore. The earliest Pāli scriptures contain germs of Mahāyāna or developed Buddhist religion; and they were brought out immediately after the Buddha's death.[64] According to them the Buddha's birth is supernatural and if he wanted he could have lived till the end of the present *kalpa*. The nature of the Buddha after his release from after-death is deep and unfathomable like the ocean.[65] The *Mahā-parinibbāna-sutta* (IV.57) mentions heaven as a reward for the good. The Kathāvatthu mentions the ideas that the Buddhas are born in all quarters of the universe, that the Buddha was superhuman in his life and that he was not really born in the world and that he did not preach the *dhamma* himself. The Pāli canon at several places speaks of the gods, Brahmā, Śakra, Māra, etc. and that the Buddha is superior to all of them; and that he was worshipped by them many times. Thus the original Buddhism itself passes into developed Buddhism. Mahāyāna

63. Charles Eliot, op. cit., vol. II, p. 64.

64. R. Kimura, op. cit., p. 59.

65. *Majjhima-Nikāya*, 1.486.

is a logical development of Hīnayāna or Theravāda; nowhere is there a sudden break as Stcherbatsky had imagined.[66]

In Mahāyāna the Buddha's idea of compassion reaches full development, according to which there is no such self in reality. So no one exists whose suffering is really his own. No suffering can be separated as "this is his," for there is no such circumscribed "he." All suffering is suffering; there is no distinction in suffering. There is no sense in trying to distinguish between "my" suffering and "your" suffering, as there is no "I" and "you." Therefore as long as there is suffering it is all one and must be removed.[67] As long as there is a creature in suffering, there can be no joy for the others. In these circumstances to set-up an ideal one's own liberation is incomprehensible. True liberation must be once for all and that for the entire universe. (Is the doctrine of *Sarva-mukti* in Advaita evolved from this?) Mahāyāna therefore sets up as an ideal that the man, who is qualified to attain *nirvāṇa* should not enter into it, but must wish, pray and strive incessantly for the deliverance of all beings. "In all lands may all the sufferings of living beings come to an end."[68] "Through all the good done by me may I become a tranquilliser of all the pains of all beings. . . . My own self and my pleasures, all my righteousness, past, present, and future, I sacrifice without regard in order to achieve the welfare of all beings."[69] It is possible that this idea of universal compassion, the idea that one can and should suffer for the sake of all beings may have been formed under the inspiration of the *Bhagavad-Gītā* ideal of *loka-saṁgraha* and the concept of *sarvabhūta hite rataḥ*. We

66. Stcherbatsky, *The Conception of Buddhist Nirvāṇa*, p. 36.

67. Winternitz, *Der Mahāyāna Buddhismus*, pp. 44, 58-60.

68. Winternitz, op. cit., p. 46.

69. *Dharma-Saṁgraha*, 14.

find a feeble echo of Mahāyāna ideal in St. Paul: "For I could wish that I myself were cursed and cut off from Christ for the sake of my brothers, those of my own race, the people of Israel."[70] Saints, who again and again voluntarily accept human existence, though they are eligible for *nirvāṇa*, are *bodhisattvas*, potentially the Buddhas. Among the *bodhisattva*s the most prominent are Avalokita and Mañjuśrī. The *bodhisattva*s are also worshipped, for they grant favours and save one from physical and moral evil.[71]

Philosophical Developments in Buddhism

In China and Japan, Nāgārjuna (second century CE) is reported to be the founder of Mahāyāna.[72] In Nāgārjuna's works quotations from many Mahāyāna *sūtra*s are found. It is therefore possible that there were Mahāyāna works prior to Nāgārjuna. Paramārtha in one of his works says that Mahāyāna *sūtra*s were used by the early Buddhists. If that is correct, the existence of Mahāyāna texts is pushed to the fourth and third century BC.[73] But none of them can be pointed out.[74] One of the earliest of them *Prajñāpāramitā*, was translated into the Chinese in CE 170; and the *Saddharmapuṇḍarīka* was translated in CE 265-316 and these have been the most popular in China and Japan. Especially *Vajracchedika* is one of the most widely used and one of the shortest treatises in the *Prajñāpāramitā*.

In the early Buddhist Pāli works we find the posing of such questions: Is the world eternal or not? Is it finite or infinite? Is *jīva* the body or something else? Is *tathāgata* after

70. Romans 9.3.

71. *Saddharmapuṇḍarika*, Sacred Books of the East, XXI, pp. 4, 406.

72. R. Kimura, *Origin of Mahāyāna Buddhism*, p. 161.

73. R. Kimura, op. cit., p. 11.

74. E.J. Thomas, *History of Buddhist Thought*, p. 283.

death existent or not?[75] To all such questions the Buddha gave neither a positive nor a negative answer. They were declared to be unrevealed questions (*avyakta*). The Buddha did not say that the soul existed, but he refuted to be called a nihilist.[76] What then must be said about the status of the soul, is it existent or not ? In the *Saṁyutta-Nikāya* (III.109) the answer is given: The body, feeling, perception, the aggregates and consciousness are impermanent; of none of them it can be said, "this is mine, I am this, this is myself." Neither can a person be said to be in the body, apart from the body or consisting of the body. Therefore a person — whether he is a *tathāgata* or an ordinary person, cannot hold to be perceived as existent even while alive. What happens when one dies? When a fire is burning, one says that it burns on account of the fuel of grass and sticks. When it is extinguished, if some body asks, where has it gone? We cannot say that it has gone in this direction or that. Even so when a *tathāgata* dies he is cut off at the root, uprooted like a palm tree and becomes like the ocean. Nothing can be said about him, whether he is reborn or not reborn, nor can both birth and rebirth be denied to him.[77] Elsewhere the Buddha says, "I do not say that there is an *ātman*, for then I am an eternalist. I do not say that there is no *ātman* that would be annihilationism. Further, to say there is no *ātman* is to admit that there is an *ātman* and then go on to deny it."[78] The Buddhist conception of an individual is that it is a compound of body, sensations, mind and thought.[79] There is no individual beyond them, or in them, or apart from them or

75. *Majjhima-Nikāya*, I.157.

76. Ibid., I.139.

77. *Majjhima-Nikāya*, I.486.

78. *Saṁyutta-Nikāya*, IV.400.

79. *Dīgha-Nikāya*, II.290.

do they together constitute the individual. It has been interpreted as the doctrine of no-soul.

The inadequacy of Buddhist theory is seen when the conception of soul is sought to be combined with that of rebirth. The Buddha was forced to admit that the group of aggregates of which an individual is made is not entirely dispersed at death, but only changed. There is no rebirth when the *khandhas* (aggregates) are completely dispersed; and this happens only when craving is destroyed. Till then an individual has a past, which can be remembered if he has the capacity. That was how the Buddha recollected his past births.[80] All this was rather confusing for the multitude who regarded the soul as a thing, an entity, just like any other thing. So the Vātsiputriyas started their doctrine of an individual and the five *khandhas*. Although the immediate followers of the Buddha and most probably the Buddha arrived at a revolutionary conception of self through an analysis of that notion, they were unable to develop it fruitfully or hold it consistently.

If the soul cannot be said to be existent or non-existent, can the body, the will and wisdom or anything for that matter be described as existent or non-existent? This was the idea that was developed in the Mahāyāna texts, especially, the *Vajracchedikā*, wherein it is stated:[81] In *nirvāṇa* when men attain complete wisdom there is no conception of phenomena as an entity, a being, a living being or a personality. If there is no entity, being or personality, it follows that there is nothing to be redeemed or redeemed from. An enlightened man should spontaneously act for the deliverance of all beings, but he should act so without depending on any conception of

80. *Majjhima-Nikāya*, I.256.

81. W. Gemmell, tr., *Diamond Sūtra*.

phenomena, for there is no such thing.[82] The Buddha is not to be perceived by the marks of his physical body, for there is no physical body. Every form or quality of life and phenomena is transient or illusive.[83] As phenomena have no permanency and reality, the concepts of being, entity, personality, etc. become meaningless. Apart from the law, there are no qualities or ideas having an existence nor are there any such coincident with the law.[84] What the Buddha adumbrated in terms of the law is an inexpressible surpassing spiritual concept. So it cannot be specifically formulated or explicitly stated as knowledge. It is neither consonant with law, nor apart from law.[85] In fact, what termed "Buddha Law" is not really to be attributed to the Buddha.[86] Words like the "good man," "the man about to be redeemed," "the man redeemed" are only descriptive terms and convenient designations. In reality there are no such things.[87]

Since entity, being and personalities are mere ideas to which no reality corresponds, they are mere nebulous and hypothetical ideas.[88] A good man should practise, "I am becoming oblivious of every idea"; but at the same time he must practise that there is no one to whom every idea is becoming oblivious. In truth there is no one to entertain an idea, nor is there anything of which an idea may be entertained.[89] Long before Gautama the Buddha was born, in

---

82. Ibid., pp. 13-14.
83. Ibid., pp. 17-18.
84. Ibid., p. 22.
85. Ibid., p. 24.
86. Ibid., p. 27.
87. Ibid., pp. 29-33.
88. Ibid., p. 54.
89. Ibid., pp. 69, 70.

another birth another Dīpaṅkara Buddha greeted him thus: "You will become Śākya the Buddha." If the law existed even then, how could Dīpaṅkara greet thus? The law is that by which spiritual wisdom is attained; and if such a law existed then how did it fail to make Gautama the Buddha even then? So there is no such law, no such wisdom; they are mere terms.[90] It is said that the Buddha knows the mental dispositions of all beings in all the worlds. How does he do it? He does it because there are no such things known as "mental dispositions," all modes of thought are unreal and illusory.[91] As such in reality there is no merit, no law or doctrine; neither any living beings to be saved, nor was there a Buddha, who preached the doctrine.[92]

The argument behind the work seems to be this: Things are produced and destroyed. In certain conditions some things begin to appear, then when the conditions are no more the things also cease to exist. Like a dream, a phantasm, a bubble, a shadow, the glistening dew, or a lightning flash, all things are impermanent and swiftly vanish.[93] As in things there is no constant nature involved, in reality there is no pure and impure, large and small, far and near, known and unknown, etc. All things are therefore nothing.

Nāgārjuna (second century CE) has presented this doctrine in a systematic form and his exposition and the mode of his presentation made him the greatest philosopher India has ever seen. He was a brāhmin of Vidarbha, lived for long in Andhra, and was highly proficient in fine arts, medicine and magic. It

---

90. Ibid., pp. 72-76.
91. Ibid., pp. 80, 81.
92. Ibid., pp. 91-92, 99-100.
93. Ibid., p. 110.

must be distinctly remembered that Nāgārjuna himself never professed to be original. His *Mūla-Mādhyamika-Kārikā* is the most important text from the philosophical standpoint, on which commentaries were written by himself and Candrakīrti. The theory of causation lays down that everything arises from another or from itself. Both these are impossible. If a thing could be caused by another, anything can be caused by anything. If a thing arises itself, that means that the thing already existed. It is also absurd to assume that there are no causes, and then everything ought to be existent; but some things are not, because they are not caused; motion and rest are fictions. We talk of passing along a path, but if we divide the path into that which has been already passed and that which is to be passed, there is nothing which is being passed over. Similarly all time may be divided into the past and the future, thus there is left no present, for time to have any meaning must have a former and subsequent. So no one is ever passing along a path. Again who is it that is passing — the passer or the non-passer? If you say the passer is passing, the sentence is redundant. You cannot, of course, say, the non-passer is passing. Nor can the passer and the passing be identified, for that would annihilate the distinction between the actor and the act, making both unreal. Nor are the passer and passing different, for a passer different from passing and passing without a passer are meaningless. So there is no motion and hence no rest.

The self-existence (*svabhāva*) of a thing is not found in the conditions (*pratyaya*) of the thing. For that which has no existence of its own, there can be no existence of others. That which has no relations cannot be related to anything else. So a thing is not related to its conditions. To posit relations between things is impossible. When a thing arises it is said there are conditions. That means so long as the thing does not arise, there are no conditions. The existent need not have cause, of the non-existent there could be no cause. When the seer cannot see himself, how can he see other things? The unseen cannot be seen; the seen also cannot be seen. Seeing does not see, unseeing also does not see. If there is no seer how can these are seen by a seer? If there are no parents, how does the son come into being? If there are no children there are no parents.

People talk of consciousness. What is consciousness? If it exists in its own right, it is useless to consider it an object. If consciousness is consciousness of an object, then it means the object exists before the consciousness exists. How is this possible, for there can be no question of relation to something non-existent. Things which have not originated cannot cease, the preceding moment disappears in the effect, so that there is no cause. The effect does not exist in anyone of the causes nor in all of them; yet if the effect arises from them why does not it arise from non-causes? Therefore to talk of causes and effects is meaningless. Neither the one nor the other exists as an entity. People talk of substances, ether, etc. What is ether that which has the properties of ether? This means that there is a "That" and there are some properties in "that." Prior to the acquirement of these properties was the ether without properties? If so, it is impossible for a propertyless thing to exist. It is also impossible that a propertyless thing should come to be propertied. A thing with properties cannot, of course, acquire properties again. So there is nothing to possess properties. Even so a thing cannot acquire qualities. It is said that there is something (or someone) prior to seeing, hearing, knowing, etc. If it or he existed prior to these entire things and perception, how it was known? If without seeing, hearing, knowing, etc. he or it existed, why cannot these be without it or him?

This mode of reasoning is applied to all sorts of things — the *skandhas*, the elements, sense-faculties, contact, extinction, action and actor, pain, truth, soul, etc. Not *saṁsāra* and *nirvāṇa*, even the Buddha and *dharma* are exempted. The *saṁskāras* (inclinations) are the elements of which all things are compounded. Compounds are impermanent for they are those that originate, stay and then dissolve. The *saṁskāras* cannot transmigrate, if they do, do they transmigrate as permanent or impermanent? Neither way is applicable to them; so they do not transmigrate. As for the individual, he does not exist apart from the *skandhas*, *āyatanas* and *dhātus*. So how can he transmigrate? The *ātman* is as real as the barren woman's son. Between one craving and another, the *ātman* is non-existent even in *saṁsāra*. So how can *ātman* transmigrate? As for *nirvāṇa*, that is another fiction. Compounds arise and dissolve into their elements; so they are not bound or released. Nor are the elements bound, for that which is not bound is free, that which is already bound cannot be bound. If the bound were released, binding and releasing will be simultaneous. The not-bound cannot be released. He who thinks "I will be getting *nirvāṇa* when I cease to crave," is an illusion of the soul. There is no cessation of *saṁsāra*, for *saṁsāra* itself is not. So *saṁsāra* is *nirvāṇa*, *nirvāṇa* is *saṁsāra*. Either everything is real or unreal. If everything is real, there is neither arising nor passing away. Real things cannot become non-existent and non-existent things cannot become real. So *saṁsāra* if it is real cannot cease to be. On the other hand if everything is unreal, there is no question of *saṁsāra* ceasing to be; it never was. Whatever is the world is *nirvāṇa*, what is *nirvāṇa* is the world. There is not the smallest difference between the two.[94] It also follows that the being of

94. *Mūla-Mādhyamika-Kārikā*, XXV, 19-20.

God is the being of the world, the being of the world is the being of God.[95]

This doctrine is found in its earliest form in *Saṁyutta-Nikāya* (XXII.9.16) itself. There the Buddha says, "I do not say beings exist, I do not say beings do not exist. I teach the middle doctrine." As the theory says nothing positively while avoiding the extremes, it has been styled the "Middle Doctrine."

As the truths developed here are impossible of comprehension by ordinary mortals, the Buddha usually did not speak about them. To the ordinary people he preached in an ordinary way. But in his teachings lay implicit the profound truths that have been later deduced and derived by the Mahāyāna doctors. The former capable of being understood by everybody are the exoteric (*vyakta*) doctrines, the latter reserved for the more advanced are the esoteric (*guhya*). This is how Mahāyānists escape the charge that what they talk is not found in the Buddha's teaching. The Mahāyāna teachers made a distinction between two truths — "that which is true for the ignorant or ordinary folk" and "that which is really truth."[96]

There has been a debate whether Nāgārjuna believed in anything absolutely real and consistent beyond this world. Walleser has described him to be a negativist. Even those who were living in Candrakīrti's time thought him to be a nihilist and Candrakīrti had to deny it.[97] Whether we propose to call Nāgārjuna a mystic or a nihilist depends on how we understand him. What is it that he has said? He has taken the

---

95. Ibid., XX.16.

96. *loka samvṛtti satya* and *paramārtha satya*.

97. See Nāgārjuna's "Kārikās" and Candrakīrti's *Prasannapada ṭikā* in Saratchandra Sarma, ed., *Mādhyamika-Vṛtti*.

current categories of thought like the real, the unreal, etc. The real is that which is always, which was, and which will be. If something is now and will not be or was not, it is not real. The negation of the two concepts of reality and unreality gives us that which is neither real nor unreal.[98] Thus we have four possible kinds of predications. Nāgārjuna took a number of concepts like motion, thing, property, senses, consciousness, soul, action, content, pain, truth, liberation, god, etc. Taken separately one by one, none of the four predications are possible of them. Each is interconnected with all the rest.[99] This being that exists. This does not mean that there is a "this" which originates a "that." The world is an interconnected whole. No single item in it can be taken apart and pronounced as, "this is it", and "this is the thing" which is permanent. Also since there is nothing permanent, there cannot be anything impermanent.[100]

Nāgārjuna has denied permanence of the world, but has he predicated unreality of it? His philosophy refuses to be straight-jacketed either as nihilism, mysticism or relativism. As for the world as a whole, that again is a convenient concept. In fact, there is no such entity as "the world as a whole." The other world and god are conceivable only in relation to this world, and are therefore like this world unreal. No idea can enter into relation with the life of this world unless it also is like the world unreal.[101] There is no transcendental state, *nirvāṇa*, for what could it transcend? There is nothing to be transcended. There can be nothing called *nirvāṇa* for either

---

98. *sadasat sadasat ceti, nobhayam ceti* — Ibid., XVIII, p. 132.

99. Ibid., XVIII, p. 134.

100. *nāsti cet śāśvataḥ kaścit, ko bhaviṣyatya śāśvataḥ* — Ibid., XXV, p. 219.

101. *antavān yadi lokaḥ syāt, para lokaḥ katham bhavet.*

there is a thing which changes or permanent.[102] Things which are changeless cannot enter into a new state called *nirvāṇa*. Things which change may well enter into it but they will come out of it as well, for it is their nature to change.[103] So it is an illusion to think that there is such a thing or state as *nirvāṇa* and that one is going to acquire or enter into it, for we have already found that "things" and "states" are mere abstractions.[104] The world should be taken as it is; nothing in it is separable from anything else. Everything is dependent on everything else and that which arises depending on the others is neither apart from them nor is it them. Each has individuality, but the individuality is not a principle separable from every other thing.[105] For this very reason nothing in the world is permanent (or self-existent) nor is anything originated. We must give up the concepts of "thing," "a thing causing another thing," etc. and views such as I am suffering, I am unhappy, from where have I come, where do I go, or this world is unhappy, what is this world, what is its destiny, etc. It was for this, for the destruction of all sorts of views that the great Gautama preached the True Law.[106]

Almost every important modern writer seems to have misunderstood Nāgārjuna. Some have understood him as saying that the world is phenomenal, unreal and contradictory;

---

102. *ya ekaḥ tatra saṁsāra, nirvāṇam kiṁ vikalpyase?* — Ibid., XVI. 10. p. 107.
103. *saṁskāraṇam na nirvāṇam, sattvasyāpi na nirvāṇaṁ* — Ibid., XVI. 4. p. 103.
104. *nirvasyāmyanu-pādāno nirvāṇaṁ me bhaviṣyati, iti yeṣām grahasteṣām upādāna mahāgrahaḥ* — Ibid., XVI. 9 p. 106.
105. *pratītya yad yad bhavati na hi tāvad tadeva tat, na cānyadapi* — Ibid., XVIII. 10 p. 134.
106. *katham va sarvabhāvānām śūnyatvāt śāśvatadayaḥ, kva kasya katamaḥ kasmāt: sambhaviṣyanti draṣṭayaḥ? sarvadṛṣṭiprhānāya yaḥ saddharmamadesayat* — Ibid., XXVII. 29, 30 p. 221.

and the real, the absolute is somewhere in the blues. Others have thought that he is a pure nihilist, denying everything, criticizing everything, but constructively and positively putting up nothing. Yet others described him as a mere sophist, a maniac spinning out a lot of verbiage. Most surprising of all is Radhakrishnan's announcement that in Nāgārjuna, "reason is condemned as defective only to make room for faith."[107] Charles Eliot writes, "Nāgārjuna leaves an impression of audacious and ingenious sophistry."[108]

Nāgārjuna's terminology is to be specially guarded against his *śūnyatā* or "void." Candrakīrti's explanation throws much light; the meaning of it is the same as that of *pratītyasamutpāda* or dependent origination. It does not mean *abhāva* or non-existence. Again since Nāgārjuna said there are two truths basing on which the Buddha preached, it is concluded that the one is opposed to the other. In fact, there is only one truth, that which presents facts as they are (*yathāvastitapadā-rthānuvāda*). The other is mere conventional truth, current in and easily understood by the ignorant multitude.[109] When the Buddha speaks of somebody attaining *nirvāṇa*, as *nirvāṇa* to be attained and so on; he is using the ordinary terms for the ordinary folk. Actually everybody must present the truth, real meaning in terms of current usage, but if current usage is found inadequate in that process, one must abandon it.[110] What has

107. S. Radhakrishnan, *Indian Philosophy*, vol. I, p. 659.

108. Charles Eliot, *Hinduism and Buddhism*, vol. II, p. 39.

109. *samantāt varaṇam saṁvṛttiḥ, ajñānam hi samantāt sarvapadārthān tatvavacchadanat saṁvṛtti-ṛtyuccyate . . . athavā saṁvṛttiḥ saṁketo, lokavyavahāra ityarthaḥ* — See Nāgārjuna's *Kārikā*s and Candrakīrti's *Prasannapada-ṭīkā* in Saratchandra Sarma, ed., *Mādhyamika-Vṛtti*, p. 180.

110. *vyavahāram anāsritya paramārtho na deśyate, paramārtham anāgamya nirvāṇaṁ nādhi gamyat* — *Mādhyamika-Vṛtti*, Ibid., XXIV.10 p. 181.

been called the doctrine of twofold truth does not indicate the doctrine of two worlds — that of phenomena and noumena. There is no such bifurcation in Nāgārjuna.

The theories of Nāgārjuna were further developed by others. In the *Laṅkāvatāra-sūtra* we find an interesting and penetrating working cut off from Nāgārjuna. Philosophers talk of awareness; but it is an abstraction. Awareness is multi-dimensional and plurality, *vijñāna*s. Through each sense a particular awareness arises. When to the eye is presented a rose, there arises the awareness of a rose; this is eye-*vijñāna*. Similarly through the ear, nose, tongue, and mind (*manas*) other *vijñāna*s arise. It is *manovijñāna* which distinguishes between the objective and subjective and determines the physical and mental. It should be noted that all these *vijñāna*s mutually condition each other and are related very intimately. It is these *vijñāna*s that discriminate and distinguish between one object and another; and it is the *manas* which basing itself on these *vijñāna*s entertains an idea of self as opposed to a real world.[111] Supposing there is no eye, would it be possible to see objects as "this" and "that"? And so would be the case with all the other senses. What if there are no senses, could there be still a distinction of "I" and "You"? So it may be said that the actual world is presented out of these *vijñāna* or awareness. In fact, it is made up of these *vijñāna* as a painting is made up of colours, canvas and plate.[112] The world is not in any of the *vijñāna* and yet the *vijñāna* produces the world. As such one may say that there is no world of multiplicity, and there is only *vijñāna* out of which the world evolves; the world is therefore one's own mind. This means that there is a "one" whose mind evolves all things. Ontology comes here to our

---

111. Suzuki, tr., *Laṅkāvatāra-sūtra*, pp. 39-41.

112. Ibid., pp. 43-44.

rescue. What is this "one"? Can any adequate and intelligible conception of "one" and "another" be formed? Notions such as element, quality, substance, etc. are fictions.[113] When these notions are done away with, it is the same reality which appears as differentiated, but which is not. The fire which burns down houses, mansions and parks is of the same uniform nature; but depending upon the length and dimensions of the material which it is consuming, differences such as big and small are seen in the flames.[114] The world is like the mirage in which springs are seen, as if they are there; animals, thirsty from the scorching heat of the summer sun run after them.[115] As children seeing the projections of the magic-lantern imagine that there are really people coming and going, and as in dreams one finds all sorts of objects, the world appears as a welter of multitudinous objects.[116] Can we therefore say that all this is non-existent and false? No, because to declare that the world is false is to accept implicitly that there is something real. To describe phenomena as non-existent or non-being is to accept noumena.[117] We have therefore to give up all sorts of polar conceptions such as subject and object, being and non-being, real and unreal, etc. These are concepts which cannot be intelligibly defined.

Another conception is now to be substituted and that is that the world is nothing but *citta*. *Citta* is used in *Laṅkāvatāra-sūtra* in the sense of "piling up" or "arrangement in order." If the world is nothing but an "ordered arrangement," of what is it the ordered arrangement? Not of entities and substances

113. Ibid., p. 11.
114. Ibid., p. 17.
115. Ibid., p. 78.
116. Ibid., p. 171.
117. Ibid., p. 171.

that have been rejected. If it is objected how can there be arrangement without something to be arranged, it can be retorted how can there be entities without relations and qualities? Due to certain tendencies (*vāsanās*) and feelings, *vijñāna* originates and it selects out of *citta*, the store of consciousness (*ālaya-vijñāna*) a world of objects and bodies. This *citta* is the world in a sequence, a flow like a river, a flame and a wind. Like a machine which goes on rolling and unrolling or a water-wheel which goes on drawing — there is this panorama of world-process, without beginning and end. From moment to moment it changes, leaving no time to ask "from what has it changed to what?" Some thinkers have described the world to be non-existent like the hare's horn. This is again a categorical mistake. The non-existence of hare's horns is asserted with reference to the existence of bull's horns. But what are bull's horns? Even they are not existent, in the sense in which they (the objectors) define existence. As such it is meaningless to say that hare's horns are non-existent as there are no bull's horns even.[118] So those who say the world of objects is real or transient are misinformed.[119] It is to be described as neither. The world is not transient nor is it permanent; things suffer every moment, changes following one another, now splitting, now dividing, succeeding one another, and combining with one another, now coming forward and now passing away."[120] As long as there is discrimination between object and object there are faulty notions of permanency and impermanency.[121] When this is done

---

118. Ibid., pp. 46-48.
119. Ibid., p. 127.
120. Ibid., p. 127.
121. Ibid., p. 188.

away with, *tathāgata* too is like the world. He is neither permanent nor impermanent.[122] He is unborn. This does not mean that *tathāgata* is a non-entity, for there is no entity or non-entity. Not being subject to birth and destruction does not mean a non-entity. *Tathāgata* is never born nor does he die. He is unborn; he is not a non-entity.[123] Once people are freed from the idea of being and non-being, there is no question of emancipation.[124] *Nirvāṇa* is not annihilation, for what is there to be annihilated? *Nirvāṇa* is not the finding of the true self, for there is no such thing; nor is it following of the true path, for there is nobody to follow and nothing to be followed.[125] All these deplorable conceptions are erroneous. *Nirvāṇa* is nothing but to understand things aright, to recognize that all that is seen is of the *citta*,[126] to know that "self," "suffering," etc. are all myths. Other than this, there is no liberation.

The *Laṅkāvatāra-sūtra* contains much mythology and some passages which seem to be meaningless. But if the kernel of thought is separated, it would be presented as above. In CE 520, Bodhidharma used it to develop a sort of Advaita. He was a south Indian, and became very important in the religion and art of Far-East. This gave rise to the Zen or Chan School of Buddhism.

Vasubandhu and Asaṅga (CE 500) of Peshawar are said to be the founders of Yogācāra School. Some say Vasubandhu lived in the time of Candragupta I. They were founders of the

---

122. Ibid., p. 187.
123. Ibid., pp. 165-66.
124. Ibid., p. 125.
125. Ibid., pp. 158-59.
126. Ibid., pp. 160, 172.

school in the same sense in which Nāgārjuna was founder of Mādhyamika. At first Vasubandhu belonged to another school and his *Abhidharmakośa* was written in that period. The theory which Vasubandhu outlines in the *Abhidharmakośa* may be briefly sketched thus: There are a number of elements which go to make up the world. These elements or *dharma*s are either compounded or uncompounded. Space and stoppage by knowledge and stoppage due to removal of the cause are the primal uncompounded *dharma*s. Space is a permanent way in which mind distinguishes objects. Compounded *dharma*s are seventy-two. They are liable to change and can be classified into five groups (*skandha*s): matter (*rūpa*), feeling (*vedanā*), perception (*saṁjñā*), inclination (*saṁskāra*s) and consciousnesses (*vijñāna*). *Rūpa* is that which changes its form under physical conditions of heat, cold, etc. The forms which *rūpa* assumes are inferentially known in thought-processes through *santhana pannatti* or formal concepts. *Vedanā* is awareness of subjective affection and is felt either pleasantly, painfully or indifferently. It may be mental or physical. *Saṁskāra*s are the inclinations or volitions, those principles which form conformations or combinations that go to build up a whole of act, speech or thought. *Vijñāna* is the totality of consciousness, which is made up of phases or types of consciousness or consciousnesses as the Buddhist works say.

The school to which Vasubandu belonged when he wrote the *Abhidharmakośa* is known as the Sarvāstivāda, which holds that everything exists. Modern expositors have deduced that Sarvāstivādins are realists in the sense that all things are said to be composed of four essentials (*mahābhūta*) — *pṛthvī, āpas, teja*, and *vāyu*. The four essentials are matter (*rūpa*) in the ultimate sense. But the composite things which are made up out of these are only names that exist in the mind. What are known to us usually as concrete things — the table, book, etc.

are only names. They exist in the mind only; but in these aggregates the four essentials really exist. The "mind" is that which is conscious of an object. It is that which is related to an object, without an object there is no subject.[127] But there is no subject which has consciousness, no permanent conscious entity which remains the same. As the object changes every moment, the subject also changes every moment. Thus there is only a sequence of states of consciousness. Each state is very complex, constantly changing and giving rise to new configurations. So both body and mind are not the same even for two consecutive moments. The current of river, though it seems to be one constant in form and identity, is nothing but a sequence of flowing. When the mind is entirely free from the course of thought (*vidhi-citta*) as in deep-sleep, it is thought-free (*vīthi-mukta*). It is then termed *bhāvāṅga*, part of being. The line that divides the thought-free part of being and thought is the *manodvāra* (door of consciousness). Outside this door are momentary states of consciousness of a particular type which constitute the stream of *bhāvāṅga*, bounded by birth and death. Death being only an ushering in of another birth, the continued flow of the stream of *bhāvāṅga* from life to life is *saṁsāra* or continual going. The stream of *bhāvāṅga* or becoming is the background, on which present conscious existence is based. The stream of becoming is not however an undercurrent on which conscious life moves. There is an interweaving of both with each other. The momentary states of consciousness are mistaken to be identical, being alike to one another in some respects such as the plane of existence, the type of the states, precedent conditions and object of consciousness. This gives rise to the false conception of an abiding soul. Even that which is presented as the "soul" —

127. *Abhidhamma-piṭaka*, VII Book, p. 2.

the "I" in self-consciousness, is like anything else variable and changing. Both the subject and object are changing, but between the two sequences there is a constant correlation. The stream of *bhavaṅga* is productive of courses of thought (*vīthi-citta*). Thought which is normal and is known as *kāma-citta*, the consciousness of desires, usually prevails on this plane of consciousness. Consciousness which is entirely free from *kāma*, *rūpa*, and *arūpa* is *lokottara-citta*, outside of all planes.

Vasubandhu also uses the word *vijñaptimātra* very often, which indicates "thought" that "which is indicated." He says that the world is sought to be explained as it appears to each individual, and as such things are found to be in terms of categories such as "real," "unreal," "being," and "non-being," etc. The nature of the world is therefore "such-ness" (*tathatā*); the world is the world. *Vāsanā*s are tendencies; *vāsanā* is therefore that which brings or introduces something into. The *ālaya-vijñāna*" contains tendencies to become something. In fact, they are spoken of as *bīja*, seeds or origins. The *ālaya-vijñāna* which by its nature contains these *vāsanā*s evolves and develops touch, mental activity, feeling, perception and will. Instead of the old words *rūpa*, *saṁskāra*s, etc. a new jargon is introduced. After this *manas* and then the function of the *manas* will develop. All this which is described as the development or transformation of consciousness is only *parikalpita*, a fabrication. Things may of course be thought to be arising in a certain order under certain conditions, but they are so considered with reference to other things (*paratantra*). But as there are no things at all of self-existence and complete in themselves, everything is to be known from the store of consciousness. To know this is to achieve complete knowledge (*pariṇispanna*). Those who tend to describe the Yogācāra school as subjective idealism should bear in mind what Vasubandhu says: when anyone sees a book or a table, or anything and says "this is nothing but *vijñaptimātra*" he is a fool. For obviously there is somebody seeing the book and the book itself. *Vijñaptimātra* is to have no contradiction of an object and a subject. One reaches that stage when one has completely abandoned the belief in an entity, "the real self" and the real thing. When one reaches that stage he is no more prone to pain. He will be happy forever. He then reaches what may be called the body of *dharma* (*dharmakāya*). It does not mean that when one reaches that stage all become one, for if they were many, how could they become one? Nor can we say that they still remain separate; that would be to accept that there are many entities, and selves.

Radhakrishnan and some others have given an account of what they call four Buddhist schools. They base themselves primarily on the *Sarvadarśana Saṁgraha* of Mādhava of CE 1400, in which four Buddhist schools are mentioned. Mādhava selects those points about the doctrines which are known to him and which he can refute. Of the four schools the first is the Vaibhāsika School. It is so called as it is based on the Chinese commentaries on *Abhidhamma* called *Vibhāsa* and *Mahāvibhāsa*. Vasubandhu wrote his *Kośa* with their help. This school is also known as the Sarvāstivāda. Sautrāntika and Sammatīya are two other schools. The Sammatīyas are important for they hold that the individual is more than a mere aggregate of the components of which he is made, though he does not exist apart. There was another school called *Mahāsāṅghika*, out of which Mahāyāna arose. Nāgārjuna and Āryadeva were the chief teachers of this school. Vasubandhu was connected with the other school, the Yogācāra also. His elder brother Asanga was another famous teacher of this school. We do not have any complete treatises on Sautrāntika and Sammatīya philosophy. What they held is to be gleaned only from accounts of their doctrines given for polemical purposes in other Buddhist and Hindu works. The other three schools are described by modern writers as mutually exclusive and conflicting systems.

Buddhist thought with its dynamism, its conceptions of movements, its distinction between the flow of organic life (*bhāvāṅga*), and the emergence of sequences of conscious moments is a wonderful structure. But to speak of Buddhist philosophy is nonsense, for what there was of it was enveloped in mythological cobweb-spinning of gods and demons, *bodhisattva*s and heavens. Over and above, it is loaded with the authority of tradition, always it had to move or rather hop on the crutches of the sayings of the "Noble One" and "the interpretations of the Elders." In spite of that, we have geniuses like Nāgārjuna and Vasubandhu, whose works are surprisingly free from mythology and the burden of past. The Buddhists made great contributions to logic.

8

Sāṁkhya and Vaiśeṣika

Development of Sāṁkhya

In the fifth and sixth centuries BC there was a great mass of speculation in India as collected in the Upaniṣads. Almost subsequent to the Upaniṣads, but more probably out of the mass of ideas contained in them, a number of theories explaining the world sprang up independently. Jainism Buddhism, and the Lokāyata are partly such. At a much later time, probably between the first century BC and the second century CE, when the Vedas together with the Upaniṣads came to be accepted as revelation and as the final and supreme repositories of truth, several people began to read their views into them and write short treatises setting forth their theories. We have as a result what are known as the six Brāhmanical systems. No doubt some of the schools like the Lokāyata refused to seek support from the Vedas and in fact spurned the Vedas as nonsense. In the revivalist period of Hinduism, the Lokāyatas, etc. were looked at a distance; they were probably persecuted as much as Jainism and Buddhism. Few dared to call themselves Lokāyatas; and their literature became extinct. Moreover in those medieval days it could appeal to few; devoid of emotional appeal, relying solely on pure reason, unwept and unregretted it died. On the other hand Jainism and Buddhism lived by becoming religions with their founders as the deities and their teachings as the revelation.

Another school of thought — though atheistic and rationalistic it was, survived because it did not openly dismiss the Vedas as nonsense; this is Sāṁkhya. Unlike Buddhism and Jainism, Sāṁkhya did not repudiate the prevalent religious practices, nor did it set up any other practices which it claimed to be superior. It is on this account that though this school survived, many of its views were freely recorded in other books; and nobody holds it as a dogma nowadays, while the Vedānta claiming to be based on revelation is so held.

Garbe has called Sāṁkhya the oldest real system of Indian philosophy.[1] Albert Schweitzer declares Sāṁkhya a wonderful achievement.[2] The origin and development of Sāṁkhya cannot be known unless we know what early Sāṁkhya was. The *Mahābhārata* mentions number, matter and twenty-four principles as the essence of Sāṁkhya.[3] Johnston has remarked that "the *Mahābhārata* passages have at least one advantage, which has not been fully appreciated. The bulk of Sanskrit philosophical literature is contained in commentaries or other works, and the object of a commentator is almost invariably to show that the particular views advocated by him are to be found in the work he is elucidating. This danger is absent from the epic's philosophical expositions, which are straightforward in statement and are not obscured by a desire to prove that old ideas and new ones are identical."[4] Unfortunately Johnston himself does not use the authority of the *Mahābhārata* to find out what early Sāṁkhya was, because he starts with the definition that "Sāṁkhya is that system which divides the object of investigation into two sides, which are

---

1. R. Garbe, *The Philosophy of Ancient India*, p. 10.
2. Albert Schweitzer, *Indian Thought and Its Development*, p. 73.
3. *Mahābhārata*, XII.1.409.
4. E.H. Johnston, *Early Sāṁkhya*, p. 5.

held widely as under. The first contains one principle — psychical and divine (Īśvara). The other consists invariably of twenty-four principles, material, mental and emotive."[5] Johnston noted that this principle "undergoes no change in its constitution, except that in early Sāṁkhya the material principles are made up of five great elements and five objects of the senses, and in the classical school of five subtle elements and five gross elements."[6] Johnston does not put the significant question; did early Sāṁkhya accept the existence of souls? If the *Mahābhārata* is a reliable guide, Pañcaśikhā, one of the earliest teachers of Sāṁkhya taught that there is no consciousness after death, everything merges in *mahat* as rivers in the ocean.[7] Even when Janaka specially puts a question about the soul after death, Pañcaśikhā answers that there can be no question of destruction or existence since there is nothing but a conglomeration of the elements, and after death there will be no consciousness.[8] The word *saṁjñā* was also used by Yājñavalkya in his statement that "after death no consciousness."[9]

This constrains us to think that early Sāṁkhya as taught by Kapila, Āsuri and Pañcaśikhā did not postulate any soul or souls. In fact, even later Sāṁkhya had no need for a soul, as

5. Ibid., p. 16.

6. Ibid.

7. *evaṁ sati ka ucchedas śāśvato va katham bhavet, svabhāvād vartamāneṣu sarvabhūteṣu hetutaḥ. yathārṇavam gata nadyo vyaktimjahati nāma ca, na tu svatam niyacchanti tadrsassatvasankasyaḥ. evaṁ sati kutha saṁjñā praetya bhāve punar-bhavet? prati sammiśrītejive gr̥hyamāne ca madhyataḥ* — *Mahābhārata*, Vavilla Edition, XII.200.42-44.

8. *ucchedaniṣṭha nehasti bhāvaniṣṭha na vidyate; ayamhyapi samahārassarīrendriya cetasam* — Ibid., 200.2.4; 200.6.

9. *pretya saṁjñā nāsti.*

according to it mind, egoism, intelligence, etc. are evolutes of matter, unless one feels there should be a knower behind knowledge, though it would be extremely difficult to explain how knowledge and knower are connected. That early Sāṁkhya did not postulate *jīva*, a separate individual principle can be known from the definitions of *jīva* found in the *Mahābhārata*. Bhāradvāja asks why we should postulate a *jīva*, when we are able to explain all the physical and psychic processes without assuming such an entity.[10] Bhr̥gu dogmatically says that when death occurs it is only the body that is destroyed; the *jīva* goes to another body.[11] He seems to hold this belief because otherwise there will be no meaning in morality. He goes on to say that *jīva* is not destroyed just as fire is not destroyed even after the sticks are burnt out.[12] Bhr̥gu objects that this is absurd; because after the fuel is consumed no fire is available, fire without fuel is annihilated.[13] Bhr̥gu says that fire is not destroyed even after all the fuel is consumed. It exists in space (*ākāśa*), but having no dwelling or container (*āśraya*) it is not visible. Even so *jīva* after death takes refuge in ether and being very subtle is invisible; but is not destroyed.[14] Bhāradvāja asks what is the nature of this *jīva* for when the body is dissected (*bhidyamne*) no *jīva* is obtained. Bhr̥gu says that it is the subject of all experience.[15] Bhāradvāja says that it is the senses and the mind which perceive and conceive, for example when the eyes are shut or ears are closed nothing can be seen or heard; when the mind is otherwise

---

10 *Mahābhārata*, XII.200.174.

11. Ibid., XII.175.1.

12. Ibid., XII.175.2.

13. Ibid., XII.175.3-4.

14. Ibid., XII.175.5,6.

15. Ibid., XII.175.15.

engaged nothing can be thought, and in sleep the *jīva* though present does not have any experience. So there is nothing that can be called a Subject which may be called *jīva*.[16] Bhṛgu again dogmatically says that in the body constituted by the five elements and made up of the five *guṇa*s there is an *ātmā* who knows and enjoys and without whom the body cannot know or enjoy.[17] Bhṛgu goes on to say he is the *ātmā*, the controller of the Universe.[18] Several definitions of *jīva* are given — *"jñānādhiṣṭitam avyaktam," "sa jīva kṣetra saṁjñākaḥ"; "mānasognīḥ śarīreṣu jīvaḥ" "Jamo rājas ca sattvam ca viddhi jīva guṇaniman."*[19] It is further said that *jīva* is the quality of the *ātman* and *ātman* of *paramātman*. This is very interesting, if the same elements or tendencies that are found in *prakṛti* characterise *jīva*, and *jīva* as the *ātman* and the latter the *paramātman*. What is the difference between matter and *paramātman*?

If the early Sāṁkhya denied any souls, what was the relation between it and the Lokāyata; and why did it later accept the existence of souls? Speyer has expressed the view that Sāṁkhya has developed from an original materialist system;[20] and Jacobi holds the same view. Disagreeing with this view, A.B. Keith remarks that Sāṁkhya can be traced to the Upaniṣads. He forgets the materialist views that are found in the Upaniṣads. Even if Sāṁkhya developed from the Upaniṣads, it can still be said to have developed from materialism. Thus A.B. Keith is forced to admit that the realist elements in Sāṁkhya may be due to the contemporary tendency

16. Ibid., XII.175.17,19.
17. Ibid., XII.175.20.
18. *lokasya vidhāyakam*.
19. Ibid., XIII.175. 31; XII.175.4, 9, 25, 31.
20. *Indische Theosophie*, p. 113.

to materialism.[21] Max Müller on the other hand believes that Sāṁkhya is an attempt to remove from the Vedānta the two startling features — denial of the reality of objective world, and negation of the individuality. He is far thinking that Sāṁkhya is a "toning down" of Vedāntic Monism.[22] Dahlmann's view is almost the same: The theory of Upaniṣads that there is one *ātman* makes bondage and liberation meaningless, as how the one *ātman*, omniscient and all-present came to be bound. Clearly the way out was to have a plurality of souls, having the same characteristics which the *ātman* in the Upaniṣads possesses, and also to accept besides that there is another principle, matter. In the end the conception of the one *ātman* — absolute and all present, was found to be superfluous for matter by itself evolved into the world of manifold objects. This supposition of Dahlmann does not work out for the difficulty that in Sāṁkhya bondage is said to be merely verbal and fictitious, *aṇumātram*.[23] If bondage is real how could it be broken? Aniruddha quotes a verse in support, "there is no bondage in the nature of things, nor does release follow from its non-existence."[24] Therefore we have the paradox of Sāṁkhya exhorting us to break up our bondage, though it never existed. The positing of plurality of *puruṣa*s has in no way removed the difficulty. We are therefore constrained to admit that Sāṁkhya started as a reaction against the *ātman* theory, which denies the validity of the reality and variety of the world; and possibly it grew out of

21. A.B. Keith, *The Religion and Philosophy of the Veda and Upaniṣads*, vol. II, p. 550.
22. Max Müller, *The Six Systems of Indian Philosophy*, pp. 229-30.
23. *Sāṁkhya-pravacana-sūtra-vṛtti*, I.58.
24. *Sāṁkhya-pravacana-sūtra-vṛtti*, I.7.

materialism.

The Sāṁkhya conception that matter or *prakṛti* is the unconscious productive principle (*prasava dharmī*) consisting of three conflicting tendencies towards (a) stability, (b) movement, and (c) inertia, is the great contribution.[25] The evolution of all things proceeds from the movement and counter movements: *sañcaraḥ partisañcaraḥ*. That which is non-existent cannot be the cause (*asada-kāraṇāt*). That which is produced must be constituted out of its material (*upādāna grahaṇāt*). Not everything can be produced from everything (*sarva sambhava bhavat*); the efficient can bring out only that which it is capable of (*saktasya sakya kāraṇāt*) and lastly the effect must contain the cause as its material (*kāraṇa bhavat*). For all these reasons there must be a real cause which is really transformed into the effect.[26] As individual objects are limited, they must have a cause which is unlimited. But the cause of them must be of the same nature as themselves, because a thing cannot have another cause of a different type. Moreover the cause must be such that it is capable of producing the effects. So we must postulate as the cause of this world that which can produce the effects by it. Lastly, in the world we see that effects are potentially existent in causes, evolve out of them and are finally resolved into them. For all these reasons we must infer that there is a cause for all the things in the world out of which they have developed and which possesses all the characteristics which these things possess and which is capable of evolving into these things by itself. Sāṁkhya goes on giving a scheme of the order for development of the world from matter. But no reason for matter is given, nor is it

---

25. *Sāṁkhya-Kārikā*, 11,13.

26. Ibid., 9.

shown how it came to be known that matter follows this order of development. Vijñānabhikṣu went to the length of saying that the order of production must be accepted on the basis of scripture.[27]

The idea that everything, conscious and unconscious, is the production of one ultimate material principle is found in the Upaniṣads. For instance, in the *Bṛhadāraṇyaka* (1.46) the idea that the Universe is the same as food and the eater of food is found; the *Taittirīya* also contains this idea (3.10.6). In the *Kauśitakī Upaniṣad* (2.13,14) and the *Chāndogya Upaniṣad* (4.3.3) attempts are made to determine what that function or element is into which all the other elements are resolved when the individual sleeps or dies and from which they again come forth when he wakes up or is reborn. We have also seen that the Upaniṣads contain speculations about the nature of the fundamental principle of the universe being water, air, or earth, etc. So from all these the main idea of the Sāṁkhya is derived, namely, (1) the ultimate principle of the world must be one, (2) it must be capable of explaining the variety of the world, and (3) it must contain within itself the principle of development. This results in the conception of *prakṛti* (or that which is before the effects) as that which is made up of three conflicting tendencies and out of the action and reaction of which everything *develops*. The theory that these *guṇa*s are inherent in everything and that they are responsible for the variety of the world on account of the varying proportions in which they enter into each is also found in the Upaniṣads.[28] It may be traced to *Chāndogya* where it is said, reality consists of three forms (*rūpa*s) from which all are constituted.[29] The idea

27. *sṛṣṭikrame śāstram eva pramāṇam sāṁkhyasāra* — Ibid., 15-16.

28. *Maitrī Upaniṣad*, 3.2; 6.10.

29. *Chāndogya Upaniṣad*, 6.4.

that multifariousness of the world can be explained through a single principle is a great advance. Further the idea that such a principle cannot be conceived as a static uniformity, but as a many-united-one registers tremendous progress in thought. Added to this, if we remember that Sāṁkhya insisted that the development of things from this principle should be self-explanatory, and no extraneous element such as God should be assumed, the boldness and vigour of Sāṁkhya speculation is surprising. Garbe's remark that it "is the most significant system of philosophy that India has produced" is not unwarranted.[30] It must be remembered that early Sāṁkhya has not recognized souls and God; and the Sāṁkhya that we meet within the *Śvetāsvatara Upaniṣad* is posterior to the early Sāṁkhya.[31] In this connection it is significant to notice that the *Kena Upaniṣad* (3.10-12; 6.7-8) mentions that the *mahān-ātman* has evolved from *avyakta*. It, of course, mentions that there is a *Puruṣa*, immanent in all.

Classical Sāṁkhya does not accept this sort of *Puruṣa*; it accepts *puruṣa*s. Because it did not want to be put on a par with the Lokāyata or because the founders of classical Sāṁkhya thought it was logically necessary to accept souls. We need not suppose that Buddhism was responsible for the origination of Sāṁkhya, because many Buddhist works mention Kapila to be the founder of Sāṁkhya; and there is much evidence in Buddhist literature to show that Sāṁkhya is pre-Buddhistic.

Whatever be the form of early Sāṁkhya, which can remain only a reasonable conjecture, classical Sāṁkhya as we have it in the earliest work extant, namely the *Sāṁkhya-Kārikā* (later part of third century) accepts a plurality of *puruṣa*s, and it

30. See R. Garbe, *The Philosophy of Ancient India*.

31. R.E. Hume, *The Thirteen Principal Upaniṣads*, pp. 8-9.

accepts this on rational grounds. The conglomeration of the evolutes of *prakṛti* which are unconscious must be for the sake of another, as unconscious things do not exist for themselves. For instance the cot, the table, etc. exist for the sake of man, not for themselves. So also *prakṛti*-evolution must be for the sake of something conscious. As there is an unconscious principle of three *guṇas*, the contradictory of it also must exist. Further, unconscious *prakṛti* must have a controlling power. As the nature of things is to be pleasing or painful, there must be somebody who enjoys them. Lastly since all desire the attainment of liberation, there must be somebody who can attain liberation.[32] So the soul exists. There are many such souls, because if there were only one soul, birth, death and action cannot be individual. When one individual dies all the others do not die, nor when one does something all the others do the same. If the soul is the same in all bodies, then all men and women will be engaged in the same activity at the same time, which is not so. Further, when one is happy, another is miserable; if the soul were one, this would not be. So there is a plurality of souls.[33] It can be seen that the proofs for the existence of the *puruṣa* start with these presuppositions; the objects of world are enjoyable (pleasing or painful), so there must be an enjoyer; the objects of the world are for the sake of somebody (*parārtha*), so there must be that somebody; people desire liberation, so there must be something to be liberated. The value and validity of these arguments is obvious. All this is directly contradicted by Īśvara Kṛṣṇa himself who goes on to say next, there is nobody bound or liberated, only it is *prakṛti* which is bound and liberated.[34] This shows that the

32. *Sāṁkhya-Kārikā*, 17.
33. Ibid., 18.
34. *Sāṁkhya-Kārikā*, 62

rationalistic early Sāṁkhya was tortured and mutilated to make it a *darśana* showing the path of salvation like all other *darśanas*. How could this be done without assuming that there is somebody to be saved? Therefore *puruṣas* are postulated. And as for the conception of *puruṣa* it was there in Yājñavalkya's utterances.[35] Like Yājñavalkya's *ātman*, Īśvara Kṛṣṇa's *puruṣa* is also a passive spectator. It does nothing, belongs to nothing; it merely sees and knows (*sākṣī* and *jñātā*). And the same views of bondage and liberation as expressed are found in the Upaniṣads.[36] There is really no bondage, yet we are exhorted to strive to cast it off. Īśvara Kṛṣṇa is only apparently rationalistic, by trying to prove there are souls because there is enjoyment and bondage. If enjoyment and bondage are only apparent and unreal, as he admits; why may not we argue that the soul is also unreal and an illusion? These contradictions of classical Sāṁkhya tend to prove that early Sāṁkhya was probably simple and thoroughly rationalistic. The irreconcilable way in which the views of Vedānta are taken over and grafted on to a theory which holds that every function — mental and physical, of man is a development of *prakṛti* goes to prove this.

Origins of Vaiśeṣika

In the *Vaiśeṣika-sūtras*, Kaṇāda formulated an atomistic realism. Nobody knows who Kaṇāda is, and when he lived or where he lived. The *Vāyu Purāṇa* says he was born in Prabhās (Saurāṣṭra). He was the son of a certain Ulūka and the disciple of one Soma Sarma. Kaṇāda means "particle-eater." It might probably be a nickname or even a title.

35. *Bṛhadāraṇyaka Upaniṣad*, 4.5.15.

36. A.B. Keith, *Sāṁkhya System*, p. 76.

Praśastapāda who expounded his system calls him Kāśyapa, i.e. he might have been born in the genealogy of Kāśyapa. Praśastapāda lived in the fifth century CE.[37] Some other scholars place him earlier.[38] Kaṇāda has been declared to be pre-Buddhist, as he does not discuss or show the influences of Buddhism. A Jaina work, *Āvaśyaka* records that a certain Rohagutta propounded an atomic theory. Dharmottara expresses an atomic view of the universe.[39] Aśvaghoṣa informs that there was an atomic theory even before the Buddha.[40] It is possible that some unknown thinkers gave rise to the atomic theory, and it is probable that they might have been Jainas. Ancient Indian writers do not appropriate the works of others and theories; and then claim them to be their own. When the Jaina work *Āvaśyaka* says that Rohagutta is its founder, due weight must be given to the statement. But Rohagutta's work that deals with atomism does not exist; and the first systematic thinker of this school of atomism is Kaṇāda. Atomistic views may have been voiced even prior to the Buddha and Rohagutta of the first century CE, who may have taught it as one of his chief doctrines. Kaṇāda may have later taken his inspiration from him and built up a system. As Nāgārjuna seems to. be familiar with the *Vaiśeṣika-sūtra*s, it is probable that Kaṇāda lived prior to him.[41] Dasgupta begins to expound Nyāya-Vaiśeṣika by saying that Buddhists upset all common sense convictions of substance and attribute, cause and effect; and that the Sāṁkhya assumptions are baseless.[42] He concludes

37. A.B. Keith, *Indian Logic and Atomism*, p. 93.

38. Faddegon, *The Vaiśeṣika System*, pp. 319-23.

39. *Nyāya-bindu-ṭīkā*, p. 86.

40. Ui, *Vaiśeṣika Philosophy*, pp. 40-41.

41. Ui, *Vaiśeṣika Philosophy* pp. 46-55.

42. S.N. Dasgupta, *History of Indian Philosophy*, vol. 1, pp. 274-75.

his introduction by saying that experience calls for a new careful reconstruction in the light of reason.[43] The implication seems to be that Nyāya-Vaiśeṣika is a reaction against Buddhism and Sāṁkhya. He expressly says that Nyāya-Vaiśeṣika discussed the doctrine of momentariness.[44] Dasgupta does not stick to the presumptions of his statements. He goes on to say that Vaiśeṣika is pre-Buddhistic.[45] His reason is that no knowledge of Buddhism is shown in the *Vaiśeṣika-sūtras*. Another argument of Dasgupta is that Vaiśeṣika supplemented metaphysics to strengthen the grounds of the Vedas."[46] Now that is quite possible and Dasgupta's points are very plausible. Why may not we think that Vaiśeṣika rose as a reaction against the sort of theories that are found in Buddhistic texts such as *Kathā-vatthu, Abhidhamma,* etc.? Could not have Kaṇāda used atomism to support Vedicism? Radhakrishnan remarks that Nyāya and Vaiśeṣika are interested mainly in averting the sceptical consequences of the Buddhist phenomenology.[47]

The Vaiśeṣika system is based on the presumption that things can be thought and named; and they do exist. So we have six categories — substance, quality, movement, genus, species and inherence. Apart from that Kaṇāda classifies space, time, soul and mind as substances, which are directly perceived. Space is the basis of the notions of east and west, far and near. Space (*ākāśa*) has to be admitted because sound which is a quality does not inhere in any perceived thing. So we have to postulate a substance space (*ākāśa*) in which sound inheres. Air is inferred from touch and as it does not inhere in

43. Ibid., p. 276.
44. Ibid., p. 310.
45. Ibid., p.305.
46. Ibid., p. 285.
47. S. Radhakrishnan, *Indian Philosophy*, vol. I, pp. 29, 177.

any substance; it is a substance by itself. Time is a continuity and unity; it is that which produces the notion of simultaneity — prior and posterior, etc. It appears to be many due to its association with changes. It is that which produces non-eternal things. The soul has to be admitted because something which corresponds to the notion of self, of "I," must exist. This is strengthened by inference, for there must be a substance in which knowledge inheres.

Genus and species are relative to the understanding *(Buddhyapekṣam)* and as being only indicates continuity, it is a genus. That by which things appear as existent is being. It is therefore different from substance, quality and movement. It has no genus and species, it is one and different from particulars as well as universals.[48]

That which is but has no cause is eternal, and is inferred by its effects. We speak of the non-eternal, which would be meaningless if there is nothing eternal. The component particles of compounds, which are produced, are eternal; they are called the atoms. Combinations of atoms are due to their *dharma*s. Atoms are qualitatively different, thus the atoms of air differ from those of earth.

Qualities are inherent in substances; they do not possess further qualities, and are not causes of contact or separation. Movement also inheres in substance; and it does not possess any quality. It is an independent cause of contact and separation. Substance is the material cause of qualities and movements, while quality is the non-material cause. Movement cannot produce substances; but a substance is the result of the contact of many atoms.

---

48. *guṇatva, dravyatva, karmatva.*

The causes of phenomena are unknown or unseen. When this unknown (*adṛṣṭa*) is absent, contact between soul and body is impossible. When the causes of phenomena are known one gets liberation. It is a fact that the contact of the soul with mind, senses and objects will result in pain and pleasure.

The above brief summary may look like a caricature, but that is all the amount of philosophy that *Vaiśeṣika-sūtra*s of Kaṇāda contain. He is interested in a lot of other things such as to whom gifts should be given, how Vedic performances produce *adṛṣṭa*, etc. Today we can scarcely call all this as philosophy. Later Vaiśeṣikas developed Kaṇāda's scheme and their physical speculations are of historical interest. They have been described in Beal's *Positive Sciences of the Ancient Hindus.*

Though later Vaiśeṣikas have attempted to define and discuss substance, movement, genus, species, etc. they have failed to develop any system of philosophy. For instance what is their world-view? The ultimate stuff of the universe is made up of atoms. But the soul, air, etc. which are deemed to be eternal are not made up of atoms. As such only material things are made up of atoms. The relationship between the spiritual entities — soul, mind, etc. and the material things made up of atoms is not explained nor are these conceptions fitted in with those of space and time which are regarded as substances. In what sense are things said to be? Do space and time, the soul, etc. exist in the sense in which a jar or a table exist? This question remains unasked in Vaiśeṣika system.

The speculations of Vaiśeṣika are of the same order of philosophical development as those of Greek atomists. An attempt to read into them the latest developments is to play havoc with history and ignore all the sound canons of critical scholarship. Radhakrishnan expounded Vaiśeṣika with reference to A.N. Whitehead's distinction between sense-data, the world of perception and scientific objects and declared that "in the Vaiśeṣika also we have" these.[49] Do such expositions and explanations arise from the same tendency which credits ancient Hindus with the discovery of aeroplane and the theory of relativity, because Vālmikī describes a Vimāna and the Veda speaks of the sun as neither rising nor setting?

A school known as Nyāya is invariably described as a Brāhmanical school of philosophy by modern scholars. The Nyāya discusses such subjects as doubt, purpose, fallacy, quibble, etc. along with means of knowledge and objects of knowledge. Its ontology is that of Vaiśeṣika. But it develops logic and epistemology. Subjects like inference, causation, authority, etc. have been discussed by Nyāya writers with consummate ability. Especially in this connection mention has to be made of Gaṅgeśa (CE 1200) and his followers who have striven hard to formulate precise definitions of concepts like probans, probandum, the relation between the two, etc. But all this is not to be mistaken for philosophy. It is logic or at the most epistemology, and has no place in a history of philosophy. No historian of Western philosophy expounded the contents of Aristotle's Organon in his work. That ought to be dealt within treatises on Logic.

---

49. S. Radhakrishnan, *Indian Philosophy*, vol. II, p. 229.

9

Schools of Vedānta

IN the middle of the fifth century CE, the central Asian tribe of White Hūṇas under Attila spread desolation throughout Europe, and invaded India. Had not Attila died in CE 453, and had the Hūṇas loved their nomadic freedom with lesser intensity, they might have played the same part as did the barbarian Greeks towards the Aegean civilization. But it was the Hūṇas with their leader Toramāṇa were responsible for the break-up of the Gupta kingdom in India. Toramāṇa consolidated his power in the Western frontier provinces as effectively as the Kuṣāṇas. His son Mihirakula (CE 470-530) persecuted the Buddhists relentlessly; but he was defeated by a confederation of princes under Yaśodharman of Mālwā as its head. Some regard Yaśodharman to be the fabled Vikrama, at whose court flourished Kālidāsa, Varāhamihira, and others.

Nobody precisely knows what happened in India for a century after Yaśodharman. We have once again a reliable history with Harṣa coming to power in about CE 606. Harṣa's power extended up to Magadha and Bengal. The kings of Kāmarūpa and Gujarat accepted him as overlord. The entire north-western India up to Indus and the whole Gangetic valley including Nepal were under him. He tried to extend his suzerainty into the south also but was defeated by the Cāḷukyan king Pulakeśin II. Harṣa was a remarkable man; he was a poet, patron of learning and kind ruler. He was a polytheist, who worshipped a number of gods — both Hindu and Buddhist. The brāhmins did not like Harṣa's worship of the Buddha and his reverence for the Buddhist paṇḍits; they plotted to murder him, and a Buddhist monastery was set on fire. Hiuen Tsang recorded these events. Harṣa's contemporary king Śaśāṅka of Bengal ruthlessly persecuted Buddhists in CE 600 and even uprooted the sacred *bo*-tree at the Buddha-Gayā. In the capital of Harṣa himself there were 100 Buddhist monasteries and 200 Hindu temples. According to Hiuen Tsang Buddhism prevailed only in Udyana, Kanauj, Ayodhyā and Magadha. But even there idolatry, ceremonial worship, growth of a class of deprived priests and monks and who resorted to magic (*tantra*) began to develop within the fold of Buddhism. If the Buddha had to come back he would not have recognized all these practices as Buddhism. The Chinese traveller I-ching describes, with evident satisfaction, the temples and images of the Buddha and the pageant of ceremonial worship. I-ching (CE 671-695) records that a Buddhist monastery in Magadha had the idol of Avalokita, a *bodhisattva*, and his wife Tārā. All this shows how Buddhism was becoming degraded into gross polytheism, magic and superstition, and how it was slowly losing its influence due to its own inner weakness and the persecution of bigoted kings and zealous brāhmin priests.

Kāśmīra-Śaivism

From Kalhaṇa's *Rājataraṅginī*, we learn that in Kashmir powerful Hindu kings ruled; and one of them was the famous Lalitāditya (CE 724), a great warrior who fought with the Tibetans and Turks and conquered Punjab and Kanauj. He was a worshipper of the sun and it was he who built the Mārtaṇḍa temple. He worshipped the Buddha also; but his successors were all Śaivaits. From early times Kashmir was occupied by Aryan tribes, it formed part of Aśoka's empire. Aśoka's son Jalauka drove out the foreign oppressors and established the Mauryan form of government. Later Kashmir formed part of Kuṣāṇa Empire and Buddhism flourished there. The third general assembly of the Buddha was convened in Kashmir at which Nāgārjuna dominated. Later the Hūṇa conqueror Mihirakula established his sway over it; he swept away Buddhism, built Śaiva temples and endowed brāhmin monasteries. Several dynasties followed each other until the Karkoṭa dynasty came to power. It endured for a longer time than others. Lalitāditya belonged to this line. At last it too was exterminated and a kinsman of the Karkoṭas, Avantivarman became the king in CE 855. He was a good and great king who ruled for about thirty years. In his regime scholars flourished and their contributions to Sanskrit literature are outstanding. Aided by his able minister Suyya, Avantivarman promoted many irrigation works. The floods were prevented; water-logged land was reclaimed; new beds were constructed for rivers to prevent inundations. The Mahāpadma Lake which used to overflow and ruin crops every year was embanked with stone, and land around it was granted to brāhmins, who were encouraged and helped to raise its level.[1] Under the Karkoṭas and Avantivarman, an interesting development in Śaivism was made by the Kashmir scholars.

A Śaiva teacher Vasugupta (CE 800) was engaged in popularizing Śaivism. But some Buddhist scholars headed by one Nāgabodhī began to criticize his views and arguments. Unable to defeat them with logic, Vasugupta composed a body of aphorisms known as *Śiva-sūtra*s, which he claimed were revealed to him by God. On these *Sūtras*, Kallaṭa wrote a

---

1. See M.A. Stein, *Introduction to Rājātaraṅgiṇī.*

detailed commentary known as *Spanda-Kārikā*. Some say that Vasugupta himself was the author of this. Later scholars like Abhinavagupta of eleventh century CE, and Kṣemarāja, among others, wrote commentaries on it and also independent expositions. Kallaṭa, Somānanda among others lived in the peaceful reign of Avantivarman.

According to Spanda system, which is based up on *Spanda-Kārikā*, the ultimate principle of the universe is consciousness, which is of the nature of vibration, a power of activity. Pure consciousness is devoid of change and modifications; it is immutable and dynamic but not static. It is this principle of vibration in theistic schools that is called God.[2] The entire world is a manifestation of the essence of this principle; by its own free will this principle has created the world. The world is not an evolution from undifferentiated pure consciousness; because what evolves ceases to remain as it was. But this principle, though it assumes diversity never ceases to retain its real nature. Moreover the unconscious alone can change, the conscious cannot change.[3] On this account the diversity of forms should not be deemed to be an appearance as something not real. For them how could the real give rise to the unreal? The ultimate principle is changeless, yet it manifests in diverse forms. It thus accomplishes the impossible.

All the diverse objects in this world are brought into being by the principle of vibration like reflections in a mirror which are not different from their originals, but appear so. Experience has the bifurcation of object and subject, the known and knower. Here the object is nothing but a creation while the subject is not the created, but itself the creator. Even the finite

2. *sarveṣu parameśvareṣu yadupasyam taditaḥ spandatatvāt nādhikam* — Kṣemarāja, *Spanda-Nirṇaya*, p. 12.

3. Ibid., pp. 13,14.

subject is one in form with the ultimate principle. So the subject is always indestructible, the objective is evanescent.[4] Every individual is in fact identical with the whole, for the whole is the total reality, which is indivisible. The multiplicities of things are originated in the Reality on account of its free will. Therefore every individual is the Reality itself; and it is the one subject who is ever, and everywhere present in all the diverse objects as the object and enjoyable.[5] This projection of itself into the object by that one principle — the conscious subject — is natural to its being. All this is known by yogic experience, the direct perception of things in full cognition (*pratyabhijñā*). By scriptural study man comes to know the ultimate reality of God. When God manifests himself before the individual, the individual by meditation on the fact "I am God" attains full cognition. That is the *summum bonum*. Then one becomes omniscient and all-doer. The most handy and yet authoritative work on the Spanda school is Kṣemarāja's *Spanda-Nirṇaya* Elaborate treatment of the system is to be found in Abhinavagupta's books.

Stated in the abstract as done above, the Spanda school may look rational and free from mythology; but in its practical aspect it conceives Śiva or God as having matted hair and a *khaṭvāṅga* (a weapon) in his hands, etc. The power or energy of God is conceived as a feminine deity, which is prayed and worshipped. All sorts of magical formulas and dubiously valuable methods of worship are encouraged by this school. It is not a school of philosophy, but a religious sect, which incidentally had a curious philosophy, which was neither fully developed nor wholly logical. The resemblances between the

4. Ibid., p. 32.

5. Ibid., p. 48.

conceptions of this school and those of Royce as developed in his conception of God are striking. But Royce's treatment is fully philosophical, while that of the Kashmirian school is nothing of the kind. The dynamic conception of reality and Advaita which we find in the Kashmirian school may be due to the Buddhist influences.

Śaivism in South India

In the third century CE, Āndhra power came to an end. Gradually the Pallavas took possession of the large tracts of the country, formerly under the Āndhras. With Kāñcī as their capital, they for sometime ruled almost the whole of peninsular India. Śivaskandavarman performed the Aśvamedha. Then the Cāḷukyas from the north claiming to be descendants of Rājpūts came. They drove out Pallavas from Vātāpi (Badāmī), who retired to their eastern and southern possessions. For two centuries (CE 550-750) the feud between the two dynasties continued. The first Cāḷukya who made the dynasty a great power was the first Kīrtivarman. It was under him that the construction of the cave temples of Bādāmī began. The most famous of Cāḷukyas is Pulakeśin who defeated Harṣa. In CE 615 he defeated the Pallavas and took over Veṅgī to which his brother Viṣṇuvardhana was appointed Viceroy. Shortly after that Viṣṇuvardhana declared himself independent and founded the house of Eastern Cāḷukyas. In the eighth century the Rāṣṭrakūṭas, a feudatory of Cāḷukyas, overthrew the Cāḷukyan power.

We had an occasion to refer to the origins of Śaivism in the far-off days of sixth century BC; and in the second century BC there was a sect of Śaivas. Śiva in the first was a tribal deity of aboriginals, who was taken up by others in view of the popularity and prevalence of his worship. Later he came to be associated with the Vedic god Rudra and finally in the

Śvetāsvatara Upaniṣad, with Rudra and Śiva. In the fourth century some Śaivas, for whom the austerity and pessimistic view of life of the Buddha had an appeal, wanted to incorporate those elements into their religion. So in the place of the Śākyamuni was set up Śiva, the supreme ascetic who lives naked in the Himalayan snows amidst a host of goblins and demi-gods, wears snakes and skulls, smears ashes of corpses and drinks poison for the benefit of the world. Elements of devotion were already there in the *Śvetāsvatara*; and so around this ideal of Śiva grew up a vigorous Śaiva movement. But this time it was in the south. The beautiful Śiva temples near Bādāmī show that Śaiva movement made much progress by the seventh century. Āndār Nambi who collected a vast mass of hymns in honour of Śiva lived in the time of Rājarāja (CE 1000). So the composers of the hymns must have lived in the preceding centuries. We have definite evidence that one of the hymn-writers Sambandhar lived in the seventh century. The Śaiva reformers wanted to have a more spiritual and ethical ideal than that of the Buddhism and Jainism, as Jainas and the Buddhists were very much prevalent then in the south. Māṇikkavāchagar, minister to one of the Pāṇḍya kings of Madurai in the sixth century, was a great Śaiva. He preached renunciation of all that is worldly and devotion to Śiva as the cure for all suffering and unhappiness. Some of the Śaiva saints were śūdras, though the more important ones were as a rule drawn from the higher castes. In the eighth century Vikramāditya II of Pulakeśin's clan built the Virūpākṣa temple at Paṭṭaḍakal. The Rāṣṭrakūṭas, specially king Kṛṣṇa who built the Kailāsa temple of Ellorā, were patrons of Śaivas.

By this time there were left no royal patrons of Buddhism in the north or south, except the Pāla kings of Magadha who came to power in CE 730, and ruled for a very long time. But the Pāla ministers were almost always brāhmins and under their patronage non-Buddha idols were installed in the Buddhist monasteries. All this demoralised the Buddhist priests; the Buddhist pantheon with rituals of magic and immoral practices was evolved, which was called Tantra. A wave of this religion went to Nepal and to further India, where the Trinity of Brahmā, Viṣṇu and the Buddha came to be worshipped. There are some Buddhists still in Orissa who are known as Saraks who gather once every year at Khaṇḍagiri to worship a four-armed Buddha.[6] Thus by the eighth century CE, Buddhism became thoroughly polytheistic. Kumārila (CE 750) was a vigorous opponent of Buddhism and Jainism. He initiated the movement of "Back to the Vedas and Vedic sacrifices." The Pūrva Mīmāṁsā, which was developed by him, is neither philosophy nor religion. It is not religion because it has no god, creator of heaven and earth; it is not philosophy because it is dogmatic through accepting Vedas as revelation. It is a ritualistic system of sacrifices and magical chants based on the belief that sacrifices performed according to the prescribed rules produce an unseen power by virtue of which man can go to heaven and enjoy great happiness. Kumārila was born and flourished in Bihar.

In Orissa at about CE 474, the Keśarī dynasty was founded and it lasted till the end of the eleventh century, occasionally losing its influence. The Keśarī kings were not patrons of Buddhism, though they may have tolerated it; for it was they who constructed the temples at Bhubaneswar and other places. Their successors, the Gaṅgas built the temples of Purī and Koṇārk. The Rājpūts who emerged as an important warrior-class in the eighth and ninth centuries were devout followers of Brāhmaṇism seeking to trace their ancestry back to the

6. N. Vasu, *Modern Buddhism*.

celebrated Hindu gods and heroes of the *Rāmāyaṇa* and the *Mahābhārata* and never liked Buddhism. The Rājpūts were a martial race delighting in battles and dangerous war-like sports; the Buddha could never be their god. Śiva in his phallic emblem (*eka-liṅga-bhagvān*) is the tutelary deity of the noblest royal house of Rājpūts of Mewar.

Śaṅkara: Advaita Vedānta

It was in the eighth century, when the Rāṣṭrakūṭas were in ascendance that Śaṅkara was born in Kaladi in the state of Kerala. He was the precocious son in a family of Nambūdri brāhmins. He became an ascetic early in life. Fables tell us that he was a violent opponent of Buddhism, Jainism and Mīmāṁsā. He sought to establish a religion. As revelation he took the three books, the *prasthāna-trāyī* — the Upaniṣads of the Vedas, the *Brahma-sūtra* and the *Bhagavad-Gītā*. He studied under Govinda a teacher, and then went to Benaras, where he composed his commentaries on the above books and is alleged to have written a number of hymns and minor books also. After winning great distinction as scholar and debater, he went about the length and breadth of India propagating the theology of Brāhmanism. He was received with deference at courts, was reverenced by the multitude and feared by the Buddhists and Jainas. Taking a leaf out of the Buddha, he established four monasteries in the four key-corners of India. The most important of them is at Śṛṅgerī in Karnataka. He died at a very young age; and his achievements are amazingly outstanding.

The mission of Śaṅkara was so successful that after the eighth century, Buddhism disappeared from south India. The Sena dynasty which succeeded the Pālas in Bengal and Bihar in CE 1038 was indifferent to the Buddhism. King Ballāl of the Sena dynasty organized Kulinism in Bengal. In 1193 a general of Qutubuddin invaded Bihar, seized the capital which was full of monasteries and priests, burnt the monasteries and dispersed the priests. In the same year the Buddhist centre of Sāranāth at Benaras was demolished and the libraries burnt. The Buddhist religion which was concentrated at certain places disappeared as soon as those centres were annihilated. But Jainism persisted for a long time in south India and Gujarat. King Amoghavarṣa (CE 815-877) was for instance a Jaina; he was a great Rāṣṭrakūṭa king, founder of the city of Manyakhet, patron of learning and a kind man. Some of the kings of south were Jainas, Rāmānuja was for example patronized by a Jaina king, who was later converted.

Sir Charles Eliot and others have argued that the works of Kumārila and Śaṅkara do not show any evidence of violent hatred of the Buddha and therefore they could not have been persecutors. If we read the writings of some of the churchmen of the middle ages in Europe who were actively associated with the inquisition and the ruthless hunting down of the heathens and heretics, we cannot imagine how they who appear so charming and so full of kind thoughts could have been such tormentors of fellow beings. It is however sufficient to note that the Buddhist works mention ruthless persecution as the cause for the disappearance of Buddhism in India; and the names of Kumārila and Śaṅkara are specially associated with that. It is quite probable that Buddhism died a natural death and the Buddhist works are only telling a mass of lies when they talk of persecution. But persecution need not always mean beheading; it may have been expropriation of the properties of the Buddhist monasteries, discouragement and prohibition of assemblages of the Buddhist monks in public places, ruling out of the books written by the Buddhists from the curriculum of the *gurukula*s and debarring the Buddhists from public offices. In the courts of the kings of those days religious debates between Buddhists and Vedic scholars and even between Śaivaites and Vaiṣṇavaites were quite common; and the defeated were either converted or banned from the region.

One of the first points to be remembered in connection with Śaṅkara is that he is not a philosopher. He is a theologian, whose first principles are drawn from scriptures. He rationalizes on the basis of scriptural statements. He does not use reason to establish anything independently; but uses it to remove contradictions of the scriptural statements and criticize statements of others. Secondly Śaṅkara is neither an absolutist nor an illusionist. He is a strict theist; in fact, a monotheist *par excellence* that India has produced.

Radhakrishnan and others while giving an exposition of Śaṅkara's doctrine often mix it up with the additions made by later teachers of his school. They do not also differentiate between the statements of his position as found in the *Brahma-sūtra-bhāṣya* and as found in his other works.

Gauḍapāda is traditionally reputed to be the master of Śaṅkara's teacher. His *Māṇḍūkya-Kārikā* is so cogent, logical and free from scriptural quotations and mythology, that we must mention him as the second great philosopher that India has produced, the first being Nāgārjuna. His argument runs thus: The world of dreams is unreal, while the waking state is considered to be real. There is no justification for regarding one of these states as more real than the other, for the one is contradicted by the other and vice versa; both the states are one.[7] Duality is an illusion; the soul through his own peculiar power (*māyā*) projects himself as the object. He imagines himself through himself.[8] This world has the same status as the snake

7. *Māṇḍūkya-Kārikā*, 2.5.

8. Ibid., 2.12.

imagined in the rope, as the city revealed in the mirage, as the circle of fire that appears when the fire-brand is revolved with speed, and as the mango tree that is grown by the juggler's trick. All these illustrations are given by Gauḍapāda. In reality since there is no duality, there is no creation, no bondage and hence no liberation.[9] Every process and relation requires two terms, but since there is no duality there is no process and no relation. The relation between the individual and the reality is that the whole may be understood with reference to the analogy of space which is present in a jar and space in general. When the jar is broken the enclosed space merges with the universal space, from which however it was never separate.[10]

With reference to causation, if cause itself is the effect, and even the cause is produced, there is no permanent thing that can be called cause. If there is identity between cause and effect, then the effect is also unproduced for it itself is cause. The effect is produced either from a produced thing or from an unborn thing. The latter is impossible; in the former case what is regarded as cause is not the cause and thus there is regression.[11] All duality is thus a vision of the mind (*manodr̥śyam*), when mind is "unminded" (*amanibhāve*) there is no duality.[12] The ultimate reality is eternal immutable consciousness (*vijñāna*) which is not of the nature of a thing (*avastutvam*).[13] It is the *vijñāna* which appears as classified, as moving and as a thing. As the movements of the fire-brand

9. Ibid., 2.32.
10. Ibid., 3.4.
11. Ibid., 4.11.
12. Ibid., 3.31.
13. Ibid., 4.45.

leave an impression of a fire-circle, so the vibrations in consciousness appear as diverse objects.[14] The vibrations in consciousness are not due to any extraneous cause and when the vibrations cease they do not go anywhere nor do they enter consciousness, even as the movements of the firebrand.[15] The end of man is to realize that there is no duality; by stilling the mind one ceases to have alternative conceptions.[16] This is not the same as sleep, for in sleep mind is annihilated, while in knowledge it is enlightened.[17] When man reaches this state he is released from all sorrow and desire and is supremely happy.

Gauḍapāda's obligations to Śūnyavāda and Yogācāra are obvious. Though at one place he expressly says that what he has been saying was not taught by the Buddha,[18] his conceptions of ultimate reality as *vijñāna*, his account of diversity in the world as due to movements in *vijñāna* and all his examples are borrowed from Buddhism. Nobody knows who this Gauḍapāda was, and tradition mentions that he preceded Śaṅkara, who is supposed to have expounded his work.

Śaṅkara's most famous work is his commentary on the *Brahma-sūtras*. Nothing is known about the author of the *Brahma-sūtras* (aphorisms) beyond the fact that he was one Bādarāyaṇa. Jaimini in his *sūtras* mentions Bādarāyaṇa; and Bādarāyaṇa mentions in his *sūtras* Jaimini; therefore they must have been contemporaries. Since Śaṅkara belonged to the eighth century and as he accords great sanctity to the *Brahma-*

---

14. Ibid., 4.47.
15. Ibid., 4.48-9.
16. Ibid., 3.34.
17. Ibid., 3.35.
18. Ibid., 4.99.

sūtras, it is probable that some centuries must have passed during which the *Brahma-sūtras* gained prestige. As we have earlier said all the *sūtra* literature must have been composed between the heyday of the Kuṣāṇa power and the end of the golden age of Guptas.

During the centuries that elapsed, the interpretation of the scriptures in the form of aphorisms (*sūtra*s) raised many perplexing problems; there were also sects questioning the authority of these *sūtra*s to interpret the Upaniṣads. Some time before Śaṅkara, Gauḍapāda has expounded a doctrine in a brilliantly succinct way, which though was influenced and in fact derived from the Buddhist works, was not alien to views expressed in the Upaniṣads. For the Buddhists, themselves, were indebted to the Upaniṣads. Gauḍapāda has developed his theory with reference to the *Māṇḍūkya Upaniṣad*. Śaṅkara took over the doctrine of Gauḍapāda and modified it, and further sought to harmonize the Upaniṣads and the *Brahma-sūtras*, in order to present a consistent view. He had a difficult task as the Upaniṣads contain different views and contradictory statements. He got over this by the ingenious device of saying that whatever did not suit his theory was said from the ordinary standpoint, while statements in accordance with his theory were from the ultimate standpoint. The device of the Buddhist scholars by which they explained away inconvenient statements of the Buddha by calling them *samvṛtti-satya* was probably known to Śaṅkara. However it must be said that Śaṅkara's theory is not primarily a development of Buddhism; it can be logically evolved from certain Upaniṣadic passages and the *Bhagavad-Gītā*. The doctrine of *māyā* is found in the *Śvetāsvatara Upaniṣad* and the *Bhagavad-Gītā*. They are as old as the earliest phases of Buddhism, if not older. As such Śaṅkara's views have been derived from the Vedānta-trilogy (*prasthāna-trāyī*): the Upaniṣads, the *Bhagavad-Gītā* and the *Brahma-sūtras*.

Śaṅkara's *magnum opus*, the *Brahma-sūtra-bhāṣya* contains the following views: In experience when man says "I am this" or "that is mine" a transfer or superimposition of the qualities of the body to the soul is made. The superimposition of the qualities of silver on the pearl-shell, etc. is recognized as an error. Such superimposition is as wrong as to say that space (*ākāśa*) is blue. All ordinary knowledge, whether religious or empirical, is vitiated by this kind of wrong superimposition (*adhyāsa*). In all perception and inference, the soul is presupposed with the attributes such as — the body, senses and individuality, etc. All our knowledge of the soul must be false for it involves the fallacy of *adhyāsa*, the superimposition of the attributes of the body on the soul. It is admitted that animals and humans behave similarly with reference to perception and empirical experience. If a cow sees a man approaching with a raised stick, it goes away; similarly if a man sees another man with a frightening face or naked sword in hand, he turns away. Since man's behaviour is not different from that of animal, he too cannot distinguish the soul from the not-soul, the body. When the scripture says that the duty of brāhmins is to sacrifice, the fallacy of *adhyāsa* is involved, for how can the soul be identified with caste and stage of life. When it is said "I am sick" or "I am blind" — it involves the fallacy of *adhyāsa*, the superimposition of the attributes of the body on the soul.

The existence of the soul is an intuitive fact, a necessary presupposition of all knowledge.[19] Its existence is implied in its very denial, for that which denies it is the soul.[20] Further we must admit an ultimate substance which is the cause of everything. Everybody knows that he is this soul which is

---

19. Introduction, *Brahma-sūtra-bhāṣya*.

20. *Brahma-sūtra-bhāṣya*, 1.1.4.

known by everybody as "I" cannot be denied. This object of the idea of soul (*ahaṁ-partyaya-viṣaya*) though real is not the ultimate reality. For this "I" of whom I am aware is the agent and enjoyer, and there are several "I's." So we have to postulate a greater than these selves, a witness of all these "I's." The soul or finite soul in us is a witness to all our actions and experiences.[21] The finite soul constrains us to postulate an Infinite Soul and though the two are related as part and whole, the two have altogether different characteristics and that is evident.[22] Śaṅkara is quite clear that the finite soul is not God, though in its essential nature the two do not differ. There is non-difference (*na-dvaita*) between the two, no identity at all.

For Śaṅkara, the Supreme Soul, *Brahman* is the ultimate reality and pure intelligence for the order and harmony in the world; and it is an intelligent principle.[23] Other than being consciousness through and through, like a salt tablet which is salty through and through, *Brahman* has no attributes. Once the existence of the ultimate reality or the greatest, *Brahman* (*bṛh* = to be great) is granted, its very idea constrains us to understand it as having purity, freedom, perfection, etc. One can only be silent regarding its attributes, as our understanding is limited. Śaṅkara nowhere makes any clear distinction between the *Brahman* as such and the *Brahman* with attributes.[24] There was no need to do this for what exists is the one *Brahman*, pure being and consciousness, devoid of all attributes. Predications are only superimposed on that as a piece of crystal placed near a red flower is spoken of as red.[25]

---

21. *ahaṁ pratyaya viṣaya kartṛvyatirekena tat sākṣī puruṣah* — Ibid., 1.1.4.
22. *pratyak-sameva jīvasya iśvar viparīta dharmatvam* — Ibid., 3.2.5.
23. *Brahma-sūtra-bhāṣya*, 2.2.1.
24. Paul Deussen, *The System of the Vedānta*, pp. 100-01.
25. *Brahma-sūtra-bhāṣya*, 3.2.15.

Between the supreme soul and the individual soul there is no ontological difference, except for the limiting adjuncts like the body, name and form, etc. which are the products of nescience. Therefore release (*mokṣa*) is not something to be effected, but ever present. He, who sees a rope in the dusk and mistakes it for a snake, will get rid of his fear as soon as he knows it to be a rope.[26] Just as we speak of the space in the jar, in the cave, in the water-vessel, etc. though space is one and indivisible, there is only one Lord in connection with various, limiting adjuncts like bodies, etc. Apart from that one principle there is no other transmigrating soul.[27] This is not to be understood in the sense that there is only one soul, for then if there is only one soul, with the emancipation of that one soul, the world-process comes to an end.[28] The fact that the individual soul is one with the supreme soul holds good only when the former attains complete knowledge and passes out of the body, becoming one with the supreme soul. Till then the individual must be deemed to be and is absolutely different from the supreme soul. This is Vācaspati Miśra's explanation of Śaṅkara's passage.[29] Some ocean water brought in a jar is not different from the ocean water, but it is not the ocean. It will be the ocean only when it is poured back into the ocean. For example, the Biblical view that man is made in God's image does not mean that man is God.

Brahman is that which is the cause of the world; It is both the material and efficient cause of the world, and though this looks impossible, it must be accepted on scriptural authority.[30]

---

26. *Brahma-sūtra-bhāṣya*, 1.4.22.
27. Ibid., 1.1.5.
28. Ibid., 3.2.21.
29. *Sacred Books of the East*, vol. XXXIV, p. 278.
30. *Brahma-sūtra-bhāṣya*, 1.4.23-27.

God is the cause of the world in the way in which clay is the cause of jars and gold of ornaments; and further he is the cause of the world by virtue of his rulership as the magician is the cause of his magical performances.[31] God is the cause of the world without undergoing whatsoever change like the magnet which moves iron without itself moving.[32] Creation of the world is not a difficult matter for God.[33] The inequalities and cruelty in the world do not point towards God's injustice. All this happens according to the law of *karma*, since creation and destruction are beginningless and since beings are given the form and station which they deserve on account of their past births.[34] God's creation is purposeless, for he has no unfulfilled desires. It is a sort of sport for him, he exercises his spontaneity thereby.[35]

Keen minds have made refinements over this position of Śaṅkara as found in his *Brahma-sūtra-bhāṣya*. But nothing creative, nothing of the nature of a substantial development over Śaṅkara is found in all these attempts. Dasgupta has patiently recorded the contributions of the teachers that followed Śaṅkara. He conceives God as pure undifferentiated being of the nature of intelligence, which is also similar to Thomas Aquinas' conception of God. Śaṅkara may not have developed his monotheism logically to its end, yet he is the one great monotheist India has produced. It is a blunder to make him out to be a philosopher and at that too an absolutist. Śaṅkara calls his theory "non-dualism," but not monism.

---

31. *Brahma-sūtra-bhāṣya*, 2.1.1.
32. Ibid., 2.22.
33. Ibid., 2.1.32-33.
34. Ibid., 2.1.34.
35. Ibid., 2.1.33.

Śaṅkara does not teach bare static unity, for that would be to teach nothing. He has only denied real multiplicity, but has not advocated absolute non-difference.[36]

Śaṅkara's followers did not remain content with his position. For them *Brahman* is the ultimate reality; it is one and is of the nature of consciousness; it is God. The soul of man is also in its essence of the same nature; it is an *aṁśa* (part) of God.[37] If so it is God itself, for a part of anything is the thing, you do not call the leg of a chair a thing and the chair a different thing. For reality is one and undifferentiated and the individual soul is not different from supreme soul, there is no liberation and none to be liberated. To understand this is liberation. This was how Śaṅkara's followers developed his position. In all this, a confusion of the finite with the infinite soul is involved; but even in Śaṅkara's interpretation there is no such confusion. Yet logic if carried out ruthlessly would compel Śaṅkara's position to be driven to this end. Śaṅkara was skilfully and imperturbably silent on the difficult points involved. But his followers being not as great as himself applied themselves with energy to these issues, which were avoided by him with foresight.

Rāmānuja: Viśiṣṭādvaita Vedānta

Towards the end of the tenth century the Rāṣṭrakūṭa power came to an end. Then a section of Cāḷukyas founded a new dynasty called the Cāḷukyas of Kalyāṇī. There were constant conflicts between the Cāḷukyas and Coḷas. The Coḷas crushed the Pallava supremacy in the south during the ninth century.

---

36. *na-khalu ananyatvamiti abhedam brumaḥ, kiṁtu bhedam vyasedhamaḥ* — Bhāmati, II.1.14.

37. *satyopi jīveśvarayoḥ aṁśamsibhave* — *Brahma-sūtra-bhāṣya*, 3.2.5.

Rāja-rāja Coḷa (CE 985) conquered Maldive and Laccadive Islands, the Ceylon and built the great Śaiva temple at Tanjore. His son Rājendra conquered the southern districts of Burma, Nicobar Islands and the Malay Peninsula. All this was accomplished by means of the Coḷa fleet. His armies penetrated into the Gangetic plain also. He was the ruler of the entire south India and Sri Lanka. At this time Muslims began to ravage north India. Cāḷukyas became powerful again. King Vikramāṅka (CE 1076), who ruled for fifty years, was a great king of the line of weak successors of Rājendra. Poet Bilhana and the Jurist Vijñāneśvar (author of *Mitākṣarā*) lived in his court. At the same time his contemporary Coḷa king Kulottuṅga I (CE 1070) regained much of the glory of his dynasty. South India under the Coḷas had a very stable government; the life of the people was just as it was in the Mauryan or Gupta periods. There was a vast administrative system, the unit being a group of villages. One sixth of the produce was collected as tax, which was paid either in gold or kind. Careful surveys of the land were made and the tax was collected strictly. Various other taxes like those on trade, salt, professions, etc. were levied. In return people enjoyed a stable and peaceful government and amenities being provided like irrigation facilities, highways, dams, etc. Within half a century after Vikramāṅka, the Cāḷukyan power did pass away; the Coḷas did not retain their glory for long after Kulottuṅga.

The Deccan was divided between the Yādavas of Devagiri, the Kākatiyas of Warangal, and the Hoyasaḷas of Dvārasamudra. These kingdoms were perpetually at war with each other and fell an easy prey to Muslims when they came to invade Deccan.

Rāmānuja was born in CE 1017, in Sri Perumbudur of Vaiṣṇava brāhmin parents. He studied under Yādava Prakāśa in Kāñcīpuram, but quarrelled with him and left. He came under the influence of Yamunācārya, a Vaiṣṇava teacher. With the help of Bodhāyana's commentary which Rāmānuja got from Kashmir, he composed his own commentary on the *Brahma-sūtras*. Rāmānuja became very famous; and large numbers of people used to flock to hear him; and many were his regular disciples. Kulottuṅga Coḷa, whom we just mentioned, was the king then and he was an ardent Śaiva. He did not like this popularity of Vaiṣṇava faith and had the eyes of two chief propagators of Vaiṣṇavism removed. One was his disciple and the other a friend of Rāmānuja. With that Rāmānuja got frightened and fled to the Hoyasaḷa kingdom of Mysore, where the king was a Jaina. That Jaina king was converted to Vaiṣṇavism by Rāmānuja; and with the king's help, Rāmānuja propagated the Vaiṣṇava faith vigorously. After Kulottuṅga's death, Rāmānuja returned from Mysore and lived till his death in Śrīraṅgam. He died in CE 1137. Rāmānuja's biography *Yatirāja-vaibhava* written by his disciple is a very straight-forward work free from the miracles.

Vaiṣṇavism is the school of Vedānta that projects Viṣṇu as the Supreme God. It traces Viṣṇu from the Vedas where he is mentioned as Āditya, a solar deity. He is he who has taken the three steps of rising, shining at the zenith and setting (*trivikrama*). Gradually the worship of the swift-moving shining sun is developed into that of the all-pervading Viṣṇu. We find another conception in the Vedas, that Nārāyaṇa as the resting place of all men. In the Brāhmaṇa portions of the Vedas, Viṣṇu is given a prominent place. The *Kaṭha Upaniṣad* (1.3.9) speaks of the abode of Viṣṇu as the goal of beings.[38] In the sixth or fifth century CE the tribal chieftain Kṛṣṇa became a prophet to his people; and he was made a divinity and

38. *viṣṇoḥ paramam padam.*

worshipped being identified with Vāsudeva, the name under which the Bhāgvatas worshipped God. Under Aryan influences this monotheism came to be combined with the Vedic cult of Viṣṇu-Nārāyaṇa. This school of devotion to God might have grown out of hero-worship and the feeling of loyalty to the dead and deified tribal chieftain. The theory of incarnations was an explanation to interpret the history of ancient heroes. The theologians of Alexandria and Antioch have conceived God after the pattern of an earthly dictator. The theory of devotion to God is not alien to the Vedas for the *R̥gveda* says that "God is like the clandestine lover of woman."[39] Vaiṣṇavism was a devotional development of the idea of the tribal chieftain as the head and protector of the people, who therefore must be respected, loved and praised. The monotheism which Vaiṣṇavas developed was clearly formulated in the *Bhagavad-Gītā* for the first time. Mahāyāna Buddhism is a phase of this monotheistic movement substituting the Buddha in the place of Viṣṇu-Kr̥ṣṇa. It was Vaiṣṇavism as found in the *Bhagavad-Gītā*, which was adopted by the Gupta emperors, who became the followers of Bhāgavatas. The *Bhagavad-Gītā* was given a congenial setting by being inserted in the great epic *Mahābhārata*, which was edited under the auspices of the Gupta emperors. With the spread of the story of the *Mahābhārata* through all parts of India, Vaiṣṇavism also spread.

Following the first Arab conquest of Sindh in CE 712, the Muslim invasions spread over north India. The priests and trading classes as well as the timid kṣatriya families began to immigrate to south India. Learned brāhmins and handicraftsmen fled from north India to the courts of Rāṣṭrakūṭa and Coḷa kings and their vassals in the South. Since the time of

---

39. *yosa jaram iva priyam.*

the Guptas, north India leaned for the most part towards Vaiṣṇavism, while south India was more favourably inclined towards Śaivism, which at the eighth century received powerful stimulus due to the appearance of Śaṅkara within its fold. Through Śaṅkara, Śaivism got a theology supplementing the agnostic philosophy of the Buddhist schools. Śaivism was austere and ascetic in its ideals with a pessimistic view of life regarding human existence, a vanity and natural phenomena impermanent and so not wholly real; and it may be a kind of Hīnayāna within Hinduism. Vaiṣṇavism was an optimistic view believing in the grace of God and devotion towards Him; and may be said as the Mahāyāna of Hinduism.

In the centuries preceding Rāmānuja, the exodus of learned men from the north to the south has given rise to the spread of Vaiṣṇava movement, which centres round the Āḷwārs. The hymns of the Āḷwārs were edited by Nāthamuni in the tenth century CE. So the chief of the Āḷwārs, Nammāḷwar, must have lived in the seventh or eighth century. It was the Vaiṣṇavism of the *Mahābhārata* and the Purāṇas which provided a stimulus to these Āḷwārs. The Purāṇas consisting of endless tales and legends of ancient kings and heroes, descriptions of sacred places of pilgrimage and sectarian wrangles were popular by then. All celebrated heroes were looked upon as God's incarnations. It is believed that God was accomplishing his own inscrutable mysterious will through battles and revolutions, overthrow of kingdoms, famines and other national catastrophes. Priests and prophets, sages and law-givers, including the Buddha were considered God's incarnations. So through every phenomenon, whether terrible or good, and in every act good or bad it was divine will that was fulfilled. It was the Itihāsa-Purāṇas and the *Bhagavad-*

Gītā that were the popular scriptures at this time. The gods of these books Śiva, Viṣṇu, and Śakti were the popular deities. It was against this background that the Āḷwārs developed the Vaiṣṇava movement and composed their hymns.

The characteristic feature of Āḷwārs' hymns is the exaggerated feeling of sinfulness which the devotee feels before God. Yāmuna, for example, speaks of himself as the vessel of thousand sins.[40] He considers himself as a shameless brute, committed every sin, reprehensible act a thousand times, but not once.[41] (Similar are the views of Karl Barth and Kierkegaard that, in sin man discovers God.) Yāmuna speaks that the individual can offer nothing to the Lord God for whatever is his belongs to the Lord's. All beings are bounded to the Lord, who is the infinite soul in the embodied soul; and the finite soul can offer nothing but himself wholly to the Lord, the infinite soul.[42]

The *Bhagavad-Gītā*, the *Śvetāsvatara Upaniṣad*, the literature of the Āḷwārs and the Purāṇas, especially the *Viṣṇu Purāṇa* determined the thought movement of Rāmānuja. Rāmānuja was greatly influenced by Śaṅkara. The conception of the soul as a part of God of which Rāmānuja makes so much was clearly stated by Śaṅkara.[43]

Theism was developed in the Upaniṣads, especially in *Kaṭha* and *Śvetāsvatara*. Even the older Upaniṣads like *Bṛhadāraṇyaka* and *Chāndogya*, view that the *ātman* is the only real; and *ātman* is in all things in the same way as the individual soul is present in the body. The *ātman* being spoken of as the inner controller

40. *aparādha sahasra bhajanam.*

41. *na ninditam karma tadasti loke sahasraso-yannamaya vyadhāyi.*

42. Yāmuna, *Stotra-ratnam.*

43. *satyapi jīveśvarayoḥ aṁśāṁsibhāve — Brahma-sūtra-bhāṣya,* 3.2.5.

(*antaryāmin*) of all things, the *Bṛhadāraṇyaka* (3.7; 4.3) speaks of the *ātman* as the ultimate light of man. Again the famous dialogue of Yājñavalkya and Maitreyī, in which he says that all earthly love is nothing but a sublimation of one's love for the *ātman* and so instead of canalizing this love in subordinate ways, one should directly seek and love the *ātman* — suggests the doctrine of devotion (*bhakti*).[44] The *Kaṭha Upaniṣad* (2.12) describes the *ātman* as that which is to be meditated as the god, *deva*. It has the characteristics of grace and election.[45] The *ātman* is not to be obtained by learning or reasoning, but by those whom he chooses.[46] The *Śvetāsvatara* (1.8; 6.23) carries this trend of thought further; it is said that the supreme is Śiva, Rudra, God, Lord (*Īśa*), the great Lord. One should have devotion towards God for man can free himself with divine grace only.

Accordingly Rāmānuja develops his theory of *Brahman* as a triad, but is nevertheless whole. *Brahman* is the one qualified by two other principles, the conscious and the unconscious. *Brahman* is present both in the souls and matter. The universe is the body of *Brahman*. *Brahman* is the soul of the souls and the world. The material world and the world of souls are different from *Brahman*, in so far as matter is an object of enjoyment, souls the enjoying subjects and *Brahman* the ruling principle. Souls and matter are non-different from *Brahman* in so far as they constitute his body and he constitutes their soul.[47] In *Brahman* are three principles: (1) matter which is unconscious, (2) souls which are conscious and atomic and (3)

44. Ibid., 2.4.5.
45. Ibid., 2.20-23.
46. *yam eva eṣa vṛṇute tena labhyaḥ.*
47. Rāmānuja, *Śrībhāṣya*, 1.1.1.

the Lord who is omnipotent and is qualified (*viśiṣṭa*) by intelligence and bliss. The totality of these three principles is *Brahman*. The Lord and the souls, the Lord and matter are related as the soul and body are related (*śarīra-śārirī* relation). All real things are included in this triad. There is no matter without souls and the Lord, nor is there a soul without matter and the Lord. Likewise the Lord is always associated with the souls and matter. Take for example a man, from a superficial viewpoint, the visible form — the body is the man. If we analyse he is, in truth, the soul that animates the body. But there is a subtler and higher principle than the Lord, who indwells the soul by controlling it. So in everything there is the triad (*traita*); nothing in the universe is unique and undifferentiated. The souls can be classified into four main groups — gods, men, animals, and non-moving things like plants. Apart from the bodies which they occupy, the souls have no distinctions.[48] Matter is the non-intelligent causal principle of the material universe. It constitutes the means for experience of pleasure and pain of souls.[49] In the *Śrībhāṣya*, Rāmānuja does not give any more account than this of matter. The souls and matter are real and are to an extent independent of *Brahman*. They are the modes (*prakāra*) of *Brahman*. The soul is a part of *Brahman*, not in the sense that it is a piece (*khaṇḍa*) cut out from him, but as a ray of light, it is a part of the source from which it issues.[50] Just as the hand-stick and earnings of a man serve as the differentiating attributes of him though they are substances, so souls and matter though they are substances can still be God's attributes (*viśeṣaṇa*). The soul is the substance of the body which is a quality of the former. This is evident because when the soul leaves, the body perishes; so the soul

48. Rāmānuja, *Śrībhāṣya*, 1.3.25.

49. Ibid., 1.4.10.

50. Ibid., 2.3.42,45.

is the substratum. The soul is the final cause of the body, because the body exists to facilitate the soul to enjoy the fruits of the actions. The body is the soul's mode because it just helps the soul to manifest as god, man or the like.[51] The individual and God, stand to each other in the relationship of part and whole, body and soul, attribute and substance. The material world also is a mode of *Brahman*.

The visible world is the effected state (*kāryāvasthā*) of *Brahman*. Before creation and after dissolution *Brahman* exists in the causal state. In the causal state of *Brahman* body and souls exist in him in a subtle condition, in the effected state they just become manifest and admit of being thought and spoken as distinct in name and form. The universe is thus an evolution, a transformation of *Brahman*, not a mere appearance of *Brahman*. But the effect, the world, is non-different from the cause.[52] When *Brahman* becomes the world, what occurs is only an act of the will of God to enter into the gross manifestations. God as such undergoes no change. The transformation of *Brahman* does not detract God's perfection; on the other hand it confirms glory. Creations and dissolutions of the universe are beginningless and endless. When *Brahman* is in the causal state, and the matter and souls are in a subtle condition; they are hardly to be distinguished. Then he wills to possess a world-body distinguished by name and form as in the previous aeon, and the body of *Brahman* (matter and souls) which is in a subtle condition gradually evolves into the manifested world, leaving *Brahman* himself unchanged.[53]

Rāmānuja writes that the world is real; all the things in the world are real. Yet non-dualism is the truth. When it is

---

51. Rāmanuja, Śribhāṣya, 1.1.1.
52. Ibid., *Śrībhāṣya*, 2.1.15; 1.1.1.
53. Ibid., 1.4.27.

said that the king of Kāśī is one without second, it does not mean that he has no wife and children, no kingdom and armies. Man is there differentiated within himself into the soul and body. When the scriptures say that *Brahman* is one without second, it means that *Brahman* is one having souls and matter for his body. Scriptural statements which teach oneness of *Brahman* indicating non-difference of *Brahman* and the souls, in the same breath assert the difference of *Brahman* and the souls.

Rāmānuja conceives *Brahman* as a person, who can will and realize his will. *Brahman* desires truth (*satyakāma*) and wills truth (*satya-saṁkalpa*); or he is one whose will is fulfilled, whose ideas are realized. *Brahman* is the supreme person for, only in his case, all ideas and wishes are realized. He is the Puruṣottama, the noblest of men. *Brahman* cannot be perceived, as he cannot be sensed. He is not like anything else in the world, so he cannot be inferred. He cannot be perceived in mystic trance, for in mystic trance one visualizes by intensely thinking of what he believes.[54] Yogic experience is only a kind of hallucination born of strenuous recollection of previously known things. Arguments such as the cosmological and teleological cannot prove God. You may be able to prove that there must be cause for this world, but you cannot prove that it is one, nor can you prove that it is auspicious, good and the highest.

Brahman can be known, otherwise what is the use of scripture? It is impossible to know a thing, which is devoid of all attributes, for then it is not a thing but nothing. Only that which has attributes can be known, *Brahman* has attributes

---

54. *nāpi yoga janyam, pūrvānubhūta viṣaya smṛti mātratvāt na prāmāṇyam iti, kuta prāmāṇyata* — Rāmānuja, *Śrībhāṣya*, 1.1.3.

and he can be known. He is not an undifferentiated unity devoid of all attributes. *Brahman* possesses infinite auspicious qualities of unsurpassable excellence. He has a divine body, not born of *karma*. His body is non-material (*aprākṛta*). Though he has a body, God is not subject to suffering. Though he has form he is formless. When the scripture describes him as having no qualities it only means that he is devoid of all inauspicious qualities.

The individual is a part (*aṁśa*) of God. The colour of a thing is a part of that thing, the species of horse is a part of horse, and a ray of light is a part of the source from which it arises. The attribute of a thing is a part of that thing. So the individual is a part and an attribute of God.[55] The soul is different from intellect, life and senses. On being conditioned (*sopādhika*) by matter, the soul enjoys suffering and pleasure.

Creation is a sport of the Lord (*krīḍa-hareḥ*). We cannot know how exactly the universe has come out of *Brahman*. For the things beyond senses, scripture is the only standard.[56] Creation and the multiplicity of objects in the world are real. How can creation, which is an act of God, the supreme reality, be unreal? Impermanence of things does not prove their unreality. And the non-existence of things at different places and times does not make them out to be fictitious. The snake seen in the rope is false because the absence of snake is experienced where the rope is at the same time and same place. Thus the experience of the world is not negated by *Brahman*-knowledge, for the *Brahman* is not the contradiction of the world. Further, if the world is an illusion we have then two principles — *Brahman* which is real, and the world which is

---

55. Ibid., 2.3.45.

56. *atīndriye arthe śāstrameva pramāṇam* — Rāmānuja, *Śrībhāṣya*, 2.1.12.

an illusion. If illusion is an illusion, Advaita theory is demolished. Whether illusion is real or unreal, according to the principle of contradiction it has to be one of these two things. Either way the Advaita will not stand.

Complete surrender of oneself to God with devotion is the first step towards the realization of God; in such *samarādhanā* which is born of complete devotion, God is perceived.[57] After learning about God's nature through scriptures, one must wish to attain God by knowing that He resides in the cave of one's heart. In this process of devotional worship three steps can be differentiated: (1) *Dhruva-Smṛti*: The nature and form of the Lord as described in the scriptures should be firmly remembered. (2) *Asakrdavṛtti*: This remembrance must be steady and continuous like an uninterrupted flow of oil. (3) *Darśana-samanakarata*: By this constant remembrance and meditation, imagination (*bhāvanā*) is sharpened; and the object of remembrance and meditation is visualized. What happens is that remembrance (*smṛti*) becomes very clear (*viṣida*); and an image of the object that is being remembered is visualized. As it possesses the character of immediate presentation it acquires the nature of perception. All this does not happen unless God's grace is obtained, for which one should surrender himself to God with firm faith. According to Rāmānuja even after release, the soul does not lose its individuality. To maintain that the individual loses its "I"-ness in release is to say that it is annihilated. Nobody would seek release if he is going to lose his personal existence. The return of the soul to God or its reunion with God is something like that of the return and reunion of the prodigal prince with his father the king.[58] The released soul goes to heaven, acquires

57. Rāmānuja, *Śrībhāṣya*, 1.2.23; 3.2.23,24.

58. Rāmānuja, *Śrībhāṣya*, 1.1.4.

a non-material body and is in every way like God.[59] The soul even then will be controlled by God; man is ever an attribute of God.

Religion has nothing to do with reason. God's existence and nature cannot be established through reasoning. God can be known only through scriptures. By remembering the scriptural description of God and ceaseless meditation on him, one can evoke a mental image of him. As this image of God, thus evoked, it may be called seeing of God. Rāmānuja sounds very modern when he says that God cannot be proved and that those who claim to see God do so by imagining very vividly what they have learnt from scriptures or teachers. Rāmānuja thought this was possible because his conception of God contains many anthropomorphic elements. His God is Nārāyaṇa; he has a body (non-material), and has a wife, *Śrīyaḥpatiḥ*. In his introduction to the *Bhagavad-Gītā-bhāṣya*, Rāmānuja mentions that his God is Nārāyaṇa, wears ornaments, uses weapons, and incarnates in human forms. So it was natural that he should suppose his God to be visible. A God like that of Śaṅkara, who is absolutely simple, undifferentiated and devoid of all attributes cannot be seen. He can only be conceived, as an electron or an atom is conceived. A God like that of Rāmānuja can be seen if one is impressionable and can with sufficient force imagine him, after hearing or reading the descriptions of him. Unless conceived anthropomorphically God cannot be seen. Therefore Rāmānuja rejected the statements that the pure-being (*viśuddha-sattā*), an undifferentiated consciousness (*nirviśeṣa cinmātram*) can only be conceived but not to be seen; and cannot be worshipped and prayed to. For Rāmānuja the religious instincts of man

59. *Brahmānubhāvaḥ na tu svarūpaikyam.*

have no need of such an abstraction; and he rejected them as a "mere nothing" and in its place substituted Nārāyaṇa-Hari, who lives in heaven, has a consort, is of transcendental beauty (*divya maṅgala vigraha*) and who enjoys the eternal charming youth (*saukumārya lāvaṇya yauvanādi ananta guṇa nidhiḥ*). Nārāyaṇa, the Lord God, hears man's prayers, runs to succour his devotees, and assumes human forms for his devotees' sake, as he did many times in days of yore. Nārāyaṇa-Viṣṇu-Kṛṣṇa is an apotheosis of the kind benevolent king or tribal chieftain, on whom one can rely and to whom one can run in difficulties. To set up some such concrete ideal and believe in it is very useful for it serves to integrate life and makes one's life meaningful.

Whether in science or religion man needs fictions. Nobody has seen the electron and shaken hands with it; none has met those things called force or ether. They are useful abstractions, which serve to integrate facts and interpret some phases of experience. If the idea of God instils meaning and purpose into life and serves to integrate personality, let it be welcomed and strengthened by all means. And from this point of view Rāmāṇuja's God is of greater use than Śaṅkara, though the latter is the more rational conception.

Accounts of Śaṅkara and Rāmānuja as found in Radhakrishnan and Dasgupta are prolonged because these authors do not distinguish between the position as found in Śaṅkara and Rāmānuja and the theories developed by their followers. Nor are the sources limited to their chief works — the commentaries on the *Brahma-sūtras*. Śaṅkara's position as found in his *Brahma-sūtra-bhāṣya* differs in some respects from that found in *Bhagavad-Gītā-bhāṣya*, *Viṣṇu-Sahasra-nāma-bhāṣya*, etc. But all these are indiscriminately used as sources; and so with Rāmānuja. In all histories of Western philosophy, Kant's thought is shown in its process of development as found in his three critiques. But in India if more than one work is alleged to be an author's, all are used indiscriminately. Again sometimes exposition is degraded into advocacy, and if the historian is not enthusiastic about a thinker, like Radhakrishnan in the case of Madhva and Rāmānuja, he is sought to be represented in unfavourable light from the beginning. This happens because all these are theologians; and treatment of them cannot be impartial as one's own sectarian loyalties clog the sub-conscious of the historian. In the case of Plato and Aristotle, Kant and Hegel among others, we do not have these difficulties, for though they discuss theological questions, they do it as philosophers, not as dogmatists.

Śaṅkara, Rāmānuja and Madhva were all the children of their time. They did not rise above the institution of caste. All of them denied to the lower castes access to *Brahman*-knowledge, which fact was invariably found in their commentaries on the *Apaśūdrādhikaraṇa* of the *Brahma-sūtras*. They took for granted the mythology of the Purāṇas — the seven worlds above and the seven below, the *devayāna* and *pitṛyāṇa*, etc. Rāmānuja's theism exercised much influence in north India through Rāmānanda, Kabīr and Nānak. Influenced by Islamic culture, all these teachers rejected caste distinctions.

Madhva: Dvaita Vedānta

After the glory of Cāḷukyas and Coḷas faded away, south India for a long time was ruled by petty kingdoms. The Yādavas ruled at Devagiri, the Kākatiyas at Warangal, and the Hoyasaḷa Ballāḷas at Dvārasamudra. They were always at feud with one another, but the people continued their ancestral modes of agricultural life in dirty poverty-stricken villages, living in meaningless toil and still more meaningless sloth. The state of the country or the adventures of chieftains did not concern them. They tilled their fragmented holdings, ate their rice-gruel, thanked Rāma for giving it and went to their beds. They produced children at an enormous rate, but did not increase the country's productivity. Nobody thought of bringing new virgin lands and forests under the plough; nobody thought of increasing the poultry, the sheep and goats and evolving them into a small industry. The north was already ravaged by the Muslims, but the invading Muslim armies did not yet cross the Vindhyas. Arab traders of course came into contact with Kerala long ago, but it had no effect.

In 1294, Alauddin crossed into Deccan and plundered Devagiri. His general Malik Kafur destroyed it in 1307 and shook the Kākatiya kingdom to its foundations. Again in 1311 Kafur returned and overran the larger part of east coast, marching as far south as Dvārasamudra. He took back to Delhi immense booty, unsettled the peaceful conditions of the south and made it convenient for Muslim adventurers to carve out kingdoms.

But before the Muslim hordes could spread all this havoc, in 1199 at Veli near Udupi was born a child in an orthodox brāhmin family; this was the celebrated Madhva. Madhva was a strong and robust boy interested more in games and sports than in studies. He was so strong in youth that he was nicknamed Bhīma. At the age of eleven, he became an ascetic and was ordained by an Advaitic hermit Acyuta, who is known as Sudhānanda. Unsatisfied with the teacher's interpretations, Madhva interpreted the scriptures in his own way. He wrote many books, toured extensively in south India propagating his views and made a pilgrimage to Badarīkāśrama in Himalayas. In Kṛṣṇa's honour, he built a temple at Udupi, which became the centre of pilgrimage for all followers of Madhva since then. Till his death at the age of 79 years Madhva led a happy and enviably peaceful life. Instead of bloody sacrifices he recommended that animal figures made out of flour (*piṣṭa pasu*) be sacrificed.

His writings are characterized by extreme brevity, vigour and manliness, as opposed to the usual oriental verbosity. Another habit of his is that when something has been said already with which he is in agreement, he never states it as his own again, and he just quotes it with approval. Often his passages are made up of a lot of short quotations from numerous works and his scholarship and the extent of his acquaintance with the mass of Vedic and Purāṇic literature is amazing.

Something of Madhva's uncompromising physical vigour is found in his logic also. There are only two principles: the necessary and the contingent; and everything falls under one of these two. All things in the world are contingent, determined and dependent on each other.[60] So the world is a contingent and a dependent on God, which is necessary and independent.[61] Both the world and God are exclusive of each other. What is not God is for ever not of God. If there is only God and nothing else, who then is making this statement and what is the ontological status of this "nothing" which is negated in God? To say that everything is God in a sense and not-God in another sense is nonsense. There are no truths, there is only truth. What is not truth is error. If mundane things are not God, well, that ends the matter; they are not of God now and finally.

---

60. *paraṇapekṣam svatantram — Tattva-sāṁkhyāna.*

61. *svatantram aśvatantram ca dvividham tatvam iṣyate, svatantrobhagavān Viṣṇuḥ — Tattva-viveka.*

God is to be known not through perception; and reason cannot establish anything finally. If one establishes God through argument, another with sharper intellect can demolish the argument. The only way to know God is through scripture. Scriptures are soul-evident, and they are the basis of all knowledge. They have no author, not even God. Scriptures (the Vedas) are eternal. If there are absolute truth and goodness and if they do not dependent on what man thinks and if they are knowable then there must be an eternal body of knowledge which can reveal them to us. The Vedas are such; they do not have human authorship for then they are fallible. God is not their author too. If God composed the Vedas and if God is to be known through them, then there is regress. If there is absolute truth there must be absolute knowledge about it. If anybody says there is no absolute truth then he need not be anxious about what is established as truth by anybody. His views are equally right with the views of others which contradict the former.[62] Thus we know from the eternal Vedas and other sources that there is God.

By the Veda, Madhva probably does not mean those works as such in the present form, but the truth-content of them. He argues that if there is absolute truth, then there is absolute knowledge of it, whether anybody knows it or not. The Vedas contain such an absolute knowledge. The Vedas have no author because nobody is known as their author; the Vedas themselves do not mention anybody as their author. Tradition knows no author or authors of the Vedas. Thus the Vedas were not composed by anybody.[63] Madhva asserts that if anywhere scripture is found to contradict experience, it is

---

62. *na dharmādisiddhiḥ syāt nityavākyam vina kvacit — Anu-vyākhyāna.*

63. *veda kartuḥ aprasiddheḥ.*

invalid; and such scripture ceases to be scripture.[64] Further, scripture has to be understood rationally, if different interpretations are possible the right one has to be determined through discussion.

For Madhva, the individual soul is of the same nature of God; but from the beginning, it is deluded by nescience and therefore in bondage. While the individual soul is the possessor of ignorance and other qualities, God is free, omniscience, omnipotence, etc. and possesses all auspicious divine qualities. Madhva says that the world is real for it is experienced. The non-existent cannot be experienced, cannot be the object of knowledge and cannot enter into causal relation; but the world is known, the objects of the world are governed by causality. Thus the world is real; and as a whole it is an effect of God. Above all, the scripture has described God as he whose will is ever fulfilled. In fact, God created the world by His "truthful-will" (*satya-saṁkalpa*). The world which is created by such a Being cannot be unreal. And if it is not unreal, it is real. It is travesty of logic to say that the world is neither real nor unreal. Impermanence of the world does not make it unreal. Except in error there is no contradiction in experience. What is experienced now and here is a fact for ever, though it may not be experienced then and there. If something is experienced and not experienced in the same locus at the same time it is contradiction. Empirical experience is therefore valid and uncontradicted.

If there are things, and there are, for they are experienced, they must have mutual relations. A thing cannot enter into relationship with itself. A thing is related to another only.

---

64. *āgamasya prabalyepi na upjīvya pramāṇa virodhe prāmāṇyam; na ca anubhava virodhe āgamasya prāmāṇyam — Viṣṇu-tattva-vinirṇaya.*

The mutual relationship of things establishes their difference. Difference is real, *satyatā ca bhedasya*. Difference of a thing is the very uniqueness of its form (*svarūpa*) from another. Truth is that which is seen (*dṛśya*), there is no knowledge without the known and knower. All knowledge is conditioned and of qualified; there is no knowledge of the unqualified. *Brahman* is knowable, that is why it is possible for scriptures to propound him. He is not manifest (*a-prasiddha*), *Brahman* is not however completely knowable. A mountain is not described with entire adequacy by words. *Brahman* is qualityless in the sense that his qualities are so many that they cannot be counted. He is the creator and ruler of the world. He is only the efficient cause, not at all the material cause. God is wholly different from the world, yet but for him the universe is not.[65] Created by an act of God's will, the universe derives its very being from God.[66] The material of the universe is *prakṛti*, eternal, insentient and characterized by *sattva, rajās* and *tamās*.

When scripture says the individual soul is *Brahman*, it only indicates the resemblance between the soul and God, not absolute identity. After knowing that the individual is entirely different from God, the great power and auspicious qualities of God and after attaining all the qualities of God, the individual soul is freed. By devotion to God, God's grace is granted, without which release cannot be attained. In heaven the saved individual acquires the same form as that of God and possesses omniscience, but remains atomic and a servant of God. The relationship between the world and God, between the soul and God is that of body and soul.[67] As the

---

65. *dravyam kṛma ca kalaśca na śānti yadupekṣaya.*

66. *prakṛtyādi sattāpradatvam can aṅgikāryam īśvarasya* — Madhva, *Sūtra-Bhāṣya*, 2.2.5.

67. *viṣṇoḥ dehat jagat sarvam avirasit* — *Tattva-viveka.*

sap and tree are different, as the bird and string are different, as the rivers and ocean, salt and pure water are different from each other so are God and soul always different.[68] As the attainment of heaven is the *summum bonum*; the true knowledge of things gives release.

Though started in the western part of peninsular India, the school of Madhva gathered momentum and spread widely. In 1486 when Sikandar Lodi was terribly persecuting Hindus, Caitanya was born in Bengal. He was the originator of a vast religious movement in Bengal and Orissa. He was influenced by the Madhva School. Madhva's school had many eminent protagonists, great dialecticians and scholars. Jayatīrtha, Vyāsatīrtha, Vyāsa Rāmācārya and Rāghavendra are the important ones. Their works like *Nyāya-sudhā, Tarka-tāṇḍavam, Nyāyāmṛtam, Taraṅganī,* and *Ṛgveda Mantrārtha-mañjarī* await translation. It was due to lack of translations that Madhva's school has failed to get the notice it deserves from popular modern exponents of Indian philosophy.

Madhva's position is far more logical than Rāmānuja's and does not go contra to experience as in Advaita. As things stand the soul and world are either God or not God. Rāmānuja says that they are not God; then they are not. To say that the soul and world are God in a sense and not God in another sense is illogical. Unlike Rāmānuja's God, Madhva's God is wholly transcendent — wholly other to man and the world; and so is more majestic in his unsurpassable and unequalled glory. Before him man and world pale into insignificance. Man can only do one thing towards such a God: fall down and worship. Only in the Israelite and the Islāmic religions do we find such an exalted conception. Unfortunately his God is also anthropomorphic with a wife, body, house (*dhāma*), etc.

---

68. *yathā pakṣī ca sūtram ca nana vṛkṣarasa yathā.*

Later Cults and Future

In every period new local deities were added to the Vedic pantheon. Cults developed around some of these and sects were formed. Disputations and adverse propaganda between these sects were prevalent. Sometimes they persecuted each other. Gradually a sort of resolution of these conflicts was achieved. A doctrine of trinity was worked out with the triads of three Vedas, the three worlds, the threefold way of *karma, bhakti* and *jñāna* and the three-time worship (*sandhyā*) of the sun at morning, midday and evening. The triple aspect of *Brahman* being real, intelligence and bliss (*sat-cit-ānanda*) and the three-fold aspect of matter — *sattva, rajas* and *tamas* — were correlated with the three aspects of the supreme God — Brahmā, Viṣṇu, and Maheśvara, in relation to the conception of the creation, preservation and dissolution of the universe. The belief that these three gods are but phases of one principle gained ground, as is evident from the beautiful prayer in Kālidāsa's *Kumārasambhava*. But that did not abolish the difference between the three and belief in the exclusive supremacy of these gods taken individually. As a result of this, the worshipper was left to choose any one of these three deities as one's patron deity without a rejection of the other two. Polytheism on a limited scale was thus introduced. This did not remain for long. Viṣṇu's *avatāra*s, the female goddess Śakti, the quasi-gods like Hanumān and many others — are among those worshipped by Hindus today. Often the same man worships two or more deities. Līlāśuka author of *Kṛṣṇa-karṇāmṛta* is a worshipper of Śiva, who chants the five-lettered mystic sentence (*pañcākṣara*), but his patron-deity is Kṛṣṇa, the lover of *gopī*s, the cow-herd of Bṛndāvan. Tulasīdās begins his *Rāmāyaṇa* with salutations to a number of Gods. Almost every Hindu adores and worships more than one god, though he may like one of them more.

The Slave kings (CE 1206-90) established and spread their rule from the Indus to the Brahmaputra; the Khiljīs and Tughlaks subjugated the Deccan; from Arakan to the Assam borders and from Himalaya to the Kṛṣṇā River, the country was resounded with the cries of "Allāho Akbar." Till the British came, except for a brief time in parts of India under the kings of Vijayanagar and the Maharattas, all these rolling centuries were one long struggle for establishing Islamic domination over these millions of *kāfirs*. A few *sultāns* and some of the Mughals might not have got it as the dominant motive, but it was always there either as a guiding idea or in the subconscious. Some are cleverer than others like Akbar, who wanted to metamorphose India to its very backbone by presenting to it a new ideology and a new God. In Akbar's case, he himself was the Holy Spirit, the bringer of the New Message.

During all these years Hinduism and Hindu culture were suppressed. The social and economic conditions of the people were not improved in any way. The Mughals gave stability to the large parts of the country, but that was not a new thing in India. The Guptas, the Kuṣāṇas, Harṣa, the Cāḷukyas, the Coḷas, the Āndhras — all these dynasties have bestowed stable governments in their regions; and the rule of some of them lasted as long as the Mughal rule. Aśoka heard of the three great southern kingdoms, Coḷa, Chera and Pāṇḍya. The Coḷas were still there in eleventh century CE. The Keśarī kings came to power in CE 474, and their dynasty lasted till the eleventh century. Bernier, a Frenchman who visited India when Shahjahan's sons were contending for power has left an account of the country's state. The emperors were weak and autocratic, his advisers were time-servers, the provincial governors were oppressive and rapacious, the rank and file were demoralized, and the peasants were crushed and trod on the earth. The centuries preceding the Mughal rule, that is from the thirteenth to the fifteenth century were worse. Even stability of government was not there. For five and half centuries after Muslim power established itself in India, India stagnated. Hindu ideals were disparaged by the rulers, Hindu women forcibly taken away, temples demolished, and nothing in exchange was given either by way of material or spiritual progress. During all these centuries no new scientific discoveries were made, no drastic measures have been extended, and possible ideal schemes have been discovered. Except for Bhāskara of twelfth century, who did something for mathematics, no original thinker was produced in all these centuries; no genius discovered any technological device. In south India under Vijayanagar kings contributions were made to Sanskrit literature, but none of it was original or outstanding. As for the Mughal rule it was barren like the eunuchs who adorned the Mughal courts.

Akbar had some Sanskrit works translated into Persian. Babar and Jehangir wrote their Memoirs. Abul Fazl has left a valuable account of Akbar's reign and Hashim Kafi Khan of Aurangazeb's history. But all this is neither science nor literature, nor philosophy. In the indigenous literature some progress was made: Kṛttivās, Kāsidas, Tukārām, Tulasīdās among others belonged to this period. But their achievements when compared to those of Kālidāsa, Bhāsa or Bāṇa are negligible.

Muslim invasions and regimes rudely disturbed India; and before it could recover from the shock, the British came. This new impact has shaken it once again. It is yet trying to understand the significance of Western modes of thought and scientific developments. And while this was happening, world politics forced the British to leave India. The myth of India's fight for independence and the myth of India's winning independence are being propagated. That however is a side issue. Every government must survive on myths. The present one has been provided a useful myth. India never fought for independence, it just got it; India did not win it. Anyway there is great scope now for unhampered creative work in every field — science, philosophy, technology, etc. But already a sort of reaction is gathering in some quarters, which can be summed up in the slogan, "Back to the bullock-cart and the rice-gruel." These people do not want English; they want to substitute in its place undeveloped languages without any kind of literature. They want Āyurveda in the place of scientific medicine, religion in the place of philosophy, superstition in the place of sane living, outmoded village polity in the place of democracy, cottage-industries in the place of industries, etc. If this reaction succeeds India will remain where it was all these six centuries or so.

Conclusion

I

MEGASTHENES (321-298 BC) has left us an account of the religion and philosophy prevalent in India of that time. The chief deities mentioned by him are Kṛṣṇa and Śiva.[1] The God of rain, the Ganges and other deities were also worshipped.[2] Herodotus mentions that there lived in India a class of people who did not kill anything, did not sow or reap and had no houses. They collected grain and herbs that grew spontaneously, boiled them and ate.[3] These must have been Jainas. Megasthenes mentions two kinds of ascetics, brāhmins and *śramaṇa*s[4] who resided in enclosed groves in front of the cities. They abstained from meat and fish, practised celibacy and spent their time in discoursing. Their usual topic was death and rebirth. They lay on straw and deer skins. The brāhmins practised austerities only for some time, after which they married. They never communicated their knowledge to their wives, afraid that the wives may leave them. The *śramaṇa*s on the other hand practised greater austerities for a longer time. They lived in forests living on leaves and wild fruits, practised

---

1. *Indiga*, Fragment XLVI.
2. Strabo, XV.1.69.
3. *Historica*, 111, 100.
4. *Indiga*, Fragment XLI.

celibacy, wore bark-garments.[5] Strabo (XV.1.61-63) mentions the gruesome austerities practised by some of these.

The Greek historians mention that the Indians held the world to be a spheroid and the deity who made and governed it has his powers diffused through all its composites. The world was created and is liable to destruction. Water is the principal element that goes to form the world and in addition to the four elements, there is a fifth element — nature, from which heavens and stars are produced. Earth is the centre of the Universe.[6] Megasthenes says that the brāhmins regarded this life as the time when the child within the womb (man?) became matured, and death as a birth into a real and happy life for philosophers.[7] The brāhmins on this theoretical presupposition underwent much discipline as a preparation for death. The brāhmins considered nothing to be either good or bad, for the same things are seen to be pleasing to some and painful to others. The activities of things are as unreal as dreams.

The accounts of Greek historians give us all the traits of Indian religion and philosophy — polytheism, austerities, obsession with rebirth and the view that life is nothing — a dream — in comparison with the life to come — the life of reality, of brāhmin which is to be got only by those who know. By the time of Megasthenes the caste system seems to have ossified for he describes as many as seven castes, and says that a man of one caste was not allowed to follow the occupation of another caste, nor were intermarriages allowed. Megasthenes also describes how there was no unity in the Indian society. Even when a war was going on, people went on ploughing in the adjacent fields as if nothing was happening.

---

5. Strabo, XV.1.60.

6. Strabo, XV.1.59.

7. *Indiga*, Fragment XLI.

II

In all histories whether of people's actions or ideas it is necessary to have a perspective; otherwise the tendency to regard the past of one particular country and people will come to be regarded as the most glorious, unsurpassed and even unparalleled. There are many Indian writers who depict India's achievements in philosophy as something unique. I remember how a colleague of mine, a Sanskrit puṇḍit, was profoundly surprised, in fact shocked, when I told him that every thought movement in India had its parallel in Europe, with the difference that when Europe is still advancing India had stopped dead.

For a century and half, after the defeat of the Persians, Greeks achieved some of the most wonderful results in every sphere of thought and culture. Herodotus gave birth to history (438 BC); Anaxagoras tried to describe the sun and stars scientifically. Power was wrested from kings and priests, and assemblies of the citizens were the ruling force. Disputation and the spirit of enquiring, after the cause and reason of everything sophistry gave birth to the Socratic spirit. Socrates was executed, but his spirit was inherited by Plato and others. Plato (427-347 BC) was the first to conceive of a Utopia, a community to be scientifically planned and worked for, and which is to be better than all the types of community that existed and exist. The social and political ills of mankind are due to our ignorance. With determined will and the necessary courage men can think out a better way of dealing with things; and a new society can be fashioned and brought into existence here and now. This was a tremendous achievement. Man dissatisfied with the present state of the world need not hanker after another world — a heaven, to be attained after death. This world can be reconstructed on a different pattern; and people can be made happy and content, provided they are sensible. That was Plato, an idealist who wanted to realize his ideal.

Then came in some ways a far greater man. Aristotle knew that before utopias were made, men needed far more knowledge, and more accurate knowledge than they had. So he set out to collect facts and systematize them. He founded political science; he was also the father of natural science. He completely rejected mythology and anthropomorphism. He was not, however, irreligious. His conception of God as the first cause, unmoved-mover in itself but moving the entire universe "as the beloved moves the lover," is a magnificent achievement. It was only some twelve hundred years later that Śaṅkara (CE 800) approached this conception in a way, but he was still ridden with mythology and scriptural authority. But Aristotle was much more than Śaṅkara, for the latter was only a theologian; and dogma guided him more than reason. On the other hand Aristotle was a rational theologian, yet the magnificent mass of his other work dwarfed his theology. The enormous output of Aristotle's clear thinking and the way he co-ordinated various branches of knowledge is surprising. Aristotle took the world as it existed and sought to understand it; he did not try to invent some nonsensical ecstatic doctrine which makes it pale into nothing. Aristotle's school and the Peripatetics were not like the wandering ascetics — the *parivrājaka*s and *śramaṇa*s of India. They were not concerned with the saving of souls and the preaching of unproved and improvable doctrines about other world and ways of reaching it. The Peripatetic people were the largest contributors to the advances made in astronomy, physics, botany, zoology, biology and history in the Hellenistic age. Aristotle inaugurated a critical and disciplined approach towards every problem. Free, precise and systematic thinking displaced the child-like methods of weird symbolism and monstrous imagery of gods, demons, the layers of worlds, etc. It is to be remembered that all this happened in Greece of the fourth century BC. It is sad but necessary to comment that in no Indian philosopher we find the Aristotelian vigour, freshness and rationalism. Even Nāgārjuna, as his biography tells us, was a magician, medicine man and alchemist. India had its astronomers — Āryabhaṭṭa of CE 476, Varāhamihira of CE 505 and Brahmagupta of CE 598; and it had its physicians and surgeons — Caraka and Suśruta of CE 80. All these made wonderful contributions to their respective sciences; some of their ideas were borrowed by the Greeks and Arabs. But what may be called the scientific spirit is foreign to all of them. Reference has already been made to Alberuni's remarks on Indian astronomers.

After the fall of Greek greatness in the days of Ptolemy I and Ptolemy II, Alexandria took over intellectual leadership. Here flourished men famous for their scientific discoveries. Eratosthenes measured the size of the earth and came within fifty miles of its true diameter. Apollonius wrote on conic sections. Hipparchus mapped the stars and catalogued them. Hero invented the first steam engine. The surgeon Herophilus, Euclid and Archimedes were their contemporaries. All this was in the third century BC in Egypt. But as with the discoveries of Varāhamihira and other Indians, the Athenian and Alexandrian achievements in science had no practical applications, nor did the common man know about these revolutionary discoveries. The world went on as it did heedless of the tremendous intellectual revolution which these energetic men wrought.

It is significant that there is nothing comparable to this sort of work in India of that period. India was then supremely indifferent to work in the spheres of technology and empirical sciences. It was centuries later that India saw its physicians and astronomers. Caraka belonged to Kaniṣka's court (first century CE), and Suśruta, the surgeon belonged probably to the same period. Kālidāsa belonged to the period of Candragupta II, the great Gupta king (CE 375). The famous astronomers Āryabhaṭṭa, Varāhamihara, and Brahmagupta came much later. Every thinking Indian must put the query to himself, why is it that interest in science was born so very late in India and why is it that the works of these few men still contain all sorts of mythologies, and patently absurd superstitions; and why is it above all that this scientific interest was still-born?

A remarkable phenomenon in the evolution of political institutions went on in Europe in the meanwhile. Before 1000 BC, Italy was a thinly populated land of mountains and forests. Non-Aryan people called the Etruscans came down upon Italy and founded Rome in 753 BC. In 510 BC, the Etruscans were expelled, and Rome became a republic with patrician families dominating plebeians. In this there was nothing unusual. The Greek republics were like that, with a large slave population at the base and the citizens with a right to vote dominating. The Indo-Aryan village establishments in north and south India were almost like that with the aristocratic families of warriors, priests and tradesmen treading under their feet the peasants and manual labourers. The village assemblies, of which modern Indian historians speak with such pride, were nothing but the gatherings of the upper well-to-do classes convened to preserve and extend their rights over the working classes. But at no time in India did the proletariat turn back and fight with the domineering priests and warriors, because over generations they were taught that caste was a divine institution, in which people were born in accordance with their actions in past births. Overthrowing of the caste system never occurred as a possibility to them. But in Rome internal history consisted of the struggle by the plebeians for freedom and equality with the patricians; and in the end the old barriers and exclusiveness of the aristocratic families were broken down and a sort of working equality was established. The extension of Roman power abroad brought Romans into contact with "outsiders" and gradually they were also given citizenship. In India we have a different phenomenon. Indians never expanded their power beyond their frontiers, excepting for occasional sway over Gandhāra or Afghanistan. Coḷa kings however conquered part of Burma, Malaya, Ceylon, and other minor islands. In every century hordes of adventurous and enterprising foreigners came and settled down in India, but in every case they were not assimilated; they came as invaders and settled down as masters. If they chose to adopt indigenous manners and customs and intermarry with the people of the land, it was because they found it to be their pleasure. To talk of their being Indianite or Hinduized or their being assimilated to the Indian way of life is nonsense. The wife of the last British Governor of Madras, Lady Nye, used to greet her Indian friends and subordinates with folded hands, and uttered the word *Namaste*, taste Indian dishes and visited temples, received as presents the fruits and flowers offered to the idols within. One cannot say that Her Excellency as being Hinduized and adapted to the glorious Indian way of life. Similarly if some of the Muslim rulers married Hindu princesses, adopted Hindu customs and read or heard Hindu literature it was because of their royal whims. I have heard of some English collectors and police officers, who evinced interest in our customs, tried to taste Indian dishes and some who patronized native women prostitutes. All this was not because they wanted to be Hinduized.

In Rome what happened was that foreigners were slowly, though not very readily, assimilated to the Roman way and granted civic rights; and these were granted as favours and received as such. India was never in a position to do so in the past; and wherever possible the natives tried to maintain their exclusiveness either through arrogance or an inferiority complex; but the foreigners forced them to yield their women and property whenever they wanted. Even after settling down the newcomers and older inhabitants lead their own segregated lives. (Witness the aloofness from the Jāṭs which the Rājpūts maintain even today. Rājpūts are the descendants of the foreign tribes of Śakas, Kuṣāṇas, Hūṇas and Gurjaras).

It should also be recorded that nothing like the wonderful growth of the Roman Empire ever occurred in India. There were the empires of Aśoka, of the Guptas and Harṣa in the north and those of Cāḷukyas and Coḷas, etc. in the south. But they were negligible in comparison with the extent of the Roman Empire; nor were they empires in the same sense. These Indian empires were only a sort of loose suzerainty, exercised by the king of a particular portion of the country over the kings of some other portions. Except that the defeated kings owed allegiance to their conqueror, the people were not affected at all by this "empire." But the growth of the Roman Empire was altogether of a different sort. Rome did not fight the states around her by destroying them, nor was it content with exercising mere nominal suzerainty. She sought the coalescence of the defeated states. The defeated cities became completely Roman in some cases by acquiring a voting share in the government, and others were self-governing with the right to marry and trade in Rome; among freshly conquered people garrisons of citizens were founded and the conquered were taught Roman ways and culture. Thus by 89 BC, the whole of Italy was Latinised, and by CE 212 all free men throughout Italy had the right to go to Rome and vote in the town-meeting in Rome. This right of citizenship was extended to all the cities and countries; and by that device the conquered were assimilated. After 240 BC, when Sicily was annexed, a novel device was thought of. It was declared an "estate" of Rome and it was exploited to make Rome rich. Thus it was Roman genius which discovered the method of colonization, which modern European nations adopted with such success. After the First Punic war the Roman farmers lost their freedom, because while they were on military service, a class of men grew up who began agricultural operations on a very extensive scale with the help of slaves; and the slave-grown produce of Sicily competed with that of the citizen farmers of Rome. The poor Roman farmer thus became a prey to his rich creditors. With the vast extension of Rome, the popular assembly, though it was in theory the assembly of all Roman citizens, became ineffectual and useless, as it was impossible for all the millions of Roman citizens to gather in an assembly and vote. Nobody thought of electing representatives and sending them to the assembly. In 73 BC, the slaves with Spartacus as their head rebelled but were cruelly put down. The outcastes in India for centuries suffered greater ignominy and equal privations, but they never rebelled. Why? Also from the time that Rome drove away its Etruscan kings in the fifth century BC, till 27 BC there was no king in Rome. The very word "king" was abhorrent to Romans. Roman republicanism killed Caesar for having dared to attempt to become king. After some years his nephew Octavian was awarded the titles of "Princeps" and "Augustus" for his having refused to be dictator. He was the first Roman emperor; the successive emperors were made and unmade by the Roman legions. They were never kings, but anyway the Senate and Assembly faded out of Rome's history and its destinies came to be in the hands of military commanders.

The Roman Empire was a colossal failure, but there is a significant question to be answered; why is it that it was Rome and Europe which first evolved the idea of a worldwide state, bound by common laws, customs and government; and why is it that even today it is Europe and America which are trying to work out that idea, while the Asian and African countries are enmeshed in their own internal problems? The Asians always had the other-worldly view; why is it that Europe was never interested so much in the world beyond (except to some extent in the brief period of the first two centuries of the Christian era)? And why is it that even today it is the Euro-Americans who are concerned with the world-view and world-government; while the dumb masses of Asia either think of their own insignificant states or of the Ideal world, the Heaven. Asia is in a dilemma; it does not know whether the world ought to embrace the West European democratic pattern or the East European communism, nor has it a third alternative. It does not in fact know that there is a world, and a world-problem requiring solution. Especially India never evolved any kind of political institution except that of tribal assembly in the far-off days and autocratic monarchy later. The reason for this was the indifference of the people towards life and ways of living; provided they had something to still their hunger they were content to lie in dazed apathy in the sweltering tropical heat.

III

Every ideology, political, philosophical or religious, arises in answer to a particular problem of a particular age and part of the country. In view of this we have to assess the contributions of Jainism, Buddhism and Bhāgavata religions.

The fundamental problem for Jainism is liberation. How can man escape from the endless rotation of rebirths? The cycle of births and deaths is taken for granted by Jainism. It only seeks a way of escape from it. Jainism accepts matter to be real; it assumes a plurality of souls. As such, contact with matter actually affects the soul. This defilement, which is a fact, cannot be removed by knowledge. If you are in a prison, you cannot get out of it by knowing that: you are within. Something must be done to cleanse the soul. So Jainism prescribes right conduct — internal and external — as the means for removing the soul's bondage. It is significant that Jaina believes the soul to be affected by matter. Classical Sāṁkhya believes the soul's bondage to be a myth. Some of the Upaniṣadic passages also regard the soul's bondage in the same way. As such though there is a lot of talk about bondage and liberation, there can really be no problem of liberation in that type of Vedānta and Sāṁkhya. They cannot at all be concerned with liberation for according to them the soul (which is immaterial) cannot at all be attached or subjected to anything worldly (material = *prākṛtika*). So for those schools the *summum bonum* is not the winning of liberation, but that of experiencing oneself to be beyond the world. This view seems to be more logical, for if at all there is something entirely immaterial, in what way and why does it get itself involved with the material? If the immaterial is the antithesis or the contradiction of the material, how can the two be connected or coexistent at any time and place? Only the absence of the one can be the invariable concomitant of the other's presence.

While in classical Sāṁkhya and Vedānta the *summum bonum* is the realization or manifestation of an ever-present state of liberation from the world, in Jainism there has to be a struggling and striving to attain liberation. While in the earlier systems ethics is of secondary importance, in Jainism it is brought to the forefront. Jainism therefore prescribes works as the means for liberation; and it places special emphasis on *ahiṁsā* (non-violence). The injunction not to harm and not to kill is mentioned only as it were by the way in the Upaniṣads. But in Jainism it is exalted above everything else. It is amusing to see the *Chāndogya Upaniṣad* (8.15) declaring that killing is forbidden everywhere "except on sacred spot," i.e, sacrificial ground. We must remember in this connection that the primitives regarded everything a sacrificial ritual, and even today every Muslim butcher utters some syllables to absolve himself before he slaughters. The *ahiṁsā* doctrine arose from an attempt to keep oneself free from all kinds of contamination. We are contaminated only when we do or think some kind of harm to somebody. So if we keep ourselves free from this by not injuring anything including the micro-organisms, we are perfect. A Jaina does not, therefore, eat meat, and does not hunt. The strict Jaina sees twice before he lays his foot lest he may trample unawares — some clod, insect or ant; he ties a cloth around his mouth and nose so that he may not breathe in any tiny organisms. He does not plough, as it is impossible to do it without killing many minute organisms in the soil. So Jainas mostly engage themselves in trade and commerce.

The chief premise of the Buddha is this: the world is evil and full of suffering. How can suffering be removed? The theories current in the Buddha's time either taught that one should practise austerities and good works or that one should know his self. The Buddha rejected both these theories. Works, whether good or bad, will not give any liberation, for one can only work in and with the world. But the world is a mass of unmitigated suffering. Nothing based on it can free us from it. So salvation through works — whether it be sacrifice or charity, penance or austerities — is of no avail. Self-mortification and such external actions attack only the effect, not the cause of suffering.[8] Nor can one attain the end by knowing, for what is to be known and by whom? There is no dead static unchangeable entity such as is known usually by the word "soul," by knowing which one can be redeemed. A flame from a wick is in fact only a constant succession of flames; they only seem to be a unity. Likewise there is no such thing as "soul" which remains static even for a moment. The Buddha's conception of reality is dynamic. (It is to be noted he does not reject "soul" and "God," but only the usual conception of them.) If liberation is not attained either through knowledge or works, what is the way for it? The Buddha's answer is that it can be had only by cessation of the will. If the will ceases to have the craving for existence and pleasure all misery ends. That is *nirvāṇa,* the coming to rest. The Buddha, of course, has not worked out how such a view can be harmonized with that of rebirth and ethical behaviour.[9]

The great contribution of the Buddha is that he was the first to clearly enunciate a positive doctrine of love. Throughout the Upaniṣads, we find the admonitions, "do not kill, do not lie," etc. Nowhere are we told expressly, "love thy neighbour," "do not harm even him, who harms you?" This very idea is foreign to the Upaniṣads. You should not, of course, hate or kill your neighbour for that defiles you; but why should you like him or love him that would be to be attached to him — a most undesirable thing when one wants to be free from every attachment. That seems to be the trend of the Upaniṣadic thought.

8. *Viśuddhimagga*, 507.

9. E.J. Thomas, *History of Buddhist Thought*, p. 105.

Many times the Buddha teaches his followers to be kind and loving. "Now this is what we must practise well. . . . We will remain friendly and sympathetic, in a temper of loving-kindness without secret malice; we will irradiate our personality with loving feelings; starting thence we will irradiate the whole world with broad, deep, unlimited feeling free from wrath and rancour."[10] "Abiding in a spirit of loving-kindness (the monk) recognizing himself everywhere in everything; he irradiates the whole universe with loving-kindness."[11] The Buddha forestalls St. Paul's, "overcome evil with good." In the Vedic religion also one is asked to do good, "give water to the thirsty" and "food to the hungry," etc. But these are only intended to confer a better life in the next birth. They do not help towards liberation, nor are they an end by themselves. Often the Vedas and the Purāṇas ask one to be charitable, but invariably the recipients of charity should be brāhmins, learned in the Vedic lore and engaged in sacrificial ritual (*śrotriya, ahitāgni*). Nowhere one finds any exhortation to serve the poor and the downtrodden, help the sick and the blind, the lepers and the mad. It is only the Buddha and his disciples who started this institution of service to the sick and the needy. In fact, the Brāhmanical scriptures detest the poor and the sick. They are deemed to have committed grievous sins in their past births, as a result of which they are suffering now. They must be allowed to work out and exhaust the effects of their sins. None should go to succour them.

According to the Buddha, goodness and kindness are not means for liberation. As such, ethics has no importance for the individual himself, for the individual attains the *summum bonum* not by doing well or thinking good, but by ceasing to

10. *Majjhima-Nikāya*, I.215.

11. *Majjhima-Nikāya*, I.445.

have the craving for existence and pleasure. So, ethical disposition is not a means towards an end as in Vedānta or Jainism. "An enlightened disciple . . . discharging the exercise of charity independent of every law," the Buddha values goodness as such, as an end in itself.[12] "An enlightened disciple ought to act spontaneously in the exercise of charity."[13] For the first time in India, goodness and kindness become absolute values subservient to nothing.

The other schools, Vedic, Sāṁkhya and Jaina are indifferent to the world and regard the earthly things to be insignificant. There can be no ethics based upon this sort of foundation. The Buddha also regarded the world as a detestable mire of suffering. Though he too emphasized the importance of "going forth" from this world, he gave equal and probably greater importance to purity of heart, of detachment from material things and he demanded of his followers that they should translate their inner perfection, poise and peace into ethical conduct. The nature of the dealings with one's fellows proves the nature of the disposition within. The Buddha's ethics, which urge a man towards perfection within — is attainable only through freedom from the world. But as in the other schools, freedom from the world need not imply the insignificance of the world. One can be aware of the world's significance and yet be free from the entire world. Freedom from the world is not a necessary corollary of the desire to be indifferent to the world; it may be sought as a means towards becoming an ethical personality — an instrument of *dharma*, in order to serve the world. Mahāyāna school, especially Śāntideva, carried this tendency to the end. An ethics of love and

---

12. W. Gemmel's, tr., *The Diamond Sūtra*, p. 60.

13. Ibid., p. 13.

compassion is the Buddha's greatest contribution.[14] He arrived at it by being extremely conscious of the world and its suffering and the need for the removal of this suffering.

In the Veda we meet with Agni, Varuṇa and Mitra as ethical divinities. Varuṇa is pre-eminently an ethical god; he is the guardian of *ṛta*, the inexorable law, which governs the whole universe. People should confess their sins to him to be forgiven. Thus in the conception of Varuṇa there was a tendency towards ethical monotheism. But it is not adhered to. Fights for supremacy between Varuṇa and Indra are described. Another direction in which a tendency towards monotheism appeared was to bring together different gods to form a composite personality (e.g. the Maruts, the Aśvins, and the Viśvedevas). In one or two hymns the one God is conceived as being called by many names. We cannot, however, be sure whether this is an assertion of monism or monotheism; and anyway there is no evolution of clear-cut monotheism from polytheism in the Vedas and the Upaniṣads. The priests were occupied with their sacerdotal power and not with the development of religious thought. They were concerned to know secrets shut off from ordinary mortals. They imagined that by incantations and sacrifices they can become one with the gods. By sacrifice one becomes a god; by a hundred horse-sacrifices one becomes the greatest of gods — Indra. So gods govern the world through spells and magic formulae. The brāhmins claimed for themselves power of the same kind that belongs to gods. They are in fact gods on earth. But the thoughtful among them studied the connection between life and self-movement, between waking, dreaming and sleeping states, between the seed and the plant, between salt and sea-water. What is it that connects these? Not surely something

14. S. Tachibana, *The Ethics of Buddhism*, p. 270.

of the same nature as the other things which we see; for had it been so, we would have seen it. So they assumed that there is a force, invisible, incorporeal, underlying all existence. From this the idea was developed that the essence of all things is something immaterial and eternal; and to realize oneness with it is the highest end of man. This supersensual essence of all things — reality as such — was called *Brahman*, the same term used for sacrificial incantation; thus showing the origin of this conception.

It can be now seen why Vedic religion and Upaniṣadic thought did not end in monotheism, but developed another way. Monotheism first appeared among Bhāgavatas. Kṛṣṇa, (the Black One) a prophetic personality of the Yādava tribe had probably much to do with the development of Bhāgavata theism. Curiously enough Bhāgavata religion is neither hostile to the Vedas nor to brāhmin priesthood, though one can be sure that its founders were not Aryan. In fact, it selected one of the comparatively obscure gods from the Vedic pantheon and identified him with Vāsudeva-Kṛṣṇa. From the *Bhagavad-Gītā* it can be learnt that Bhāgavatas did not exaggerate the importance of Veda, nor did they make it the sole authority and repository of revelation. At one place it says that unless one becomes indifferent to the ritual and jargon of the Veda, one cannot arrive at truth.[15]

The theism of Bhāgavatas has certain differentiating traits from that of Christianity and Islam. Monotheism as found in the Bhāgavata or Śaiva religions does not do away with gods. According to them God is worshipped in gods; it is the one and only God who manifests himself as Indra, Brahmā, etc. The one, and only God, is above and far beyond all these manifestations. He is Bhagavān, the Supreme Lord. God is

15. *yadā gantāsi nirvedam sṛtavyasya sṛtasya ca.*

not the creator of the world, in the sense that he brings it out of nothing; nor is he beside and beyond the world. The universe proceeds from God's nature (*daiva-śakti*) as from a primal cause. This does not mean that God becomes the world. God never becomes, he is forever immutable. Nevertheless he is immanent in the world, but at the same time transcendent to it. Individuals can become like God (*sādharmya*), they never can become God. The way towards this is complete self-surrender to God with loving adoration. God then lifts us from ourselves and assimilates us to his likeness. Quietism is very much foreign to these religions. Nobody should withdraw from ordinary life; one is expected to maintain devotion to God in thought as well as in deed. The world is not a meaningless chaos; being the Lord's creation it is purposive, and so human activity has a meaning, has a task to fulfil in this world.[16] As distinguished from the ideal of the absorption of the individual in the Absolute, found in certain Upaniṣadic passages, the goal of these religions is attainment by way of harmonious relationship with the Divine. Necessarily, therefore, ritual, sacrifice and magic are rejected. By slaughtering animals and burning them on the altar or by renouncing everything and forcing oneself into vacant thought, the Divine cannot be attained. The Divine is to be attained by worshipping him through one's daily duties.[17] For such a religion as this, loving compassion and kind sentiments towards every being become one's duty, for the same Lord is present in all beings[18] God is to be reached through his grace

---

16. See the beautiful stories of Rantideva, Ambarīṣa, Dhruva, and Prahlāda among others in *Śrīmad Bhāgavata*.

17. *sva karmaṇātamobhyarcya siddhim vidanti* — *Śrīmad Bhāgavata*, IV.25-29.

18. *samo 'haṁ sarvabhūteṣu* — *Bhagavad-Gītā*, 9.29.

only.[19] The Bhāgavata religion therefore ends in cultivating self-devotion to God in activity, as opposed to Vedic ritual, Upaniṣadic quietism and Jaina asceticism.

The great scripture of Bhāgavata religion, the *Bhagavad-Gītā*, formulates a profound and original doctrine in ethics. The contribution of *Bhagavad-Gītā* to ethics cannot be overrated. If liberation is to be free from the world, how is it to be accomplished? Can it be at all accomplished? Creation and maintenance of the world is a kind of activity. If God himself is active, the universe owes its existence to that activity. If the order of the universe requires activity, can man, subject to that order, free himself from it? So long as one lives, one cannot be without activity.[20] Therefore it must, once for all, be recognized that at least work for the preservation of life and natural duties can never be laid aside. If God himself is active, surely man cannot remain inactive. But on the other hand liberation is to be had only by rising above the world, and by freeing oneself from the world. Here is a dilemma. It can only be resolved by freeing oneself from the world from within as it is not practicable to do so outwardly. He truly is inactive who is performing actions as if he is not performing them. Performance of works should be grounded in inward renunciation of the world. But what should man do? He must fulfil those duties which belong to his station and nature.[21] Natural obligations (*sahaja karma*) should be fulfilled for their own sake, not influenced by any ends to be gained thereby (*mā phaleṣu kadācana*). Is not man an automation, swayed by forces, psychological and physical? How then can he choose to do any particular thing and avoid another? In short, how is

19. *yadayam anugṛhnāti — Śrīmad Bhāgavata*, IV.29,46.

20. *Bhagavad-Gītā*, 3.8.

21. *svabhāva niyatam karma*.

freedom of will to be reconciled with man's bondage? The *Bhagavad-Gītā* answers that man should get rid of the false notion that it is he that does. The real doer, the "master of all action" (*karmādhyakṣa*) is God. So by inculcating self-surrender to God, man accomplishes what God does through him. For the *Bhagavad-Gītā* the one question which a man should put to himself is, does a particular task come to him as a duty to be fulfilled; and if so, is he accomplishing it in complete self-surrender to God? Inner renunciation enables one to be capable of the highest activity in self-devotion to the supreme end. Action is unavoidable but it must be transcended. Action is justified only when it is performed with love and devotion to God. A householder who does so attains liberation, but not the anchorite who has gone forth from the world to sit in vacant stupor. With a lot of repetition and looseness it is this valuable strand of thought which the *Bhagavad-Gītā* seeks to unroll. Written in simple and straight language the kernel of the *Bhagavad-Gītā*'s meaning can be reached easily, but for the fact that a lot of medieval commentators have read their own views into it. Rāmānuja, Tilak and Aurobindo have to a large degree managed to keep themselves faithful to the purport of *Bhagavad-Gītā* in their works on it.

It is surprising that a book of this sort should have been in existence by about the third century BC. No doubt the *Bhagavad-Gītā* has come down to us as part of *Mahābhārata*; but it must have been merely fitted into that vast epic, though alterations and additions may have been made, which originated Bhāgavata religion. Dasgupta believes the *Bhagavad-Gītā* to be pre-Buddhistic.[22] It is tempting to comment that Hinduism and even Vaiṣṇava sect could not keep themselves strictly to

---

22. S.N. Dagupta, *History of Indian Philosophy*, vol. II, p. 549.

the monotheism and ethical doctrines of the *Bhagavad-Gītā* and thus sustained a great loss.

IV

Kauṭilya's *Arthaśāstra* gives us the glimpses of the life of people under the Mauryans; and we have no reason to believe that it differed greatly under the Kuṣāṇas. Greek accounts and Kauṭilya's work tell us that Mauryan rule was dictatorial, exclusively based on military force and secret police. Passages of the *Arthaśāstra* dealing with punishment of criminals and torture of prisoners to elicit confessions are gruesome and show the Mauryan rulers and Cāṇakya as the forerunners of Nazi and Communist dictators. But Candragupta and Cāṇakya may have largely borrowed all this from Darius I. Kauṭilya regarded the tribal republican form of government as an evil. He nowhere mentions the elected assemblies, which were so popular before the Mauryans came to power. Brāhmins were not to be tortured even when they were found to have committed the worst crimes. At the most, their property could be confiscated and be forced to work in the mines. Ascetic organizations as well craft-guilds were frowned upon; they were not allowed to exist except in a few allotted places. Slavery was not tolerated, but the law allowed one to sell one's children when one was starving or when one had to pay taxes. All sorts of taxes were levied; even temple treasuries were not excepted. A large standing army was maintained. Irrigation, highways and cattle-welfare were also not neglected. In short, the government was a dictatorial and ruthless one; all the resources of the country such as agriculture, fisheries, commerce including foreign trade were encouraged. But the common people were not allowed to benefit thereby. A large part of the produced wealth was taken away by means of taxes. Revenue thus derived was utilized for the luxuries of the royal household and for maintaining a large standing army. Secret police played a great part in upholding such a type of government. Prostitution was a recognized institution.[23]

The life under the kings of south India was also not different as shown by the accounts of the Coḷas that we have. Taxes were many, oppression was much and punishments for alleged offences were severe. But in the village assemblies were allowed to exist; and in the matter of day-to-day administration of justice they were allowed to play a considerable part.[24] Under the Coḷas a brāhmin accountant got 200 *kalams* of paddy per year, an under-accountant got much less. Temple watchmen were paid 100 *kalams* per year. Thus a brāhmin got sixteen rupees and two-thirds and a śūdra eight rupees and one-third per month, supposing the price of paddy was one rupee four annas per *kalam*.[25] If this was the condition of people with stable incomes, the appalling poverty and misery of agricultural labourers, and the lowest castes can well be imagined. And we should not forget that this was when stable governments like the Mauryans, the Guptas, the Coḷas and the Āndhras, etc. existed. When there were no stable governments, when robbers, bandits and foreign invading armies roamed at large, the anguish and the insecurity of the people was unparalleled. No doubt all this formed a fertile ground for propounding the theory that this world is an illusion and that somewhere far beyond this world were the happy sunlit regions, where one can sport with nymphs and eat sweet milk porridge, fruits and other delicacies. To be qualified to reap these great rewards one

23. N.V. Ramanayya, *The Eastern Cāḷukyas*, p. 287.

24. S.K. Aiyangar, *Ancient India*, Chap. VI.

25. Ibid., p. 190.

must, of course, worship the gods and reverence the gods on earth — the brāhmins. This is the "philosophy of the Purāṇas."

There is a legend that somewhere in the eighth century BC, Agastya followed by a lot of northern colonisers trekked to south India, felled the jungles, and established agriculture and homesteads. Just as the tribal kingdoms of Śūrasenas, Kurus, Licchavis, Kośalas among others arose in north India, so in the south three kingdoms gradually gained ascendancy — Coḷa, Pāṇḍya and Chera. Aśoka's edicts mention these. Aśoka's empire extended up to Mysore. Between the far south and the north, there were the Āndhras. Under Aśoka the Āndhras were not very important. But in the long years that followed Aśoka's death, Āndhra power grew and they were masters of all Dakṣiṇa (Deccan) from sea to sea. In the second century BC, Āndhras possibly helped the king of Kaliṅga to invade Magadha. In 27 BC, Āndhras overthrew the Kaṇvas and extended their sway over Magadha. Gradually to the south-east of the Āndhras, another power, that of Pallavas developed. In spite of mutual rivalries, the southern powers of Coḷa, Pāṇḍya and Chera helped the Āndhras whenever a north Indian or a western power had to be countered. After that for a long period nothing is known. Then we find the Pallavas prominent in the south, the Cāḷukyas in the Deccan and the Guptas in the north.

Āndhras built monasteries for the Buddhist missions of Aśoka; the *stūpa*s of Amarāvatī are an evidence for this. Even after Mauryan power ended, Āndhras continued to be patrons and followers of Jainism and Buddhism. There is no reliable answer to the question why did the Kuṣāṇa and Āndhra powers collapse? A lot of conjectures and hypotheses have been advanced. The grandson of a petty chieftain of Gosambī married a princess of the Licchavis of Vaiśālī; and with the help of the Licchavis and other clans he became ruler of Magadha in CE 308. This was a man called Candragupta. In about twenty years Candragupta became the overlord of the entire valley covered by the Ganges and the Jamunā. After him his son Samudragupta extended the Gupta Empire up to Kāñcī. He pushed back the Kuṣāṇas to the Indus; and superseded the influences of Hellenism and Buddhism, and revived the Vedic sacrificial religion. His son and successor, Candragupta II extended the empire further, conquering Mālwā and Kaṭhiāwār. He may be the fabled Vikramāditya of Indian folk-lore.

I am inclined to think that what are known as the six Brāhmanical systems of Hinduism were developed in the period extending from the last stages of Kuṣāṇa power to the end of the "golden days" of Guptas, i.e, till the days of Kumāragupta and Skandagupta, the successors of Vikramāditya. The Guptas were great Bhāgavatas.

During this period the brāhmins again emerged as the dominant leaders of society. The *Mahābhārata* composed in this period makes even Kṛṣṇa a devotee of brāhmins and cows (*go-brāhmaṇa bhakta*). Many times he is said to have washed the feet of brāhmins and sprinkled the water on his head and wetted his throat with it (*ācamana*). The brāhmin leaders incorporated the *Bhagavad-Gītā* in the setting of the *Mahābhārata*. Kṛṣṇa, leader of men and man of action, is depicted as rising from a tribe of cowherds. He delivered his people from the tyranny of Kaṁsa, freed the land from demons and goblins, and established the new-age under Dharmarāja, "the king of virtue." Thus he is put in contrast to that wandering ascetic Gautama, who begged from house to house and exhorted people to do likewise. On the other hand Kṛṣṇa calls the youth to do their duties befitting to their life-stage and caste. In the

Mahābhārata are brought together the traditions and legends of the ancient times as preserved in the accounts of the brāhmin priests and ascetics. A sort of mass religion was sought to be manufactured by recognizing all sorts of cults, creeds and practices as lawful and equally good. Thus the worship of Śiva, of Viṣṇu, of the mother-goddess, Durgā are recognized and mentioned with as much respect as the Vedic sacrificial religion. Probably the Gupta emperor and his clever ministers consciously commissioned the composition of such a work as the *Mahābhārata* in an attempt to unite the heterogeneous tribes and clans of their empire, following different customs with conflicting beliefs.[26] If so the sponsors and editors of *Mahābhārata* attained as much success as Kabīr, Akbar and the early Sikh *gurus* attained in their attempts to evolve a religion out of Islam and Hinduism. The moderns — Ramakrishna, Vivekananda and Radhakrishnan — have the same idea — that of evolving a universal religion with its content formed out of the common points between the various religions. In essence this idea or ideal has its roots in the same tendency which propelled Hitler, Stalin and some of the American leaders to found and propagate a common ideology throughout all the parts of the globe. Vivekananda for example wanted to have a new society in which the Western and Eastern elements are fused but to the very backbone in culture and instincts it should be Hindu. He wants a new religion but its mind shall be Hindu and its body Islamic.[27] Aurobindo wants a new world but the key to the new world lies through a rediscovery and a reinterpretation of what the ancient *ṛṣis* taught; and this discovery and interpretation must be that of Aurobindo. Radhakrishnan's wish that there should be a great

26. Nivedita, *Footfalls of Indian History*, p. 180.
27. See his letters.

spiritual awakening throughout the whole world on the principles of Vedānta-Śaṅkarite version of it as interpreted by himself, of course, has already been referred to. Yes, Stalin also wants a new world; all the nations and the peoples shall have equal rights and responsibilities, but the rights and responsibilities shall be based on the principles laid down by that great prophet Marx and as interpreted by his all-knowing disciple Stalin, and as decreed by the heaven, Russia.

V

The significant period of original thought in India is that which began somewhere before 500 BC, and ended about CE 1200. After this, creative thinking is replaced by exposition and criticism. As Radhakrishnan wrote, the following period has much in it to lend countenance to the charge that "it is not sufficiently dry and virile to rise above grotesque imagination and puerile mythology."[28]

One legitimate question which we have to honestly answer is, has there been an evolution of philosophy in India, in the sense in which we at least ought to understand the term now? Indian thought is governed by a practical motive to secure release from transmigration. The only exceptions to this are Lokāyata and early Sāṁkhya. Again the separation between philosophy and religion which is so very necessary has never been made in India. There arose no Thomas Aquinas in India, followed later by Bruno and Descartes. Even famous contemporary Indians have no clear idea of what philosophy is, they still confuse it with religion.[29] Dasgupta and Wadia understand that philosophy is not theology as is evidenced

---

28. S. Radhakrishnan, *Indian Philosophy*, vol. II, p. 771.
29. Vide M.R. Jayakar's amazing assertion that "Indian philosophy was an elixir to be drunk from day to day" Dec. 27, 1951, Poona.

from their contributions in Contemporary Indian Philosophy. But Dasgupta never keeps this distinction clearly in mind in his *History of Indian Philosophy*. So long as astrology was not separated from astronomy and alchemy from chemistry, there was no notable progress in astronomy and chemistry. Unless philosophy is emancipated from the threshold of dogma and based on reason, it is not genuine philosophy. This has not been done in India.

The rigid caste distinctions and the exclusiveness in which the two higher classes shut themselves up denied them all contact with technical knowledge. As clear independent thought was always suppressed and subordinated to dogma and as the belief in *karma* was always there, there was no conception of progress. As a result of this, better forms of political institutions or even ideas of a better state of affairs were never evolved in India. Preoccupation with the other world and means of reaching it closed peoples' eyes to the ethical problems. Ethics in Indian thought is very simple; you just do what the Veda says and you go to heaven. In other schools different conceptions govern: "Consult the brāhmin and then do what you want." Earthly life and moral relations are simply absent for the Indian thinkers. "Systematic ethical reflection cannot be found in it."[30]

Indian thought never had any contact with the ideas of physical-mathematical sciences. It is thus comparable to early Greek philosophy and Medieval philosophy. Mythology, random thinking and absence of system are the characteristics of every Indian work. Not even Śaṅkara, Rāmānuja and Madhva are free from this. Nāgārjuna in his *Mādhyamika-Kārikā*, Gauḍapāda in his *Kārikā*s and Īśvara Kṛṣṇa are almost free

---

30. S. Radhakrishnan, *Eastern Religions and Western Thought*, p. 96.

from this. Their thought is rational, sane and virile. On the other hand descriptions of *brahmaloka*, *vaikuṇṭha*, the way of gods (*devayāna*), the way of fathers (*pitṛyāna*) and eschatology flood the *bhāṣya*s of Śaṅkara, Rāmānuja and Madhva. In all this Indian thought has nothing in common with modern Western thought.

Contact with the spirit of the West has shaken the belief in the fundamental presuppositions of the traditional schools of thought in India. If there has to be any development, the problems have to be stated afresh and new answers to be sought. Past solutions cannot be repeated, for they have lost their relevance. For all this those engaged in the pursuit of philosophy in India have to come into greater touch with contemporary developments in all the branches of knowledge — the anthropological, political, social and natural sciences. Greater encouragement has to be given to the study of modern philosophers. Misguided patriotism should not lead to neglect of their study and turn back to the hocus-pocus philosophy of the past. From this point of view a study of Bertrand Russell or Bradley is infinitely more useful than the matter of dubious value contained in Śaiva Siddhānta and Pūrva Mīmāṁsā, etc. It is simply staggering to find all sorts of things included in the curriculum of philosophy in Indian universities. If they want to promote study of things like Śaiva Siddhānta and Śāktism, etc. why do not they start a faculty of theology or of comparative religion? Nobody wishes to discourage such studies, but let them not call it philosophy. There are some academicians, who want to intensify the courses in the Indian schools and decrease the emphasis on modern philosophy till it dwindles into nothing. They are guided by the same motives which prompt some people to substitute the study of Āyurveda in the place of modern medicine. We have to be grateful for they have not yet begun demanding the substitution of Vaiśeṣika physics in the place of physics. . . . The aim and methodology of each branch of knowledge must be universal and objective; otherwise it becomes mere subjective fancy opinion, and will have no value.

In spite of the enthusiasm of the early scholars like Max Müller and Deussen among others, Indian thought has brought little striking change in the course of modern philosophy. Some may put forward the argument that approval or disapproval of European or American thinkers does not decide the value of any work. But I ask, will not the views of an Einstein or a De Broglie in the field of physics and that of a Haldane in biology count for something? Some famous Indians nowadays advocate that what they call a world-philosophy should be evolved, through a synthesis of Western and Indian philosophy. In philosophy we have different interpretations of the same facts, as we have in physics. Of course, from the final and absolute standpoint there can only be one world-view logically tenable. But nobody knows which that is, and so we have diverse efforts and different standpoints. Any sort of cheap compromise or easy eclecticism will destroy the philosophic effort and endeavour.

I do not at all plead that the study of the history of "Indian philosophy" should be discarded. India's achievements in philosophy do not form an unimportant part in the total history of human thought. Through Buddhism Indian thought has influenced Asia in the same way in which Greece has influenced the West. Again, there are countless parallelisms between Indian and Western thought. Much light will be thrown upon the nature of the problems and their possible solutions by a study of the way in which the same problems have been stated and solutions attempted by different thinkers in the East and the West.

If India is not to remain stagnant in the domain of philosophy a clear conception of what philosophy is and how progress is possible in it should emerge. In this teachers in Indian universities have to do much. History of philosophy should be distinguished from philosophy; theology should have nothing to do with philosophy. Translation and interpretation of some old Pāli or Sanskrit text or an exposition of some old quasi-philosophical school like the Trika or the Acintyabhedābheda should not be mistaken as a contribution to philosophy. Post-graduate students working in research departments should be encouraged to study old systems with a critical and comparative spirit and they should be urged to develop a fresh viewpoint of their own with regard to every problem and its possible solution. A translation of Varāhamihira or Āryabhaṭṭa with index, footnotes and introduction is not regarded by anyone as research in astronomy or as a contribution to development in astronomy. Such a work has its value, but that is purely historical. Similarly translation of some work of Vidyāraṇya, Vedānta Deśika or Abhinavagupta, though it is ornamented with footnotes, index, glossary and introduction cannot be regarded as a contribution towards the advancement of philosophy. In every instance critical comparative studies should be made; and though difficult every endeavour should be made to make some improvement over past achievements. This is much more difficult than translation and exposition. But difficulties should not deter us from progressing. One more point, the modern technological devices help us to counter these effects of the physical environment to a large extent. Thus even in sweltering summer one can nowadays be under the electric fan, and universities and factories can install air-conditioning. Diet can be made more balanced and nourishing. And so the physical conditions which imposed limitations on the spirit and thought of our forefathers need not any more hamper us. Given the courage and vision, the future is full of promise, "The problem facing Indian philosophy today is whether it is to be reduced to a cult, restricted in scope and with no application to the present facts, or whether it is to be made alive and real, so as to become what it should," so wrote the celebrated scholar, Radhakrishnan.[31] And thereby he implies that it is not "what it should be." This book is an attempt to show that it is this ideal, which should be for us and this could be done only by taking into account the immensely increased knowledge in modern science.

---

31. S. Radhakrishnan, *Indian Philosophy*, vol. II, p. 780.

Index